Lecture Notes in Artificial Intel

T0250562

Edited by J. G. Carbonell and J. Siekmann

Subseries of Lecture Notes in Computer Science

Olfa Nasraoui   Osmar Zaïane
Myra Spiliopoulou   Bamshad Mobasher
Brij Masand   Philip S. Yu (Eds.)

Advances in Web Mining and Web Usage Analysis

7th International Workshop
on Knowledge Discovery on the Web, WebKDD 2005
Chicago, IL, USA, August 21, 2005
Revised Papers

 Springer

Series Editors

Jaime G. Carbonell, Carnegie Mellon University, Pittsburgh, PA, USA
Jörg Siekmann, University of Saarland, Saarbrücken, Germany

Volume Editors

Olfa Nasraoui
Speed School of Engineering, Louisville KY 40292
E-mail: olfa.nasraoui@louiswville.edu

Osmar Zaïane
University of Alberta, Edmonton, AB, T6G2E8, Canada
E-mail: zaiane@ualberta.ca

Myra Spiliopoulou
Otto-von-Guericke-University Magdeburg, Germany
E-mail: myra@iti.cs.uni-magdeburg.de

Bamshad Mobasher
School of Computer Science, Chicago, IL 60604, USA
E-mail: mobasher@cs.depaul.edu

Brij Masand
Data Miners Inc., , Boston, MA 02114, USA
E-mail: brij@data-miners.com

Philip S. Yu
IBM T. J. Inc., N.Y. 10598, USA
E-mail: psyu@us.ibm.com

Library of Congress Control Number: 2006933535

CR Subject Classification (1998): I.2, H.2.8, H.3-5, K.4, C.2

LNCS Sublibrary: SL 7 – Artificial Intelligence

ISSN   0302-9743
ISBN-10   3-540-46346-1 Springer Berlin Heidelberg New York
ISBN-13   978-3-540-46346-7 Springer Berlin Heidelberg New York

Springer is a part of Springer Science+Business Media

springer.com

© Springer-Verlag Berlin Heidelberg 2006
Printed in Germany

Typesetting: Camera-ready by author, data conversion by Scientific Publishing Services, Chennai, India
Printed on acid-free paper   SPIN: 11891321   06/3142   5 4 3 2 1 0

Preface

This book contains the postworkshop proceedings of the 7th International Workshop on Knowledge Discovery from the Web, WEBKDD 2005. The WEBKDD workshop series takes place as part of the ACM SIGKDD International Conference on Knowledge Discovery and Data Mining (KDD) since 1999.

The discipline of data mining delivers methodologies and tools for the analysis of large data volumes and the extraction of comprehensible and non-trivial insights from them. Web mining, a much younger discipline, concentrates on the analysis of data pertinent to the Web. Web mining methods are applied on usage data and Web site content; they strive to improve our understanding of how the Web is used, to enhance usability and to promote mutual satisfaction between e-business venues and their potential customers.

In the last years, the interest for the Web as medium for communication, interaction and business has led to new challenges and to intensive, dedicated research. Many of the infancy problems in Web mining have now been solved but the tremendous potential for new and improved uses, as well as misuses, of the Web are leading to new challenges.

The theme of the WebKDD 2005 workshop was "Taming Evolving, Expanding and Multi-faceted Web Clickstreams." While solutions on some of the infancy problems of Web analysis have reached maturity, the reality poses new challenges: Most of the solutions on Web data analysis assume a static Web, in which a solitary user interacts with a Web site. It is prime time to depart from such simplifying assumptions and conceive solutions that are closer to Web reality: The Web is evolving constantly; sites change and user preferences drift. Clickstream data that form the basis of Web analysis are, obviously, streams rather than static datasets. And, most of all, a Web site is more than a see-and-click medium; it is a venue where a user interacts with a site owner or with other users, where group behavior is exhibited, communities are formed and experiences are shared. Furthermore, the inherent and increasing heterogeneity of the Web has required Web-based applications to more effectively integrate a variety of types of data across multiple channels and from different sources in addition to usage, such as content, structure, and semantics. A focus on techniques and architectures for more effective exploitation and mining of such multi-faceted data is likely to stimulate a next generation of intelligent applications. Recommendation systems form a prominent application area of Web analysis. One of the emerging issues in this area is the vulnerability of a Web site and its users towards abuse and offence. "How should an intelligent recommender system be designed to resist various malicious manipulations, such as schilling attacks that try to alter user ratings to influence the recommendations?" This motivates the need to study and design robust recommender systems. WebKDD 2005 addressed these emerging aspects of Web reality.

In the first paper, *Mining Significant Usage Patterns from Clickstream Data*, Lu, Dunham, and Meng propose a technique to generate significant usage patterns (SUP) and use it to acquire significant "user preferred navigational trails." The technique uses pipelined processing phases including sub-abstraction of sessionized Web clickstreams, clustering of the abstracted Web sessions, concept-based abstraction of the clustered sessions, and SUP generation. Using this technique, valuable customer behavior information can be extracted by Web site practitioners. Experiments conducted using J.C.Penney Web log data demonstrate that SUPs of different types of customers are distinguishable and interpretable.

In the second paper, *Using and Learning Semantics in Frequent Subgraph Mining*, Berendt addresses the need for incorporating background knowledge into graph mining and for studying patterns at different levels of abstraction, by using taxonomies in mining and extending frequency / support measures by the notion of context-induced interestingness. Semantics are used as well as learned in this process, and a visualization tool is used to allow the user to navigate through detail-and-context views of taxonomy context, pattern context, and transaction context. A case study of a real-life Web site shows the advantages of the proposed solutions.

In the third paper, *Overcoming Incomplete User Models in Recommendation Systems via an Ontology*, Schickel and Faltings propose a new method that extends the utility model and assumes that the structure of user preferences follows an ontology of product attributes. Using the MovieLens data, their experiments show that real user preferences indeed closely follow an ontology based on movie attributes. Furthermore, a recommender based just on a single individual's preferences and this ontology performs better than collaborative filtering, with the greatest differences when few data about the user are available. This points the way to how proper inductive bias (in the form of an ontology) can be used for significantly more powerful recommender systems in the future.

The fourth paper, *Data Sparsity Issues in the Collaborative Filtering Framework* by Grcar, Fortuna, Mladenic, and Grobelnik gives an overview of collaborative filtering approaches, and presents experimental results that compare the k-nearest neighbor (kNN) algorithm with support vector machines (SVM) in the collaborative filtering framework using data sets with different properties. Experiments on two standard, publicly available data sets and a real-life corporate data set that does not fit the profile of ideal data for collaborative filtering lead the authors to conclude that the quality of collaborative filtering recommendations is highly dependent on the sparsity of available data. Furthermore, they show that kNN is dominant on data sets with relatively low sparsity while SVM-based approaches may perform better on highly sparse data.

The fifth paper focuses on the multi-faceted aspect of Web personalization. In *USER: User-Sensitive Expert Recommendations for Knowledge-Dense Environments*, DeLong, Desikan, and Srivastava address the challenge of making relevant recommendations given a large, knowledge-dense Web site and a non-expert user searching for information. They propose an approach to provide recommendations to non-experts, helping them understand what they need to know, as opposed to what is popular among other users. The approach is user-sensitive in that it adopts a "model of learning" whereby the user's context is dynamically interpreted as they browse, and then leveraging that information to improve the recommendations.

In the sixth paper, *Analysis and Detection of Segment-Focused Attacks Against Collaborative Recommendation*, Mobasher, Burke, Williams, and Bhaumik examine the vulnerabilities that have recently been identified in collaborative filtering recommender systems. These vulnerabilities mostly emanate from the open nature of such systems and their reliance on user-specified judgments for building profiles. Hence, attackers can easily introduce biased data in an attempt to force the system to "adapt" in a manner advantageous to them. The authors explore an attack model that focuses on a subset of users with similar tastes and show that such an attack can be highly successful against both user-based and item-based collaborative filtering. They also introduce a detection model that can significantly decrease the impact of this attack.

The seventh paper, *Adaptive Web Usage Profiling*, by Suryavanshi, Shiri, and Mudur, addresses the challenge of maintaining profiles so that they dynamically adapt to new interests and trends. They present a new profile maintenance scheme, which extends the relational fuzzy subtractive clustering (RFSC) technique and enables efficient incremental update of usage profiles. An impact factor is defined whose value can be used to decide the need for recompilation. The results from extensive experiments on a large real dataset of Web logs show that the proposed maintenance technique, with considerably reduced computational costs, is almost as good as complete remodeling.

In the eigth paper, *On Clustering Techniques for Change Diagnosis in Data Streams*, Aggarwal and Yu, address the challenge of exploring the underlying changing trends in data streams that are generated by applications which are time-changing in nature. They explore and survey some of their recent methods for change detection, particularly methods that use clustering in order to provide a concise understanding of the underlying trends. They discuss their recent techniques which use micro-clustering in order to diagnose the changes in the underlying data, and discuss the extension of this method to text and categorical data sets as well community detection in graph data streams.

In *Personalized Search Results with User Interest Hierarchies Learnt from Bookmarks*, Kim and Chan propose a system for personalized Web search that incorporates an individual user's interests when deciding relevant results to return. They propose a method to (re)rank the results from a search engine using a learned user profile, called a user interest hierarchy (UIH), from Web pages that are of interest to the user. The users interest in Web pages will be determined implicitly, without directly asking the user. Experimental results indicate that the personalized ranking methods, when used with a popular search engine, can yield more potentially interesting Web pages for individual users.

We would like to thank the authors of all submitted papers. Their creative efforts have led to a rich set of good contributions for WebKDD 2005. We would also like to express our gratitude to the members of the Program Committee for their vigilant and timely reviews, namely (in alphabetical order): Charu Aggarwal, Sarabjot S. Anand, Jonathan Becher, Bettina Berendt, Ed Chi, Robert Cooley, Wei Fan, Joydeep Ghosh, Marco Gori, Fabio Grandi, Dimitrios Gunopulos, George Karypis, Raghu Krishnapuram, Ravi Kumar, Vipin Kumar, Mark Levene, Ee-Peng Lim, Bing Liu, Huan Liu, Stefano Lonardi, Ernestina Menasalvas, Rajeev Motwani, Alex Nanopoulos, Jian Pei, Rajeev Rastogi, Jaideep Srivastava, and Mohammed Zaki. O. Nasraoui gratefully acknowledges the support of the US National Science Foundation as part of NSF CAREER award IIS-0133948.

June 2006

Olfa Nasraoui
Osmar Zaane
Myra Spiliopoulou
Bamshad Mobasher
Philip Yu
Brij Masand

Table of Contents

Mining Significant Usage Patterns
from Clickstream Data*

Lin Lu, Margaret Dunham, and Yu Meng

Department of Computer Science and Engineering
Southern Methodist University
Dallas, Texas 75275-0122, USA
{llu, mhd, ymeng}@engr.smu.edu

Abstract. Discovery of usage patterns from Web data is one of the primary purposes for Web Usage Mining. In this paper, a technique to generate Significant Usage Patterns (SUP) is proposed and used to acquire significant "user preferred navigational trails". The technique uses pipelined processing phases including sub-abstraction of sessionized Web clickstreams, clustering of the abstracted Web sessions, concept-based abstraction of the clustered sessions, and SUP generation. Using this technique, valuable customer behavior information can be extracted by Web site practitioners. Experiments conducted using Web log data provided by J.C.Penney demonstrate that SUPs of different types of customers are distinguishable and interpretable. This technique is particularly suited for analysis of dynamic websites.

1 Introduction

The detailed records of Web data, such as Web server logs and referrer logs, provide enormous amounts of user information. Hidden in these data is valuable information that implies users' preferences and motivations for visiting a specific website. Research in Web Usage Mining (WUM) is to uncover such kind of information [10]. WUM is a branch of Web mining. By applying data mining techniques to discover useful knowledge of user navigation patterns from Web data, WUM is aimed at improving the Web design and developing corresponding applications to better cater to the needs of both users and website owners [20]. A pioneer work proposed by Nasraoui, *et al.*, used a concept hierarchy directly inferred from the website structure to enhance web usage mining [25, 26]. The idea is to segment Web logs into sessions, determine the similarity/distance among the sessions, and cluster the session data into the optimal number of components in order to obtain typical session profiles of users. Our work will extend to analyzing dynamic websites.

A variety of usage patterns have been investigated to examine the Web data from different perspectives and for various purposes. For instance, the maximal frequent forward sequence mines forward traversal patterns which are maximal and with backward traversals removed [9], the maximal frequent sequence examines the sequences

---

* This work is supported by the National Science Foundation under Grant No. IIS-0208741.

O. Nasraoui et al. (Eds.): WebKDD 2005, LNAI 4198, pp. 1–17, 2006.

that have a high frequency of occurrence as well as being maximal in length [24], sequential patterns explore the sequences with certain a support that are maximal [1], and user preferred navigational trails extract user preferred navigation paths [5] [6].

In this paper, a new data mining methodology that involves exploring the Significant Usage Patterns (SUP) is introduced. SUPs are paths that correspond to clusters of user sessions. A SUP may have specific beginning and/or ending states, and its corresponding normalized product of probabilities along the path satisfies a given threshold. SUP is a variation of "user preferred navigational trail" [5] [6]. Compared with earlier work, SUP differs in the following four aspects:

1. SUP is extracted from clusters of abstracted user sessions.
2. Practitioners may designate the beginning and/or ending Web pages of preferences before generating SUPs. For example, you may only want to see sequences that end on a purchase page.
3. SUPs are patterns with normalized probability, making it easy for practitioners to determine the probability threshold to generate corresponding patterns.
4. SUP uses a unique two-phase abstraction technique (see sections 3.1 & 3.3).
5. SUP is especially useful in analysis of dynamic websites.

We assume that the clickstream data has already been sessionized. The focus of this paper will be on abstracting the Web clickstream, clustering of abstracted sessions and generation of SUPs.

The rest of the paper is organized as follows. Section 2 discusses the related work. The methodology related to the alignment, abstraction, and clustering of Web sessions is provided in Section 3. Section 4 gives the analysis of experimental results performed using Web log data provided by J. C. Penney. Finally, conclusive discussions and perspectives for future research will be presented.

2   Related Work

Work relevant to the three main steps involved in mining SUPs: URL abstraction, clustering sessions of clickstream data, and generating usage patterns, are discussed in detail in the following subsections. We conclude each subsection with a brief examination of how our work fits into the literature.

2.1 URL Abstraction

URL abstraction is the process of generalizing URLs into higher level groups. Page-level aggregation is important for user behavior analysis [20]. In addition, it may lead to much more meaningful clustering results [4]. Since behavior patterns in user sessions consist of a sequence of low level page views, there is no doubt that patterns discovered using exact URLs will give fewer matches among user sessions, than those where abstraction of these pages is performed. Web page abstraction allows the discovery of correlations among user sessions with frequent occurrences at an abstract concept level. These frequent occurrences may not be frequent when viewed at the precise page level. In addition, many pages in a specific web site may be semantically equivalent (such as all colors/sizes of the same dress) which makes web page generalization not only possible, but also desirable.

In [4], concept-category of page hierarchy was introduced, in which web pages were grouped into categories, based on proper analytics and/or metadata information. Since this approach categorizes web pages using only the top-most level of the page hierarchy, it could be viewed as a simple version of generalization-based clustering. A generalization-based page hierarchy was described in [11]. According to this approach, each page was generalized to its higher level. For instance, pages under /school/department/courses would be categorized to "department" pages and pages under /school/department would be classified as "school" pages. Spiliopoulou et al. employed a content-based taxonomy of web site abstraction, in which taxonomy was defined according to a task-based model and each web page was mapped to one of the taxonomy's concepts [22]. In [18], pages were generalized to three categories, namely administrative, informational, and shopping pages, to describe an online nutrition supply store.

In our study, two different abstraction strategies are applied to user sessions before and after the clustering process. User sessions are sub-abstracted before applying the clustering algorithm in order to make the sequence alignment approach used in clustering more meaningful. After clustering user sessions, a concept-based abstraction approach is applied to user sessions in each cluster, which allows more insight into the SUPs associated with each cluster. Both abstraction techniques are based on a user provided site concept hierarchy.

2.2 Clustering User Sessions of Clickstream Data

In order to mine useful information concerning user navigation patterns from clickstream data, it is appropriate to first cluster user sessions. The purpose of clustering is to find groups of users with similar preferences and objectives for visiting a specific website. Actually, the knowledge of user groups with similar behavior patterns is extremely valuable for e-commerce applications. With this knowledge, domain experts can infer user demographics in order to perform market segmentations [20].

Various approaches have been introduced in the literature to cluster user sessions [4] [7] [11] [16] [23]. [7] used a mixture of first-order Markov chains to partition user sessions with similar navigation patterns into the same cluster. In [11], page accesses in each user session were substituted by a generalization-based page hierarchy scheme. Then, generalized sessions were clustered using a hierarchical clustering algorithm, BIRCH.

Banerjee et al. developed an algorithm that combined both the time spent on a page and Longest Common Subsequences (LCS) to cluster user sessions [4]. The LCS algorithm was first applied on all pairs of user sessions. After each LCS path was compacted using a concept-category of page hierarchy, similarities between LCS paths were computed as a function of the time spent on the corresponding pages in the paths weighted by a certain factor. Then, an abstract similarity graph was constructed for the set of sessions to be clustered. Finally, a graph partition algorithm, called Metis, was used to segment the graph into clusters.

The clustering approach discussed in [16] [23] was based on the sequence alignment method. They took the order of page accesses within the session into consideration when computing the similarities between sessions. More specifically, they used the idea of sequence alignment widely adopted in bio-informatics to measure the similarity between sessions. Then, sessions were clustered according to their similarities. In [16], Ward's clustering method [15] was used, and [23] applied three clustering algorithms, ROCK [13], CHAMELEON [17], and TURN [12].

The clustering approach used in our work is based on [16] [23], however, a sub-abstraction is first conducted before the similarities among Web pages are measured. Then the Needleman-Wunsch global alignment algorithm [21] is used to align the abstracted sessions based on the pagewise similarities. By performing a global alignment of sessions, the similarity matrix can be obtained. Finally, the nearest neighbor clustering algorithms is applied to cluster the user sessions based on the similarity matrix.

2.3 Generating Usage Patterns

Varieties of browsing patterns have been investigated to examine Web data from different perspectives and for various purposes. These patterns include the maximal frequent forward sequence [9], the maximal frequent sequence [24], the sequential pattern [1], and user preferred navigational trail [5] [6].

Table 1. A comparison of various popular usage patterns

	Clustering	Abstraction	Beginning/ending Web page(s)	Normalized
Sequential Pattern	N	Y*	N	-
Maximal Frequent Sequence	N	N	N	-
Maximal Frequent Forward Sequence	N	N	N	-
User Preferred Navigational Trail	N	N	N	N
Significant Usage Pattern	Y	Y	Y	Y

* Abstraction may be applied to some of the patterns, i.e. in [2], but not all, i.e. in [19].

The usage pattern proposed in [5] [6] are the most related to our research. [5] proposed a data-mining model to extract the higher probability trails which represent user preferred navigational paths. In that paper, user sessions were modeled as a Hypertext Probabilistic Grammar (HPG), which can be viewed as an absorbing Markov chain, with two additional states, start (S) and finish (F). The set of strings generated from HPG with higher probability are considered as preferred navigation trails of users. The depth first search algorithm was used to generate the trails given specific support and confidence thresholds. Support and confidence thresholds were used to control the quality and quantity of trails generated by the algorithm. In [6], it was proved that the average complexity of the depth first search algorithm used to generate the higher probability trails is linear to the number of web pages accessed.

In our approach, SUPs are trails with high probability extracted from each of the clusters of abstracted user sessions. We use the normalized probabilities of occurrence to make the probabilities of SUPs insensitive to the length of the sessions. In addition, SUPs may begin and/or end with specific Web pages of user preferences. Table 1 provides a comparison of SUPs with other patterns.

3 Methodology

Our technique uses pipelined processing phases including sub-abstraction of session-ized Web clickstream, clustering of the abstracted Web sessions, concept-based abstraction of the clustered sessions and SUP generation.

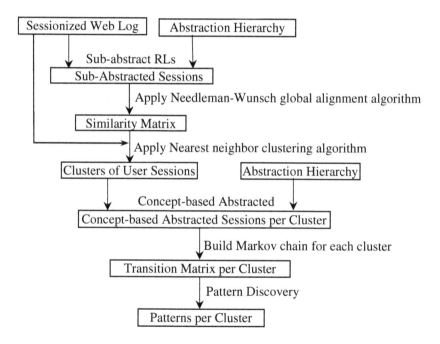

Fig. 1. Logic flow to generate SUPs

To generate SUPs, first, a sequence alignment [16] [23] approach based on the Needleman-Wunsch global alignment algorithm [21] is applied to the sessionized abstracted clickstream data to compute the similarities between each pair of sessions. This approach preserves the sequential relationship between sessions, and reflects the characteristics of chronological sequential order associated with the clickstream data. Based on the pairwise alignment results, a similarity matrix is constructed and then original un-abstracted sessions are grouped into clusters according to their similarities. By applying clustering on sessions, we are more likely to discover the common and useful usage patterns associated with each cluster. Then, the original Web sessions are abstracted again using a concept-based abstraction approach and then a first order Markov chain is built for each cluster of sessions. Finally, the SUPs with a normalized product of probability along the path that is greater than a given threshold are extracted from each cluster based on their corresponding Markov chain. This process is illustrated in Fig 1. A more detailed description of each step is provided in the following subsections.

3.1 Create Sub-abstracted Sessions

In this study, we assume that the Web data has already been cleansed and sessionized. Detailed techniques for preprocessing the Web data can be found in [8].

A Web session is a sequence of Web pages accessed by a single user. However, for the sequence alignment result to be more meaningful, we abstract the pages to produce sub-abstracted sessions. We use the term "sub-abstracted" instead of "abstracted" session, because we do not use a typical abstraction approach, but rather a concept-based abstraction hierarchy, e.g., Department, Category, and Item in e-commerce Web site, plus some specific information, such as Department ID, Category ID in the abstracted session. Thus parts of the Web page URL are abstracted and some are not. With this approach, we preserve certain information to make Web page similarity comparison more meaningful for that session alignment described below. A URL in a session is mapped to a sub-abstracted URL as follows:

URL -> {<Concept hierarchy keyword> <Unique ID> <|>}

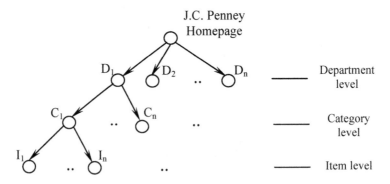

Fig. 2. Hierarchy of J.C. Penney Web site

Example 1. Based on the hierarchical structure of J.C. Penney's Web site, each Web page access in the session sequence is abstracted into three levels of hierarchy, as shown in Fig 2, where D, C, I are the initials for Department, Category, and Item respectively, 1, 2, ..., n represent IDs, and vertical bar | is used to separate different levels in the hierarchy.

The following is an example of a sub-abstracted session with the last negative number representing the session id (Web pages that do not belong to any department are abstracted as P which stands for general page):

D0|C875|I D0|C875|I P27593 P27592 P28 -507169015

3.2   Session Sequence Alignment

The Needleman-Wunsch alignment algorithm [21] is a dynamic programming algorithm. It is suitable to determine the similarity of any two abstracted sessions and we adopt it in this paper. The basic idea of computing the optimal alignment of two sequences, X1...Xm and Y1...Yn, using Needleman-Wunsch alignment algorithm is illustrated in Fig 3. Suppose $A(i, j)$ is the optimal alignment score of aligning X1... Xi with Y1... Yj. If we know the alignment scores of $A(i-1, j-1)$, $A(i-1, j)$, and $A(i, j-1)$, then $A(i, j)$ can be computed as $A(i, j) = \max[A(i-1, j-1)+s(Xi, Yj); A(i-1, j)+d; A(i, j-1)+d]$, where $s(Xi, Yj)$ is the similarity between Xi and Yj, d is the score of aligning Xi with a gap or aligning Yj with a gap. That is, an entry $A(i, j)$ depends on three other entries as illustrated in Fig 3. Therefore, we can carry out the computation from upper left corner to lower right corner, $A(m,n)$, which is the optimal alignment score between X1...Xm and Y1...Yn. Initially, as shown in Fig 3, set: (1) $A(0,0)=0$, since it corresponds to aligning two empty strings of X and Y; (2) $A(i, 0)=-d*i$, for i = 1...m, which corresponds to aligning the prefix X1... Xi with gaps; (3) Similarly, $A(0,j)=-d*j$, for j = 1...n.

		Y_1	...	Y_{j-1}	Y_j	...	Y_n
	0	-d	...	-(j-1)d	-jd	...	-nd
X_1	-d						
...	...						
X_{i-1}	-(i-1)d			$A(i-1, j-1)$	$A(i-1, j)$		
X_i	-id			$A(i, j-1)$	$A(i, j)$		
...	...						
X_m	-md						$A(m, n)$

Fig. 3. Computing optimal alignment of two sequences using Needleman-Wunsch algorithm

When taking the hierarchical representation of Web pages into consideration, it is reasonable to assume that higher levels in the hierarchy, which have more importance in determining the similarity of two Web pages, should be given more weight. To reflect this in the scoring scheme, first, the longer page representation string in the two Web page representations is determined. Then, a weight is assigned to each level in the hierarchy and its corresponding ID (if any) respectively: the lowest level in longer page representation string is given weight 1 to its ID and weight 2 to its abstract level, the second to the lowest level is given weight 1 to its ID and weight 4 to its abstract level, and so forth. Finally, the two Web page representation strings are compared from the left to the right. Comparison stops at the first pair which are different. The similarity between two Web pages is determined by the ratio of the sum of the weights of those matching parts to the sum of the total weights. The following is an example of computing the similarities between two Web pages:

Page 1: D0|C875|I weight=6+1+4+1+2=14
Page 2: D0|C875   weight=6+1+4+1=12
Similarity=12/14=0.857

Therefore, the similarity value of two Web pages is between 0 and 1, the similarity is 1 when two Web pages are exactly the same, and 0 while two Web pages are totally different.

The scoring scheme used in this study for computing the alignment of two session strings is the same as in [23]. It is defined as follows:

if matching //a pair of Web pages with similarity 1
        score = 20;
else if mis-matching //a pair of Web pages with similarity 0
        score = –10;
else if gap   //a Web page aligns with a gap
        score = –10;
else   //the pair of Web pages with similarity between 0 and 1
        score = –10 ~ 20;

Then, the Needleman-Wunsch global alignment algorithm can be applied to the sub-abstracted Web session data to compute the score corresponding to the optimal alignment of two Web sessions. This is a dynamic programming process which uses the Web page similarity measurement mentioned above as a page matching function. Finally, the optimal alignment score is normalized to represent the similarity between two sessions:

$$\text{Session similarity} = \frac{optimal\ alignment\ score}{length\ of\ longer\ session}. \qquad (1)$$

Example 2. Fig 4 provides an example for computing the optimal alignment and the similarity for the following two Web sessions (session ids are ignored in the alignment):

P47104 D0|C0|I D469|C469 D2652|C2652
D469|C16758|I D0|C0|I D469|C469

Thus, the optimal alignment score is 32.1 and the session similarity = 32.1/4 = 8.025

	P47104	D0|C0|I	D469|C469	D2652|C2652
	0	-10	-20	-30	-40
D469|C16758|I	-10	-10	5.7	-4.3	-14.3
D0|C0|I	-20	-20	10	17.1	7.1
D469|C469	-30	-30	0	30	32.1

Fig. 4. Computing Web session similarity for Example 2

3.3 Create Concept-Based Abstracted Sessions

After the original Web sessions are clustered using a sequence alignment approach, Web sessions are abstracted again using a concept-based abstraction approach.

In this approach, we adopt the same abstraction hierarchy introduced in Section 3.1, which contains Department (D), Category (C), Item (I), and General page (P) in the hierarchy. However, the abstracted page accesses in a session will be represented as a sequence like: P1D1C1I1P2D2C2I2..., in which each of Pi, Di, Ci, and Ii (i=1, 2...) represents a different page. For example, D1 (element) and D2 (element) indicate two different departments. The same applies to Pi, Ci and Ii. In addition, it is also important that for different sessions, the same page may be represented by different elements. For example, the shoe department may be represented by D1 in one session, and by D2 in another session. The definition of element is based on the sequence of page accesses that appear in a session. In the Markov chain, each of these elements will be treated as a state.

A URL in a session is mapped to a concept based abstracted URL as follows:

URL -> <Concept hierarchy keyword> <Unique ID for this concept in this session>

Thus each URL is associated with the lowest level of concept in representing that URL in the concept hierarchy and a unique ID for that specific URL within the session.

By abstracting Web sessions in such a way, it allows us to ignore the irrelevant or detailed information in the dataset while concentrating on more general information. Therefore, it is possible for us to find the general behavior in a group as well as to identify the main user groups.

Example 3. The example given below illustrates the abstraction process in this step (the last negative number representing the session id):

Original session: D7107|C7121 D7107|C7126|I076bdf3 D7107|C7131|I084fc96
    D7107|C7131 P55730 P96 P27 P14 P27592 P28 P33711 -505884861

Abstracted session: C1 I1 I2 C2 P1 P2 P3 P4 P5 P6 P7 -505884861

3.4 Generating Significant Usage Patterns

Based on the pairwise session similarity results computed according to the above-mentioned techniques, a Web session similarity matrix is constructed. Then, a clustering algorithm can be applied to the matrix to generate clusters. For simplicity, the nearest neighbor clustering algorithm is used in this study. A detailed example of this algorithm can be found in [10].

Upon generating clusters of Web sessions, we represent each cluster by a Markov chain. The Markov chain consists of a set of states and a transition matrix. Each state in the model represents a concept-based abstracted Web page in a cluster of Web sessions, with two additional states representing the "start" state and the "end" state. The transition matrix contains the transition probability between states. Example 4 illustrates this step.

Example 4. Fig 5 (a) contains a list of concept based abstracted sessions in a cluster. Assume that each number in the session sequence stands for an abstracted Web page, and it is represented as a state in the Markov chain. In addition, a Start (S) and an End (E) states are introduced in the model and treated as the first and the last states for all sessions in the cluster respectively. Fig 5(b) shows the corresponding Markov chain for the sessions listed in Fig 5 (a). The weight on each arc is the transition probability from the state where the arc going out to the state where the arc pointing to. The transition probability is computed as the number of corresponding transition occurred divided by the total number of out transitions from the state where the arc leaving.

(1) 1, 2, 3, 5, 4
(2) 2, 4, 3, 5
(3) 3, 2, 4, 5
(4) 1, 3, 4, 3
(5) 4, 2, 3, 4, 5
     (a)

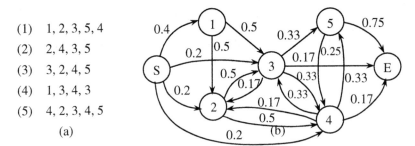

Fig. 5. Example of building a Markov chain for a cluster of abstract sessions

The Markov chain used here is first-order. Using the Markov property, the model assumes that the Web page a user visits next is fully dependent on the content of Web page that the user is currently visiting. Research shows that this is reasonable for Web page prediction [14]. The transition matrix for the Markov chain records all the user navigation activities within the Web site and it will be used to generate SUPs.

Definition 1. A "*path*" is an ordered sequence of states from the Markov chain. The first state in the sequence is identified as the "*beginning state*", and the terminating state is called the "*end state*".

Definition 2. Given a path in the Markov chain, the "*probability of a path*" is:

> *Case 1 (Beginning state identified by user)*: Product of transition probabilities found on all transitions along the path, from beginning to end state.
> *Case 2 (Beginning state not given)*: Product of transition probabilities found on all transitions along the path times the transition probability from the Markov chain *Start* state to the beginning state in the path.

Suppose, there exits a path S1→ S2→... Si→...→ Sn, according to Definition 2, the probability of the path, P, is defined as:

$$P = \prod_{i=1}^{n-1} P_{t_i} \text{ , where } Pt_i \text{ is the transition probability} \tag{2}$$

between two adjacent states.

To illustrate the two cases stated in the definition, we use Example 4, path 1→2→3→4. If state 1 is given by the user, the probability of this path is 0.5×0.5×0.33=0.0825; otherwise, the probability is 0.4×0.5×0.5×0.33=0.033. The purpose of distinguishing between these two scenarios is that: (1) Case 1: if a user only gives the end Web page, we assume that the user is more interested in the patterns that lead to that specific end page from the very beginning where Web visitors entering the Web site; (2) Case 2: if a practitioner provides both beginning and ending Web pages, we interpret that user is likely interested in viewing patterns occurring between those two pages.

Considering that the final probability of a path is exponential to the length of the path, in order to set a general rule to specify the probability threshold for generated paths, it is necessary to normalize the probability of a path to eliminate the exponential factor. Therefore, the normalized probability of the path, P_N, is defined as:

$$P_N = \left(\prod_{i=1}^{n-1} P_{t_i} \right)^{\frac{1}{n-1}} , \text{ where } Pt_i \text{ is the transition probability} \tag{3}$$

between two adjacent states.

Definition 3. A SUP is a path that may have a specific beginning and/or end state, and a normalized probability greater than a given threshold θ, that is, $P_N > \theta$.

Example 5. To illustrate the concept of SUP, again, we use the above example. Suppose we are interested in patterns with $\theta > 0.4$, ending in state 4, and under two different cases, one is beginning with state 1 and the other one leaves the beginning state undefined. The corresponding SUPs generated under those two circumstances are listed in Table 2. They are generated based on the transition matrix using Depth-first search algorithm.

Table 2. Example of SUPs

$\theta > 0.4$, end state is 4		$\theta > 0.4$, beginning state is 1, end state is 4	
SUP	θ	SUP	θ
S→1→2→3→4	0.45	1→2→3→4	0.46
S→1→2→3→5→4	0.53	1→2→3→5→4	0.56
S→1→2→4	0.46	1→2→4	0.5
S→1→3→4	0.43	1→3→4	0.45
S→1→3→5→4	0.53	1→3→5→4	0.58
S→2→3→5→4	0.45		
S→3→5→4	0.43		

4   Experimental Analysis

4.1   Clickstream Data

The clickstream data used in this study were provided by J. C. Penney. The whole dataset contains one day's Web log data from jcpenney.com on October 5, 2003. After preprocessing of the raw log data, each of the recorded clicks was broken down into several pieces of information. The key pieces of information include category ID, department ID, item ID, and session ID.

On this specific day, 1,463,180 visitor sessions were recorded. However, after removing the sessions generated by robots, we ended up with 593,223 sessions. The resulting sessions were separated into two super groups: sessions with purchase(s) and those without any purchases. The experiments conducted here use the first 2,000 sessions from both purchase and non-purchase groups, with the assumptions that the sessions from different time frames within a day are equally distributed and 2,000 sessions from each cluster are large enough to draw conclusions. An alternative method is to sample the large Web logs.

4.2 Result Analysis

The range of the similarity scores of the sub-abstracted Web sessions in the similarity matrix generated by using Needleman-Wunsch global alignment algorithm is from -9.4 to 20 for the purchase group and –10 to 20 for the non-purchase group. The average scores are 3.3 for the purchase group and –0.8 for the non-purchase group, respectively. Recall that the similarity scores are between -10 and 20. These scores are consistent with the scoring scheme used in this study. After trying different thresholds for the nearest neighbor clustering algorithm, we found that with a threshold of 3 for purchase sessions and a threshold of 0 for non-purchase sessions, both of the groups result in 3 clusters and these results give better clustering results. The average session length in the resulting clusters for both purchase and non-purchase clusters are shown in Fig 6. From the figure, it is obvious that on average purchase sessions are longer than those sessions without purchase. This illustrates that users usually request more page views when they are about to make a purchase than when they visit an online store without purchasing. This can be explained by the fact that users normally would like to review the information as well as to compare the price, the quality and etc. for the product(s) of their interest before buying them. In addition, users need to fill out the billing and shipping information as well to commit the purchase. All these factors could lead to a longer purchase session.

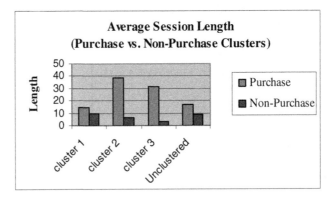

Fig. 6. Average session length

Table 3 lists the SUPs generated from each of the three different clusters in the non-purchase super-group. In order to limit the number of SUPs generated from each cluster, we applied different probability threshold to each cluster. From the results in

Table 3, it is easy to distinguish patterns among three clusters. In cluster 1, users spend most of their time browsing between different categories. By looking into the sessions in this cluster, we notice that most of the sessions request product pages at some point. However, these kinds of patterns are not dominant when we require a threshold $\theta > 0.3$. When we lowered the threshold to $\theta > 0.25$, the generated SUPs also include the following:

$$S\text{-}C1\text{-}C1\text{-}C2\text{-}C3\text{-}C4\text{-}C5\text{-}C5\text{-}I1\text{-}E$$
$$S\text{-}C1\text{-}C1\text{-}I1\text{-}C1\text{-}C2\text{-}C3\text{-}C4\text{-}C5\text{-}E$$
$$S\text{-}I1\text{-}C1\text{-}C2\text{-}C3\text{-}C4\text{-}C5\text{-}C6\text{-}C7\text{-}E$$

Table 3. SUPs in non-purchase cluster

Cluster No.	No. of Sessions	Threshold (θ)	Average Session Length	No. of States	SUPs
1	1746	0.3	9.6	98	1. $S\text{-}C_1\text{-}C_1\text{-}C_2\text{-}C_3\text{-}C_4\text{-}C_5\text{-}C_6\text{-}C_7\text{-}E$ 2. $S\text{-}C_1\text{-}C_1\text{-}C_2\text{-}C_3\text{-}C_4\text{-}C_5\text{-}E$ 3. $S\text{-}C_1\text{-}C_1\text{-}C_2\text{-}C_3\text{-}E$ 4. $S\text{-}C_1\text{-}C_2\text{-}C_3\text{-}C_3\text{-}C_4\text{-}C_5\text{-}C_6\text{-}C_7\text{-}E$ 5. $S\text{-}C_1\text{-}C_2\text{-}C_3\text{-}C_4\text{-}C_4\text{-}C_5\text{-}C_6\text{-}C_7\text{-}E$ 6. $S\text{-}C_1\text{-}C_2\text{-}C_3\text{-}C_4\text{-}C_5\text{-}C_5\text{-}C_6\text{-}C_7\text{-}E$ 7. $S\text{-}C_1\text{-}C_2\text{-}C_3\text{-}C_4\text{-}C_5\text{-}C_6\text{-}C_6\text{-}C_7\text{-}E$ 8. $S\text{-}C_1\text{-}C_2\text{-}C_3\text{-}C_4\text{-}C_5\text{-}C_6\text{-}C_7\text{-}C_7\text{-}E$ 9. $S\text{-}C_1\text{-}C_2\text{-}C_3\text{-}C_4\text{-}C_5\text{-}C_6\text{-}C_7\text{-}C_8\text{-}E$ 10. $S\text{-}C_1\text{-}C_2\text{-}C_3\text{-}C_4\text{-}C_5\text{-}C_6\text{-}C_7\text{-}E$ 11. $S\text{-}C_1\text{-}C_2\text{-}C_3\text{-}C_4\text{-}C_5\text{-}C_6\text{-}E$ 12. $S\text{-}C_1\text{-}C_2\text{-}C_3\text{-}C_4\text{-}C_5\text{-}E$ 13. $S\text{-}C_1\text{-}C_2\text{-}C_3\text{-}C_4\text{-}E$ 14. $S\text{-}C_1\text{-}C_2\text{-}C_3\text{-}E$
2	241	0.37	6.6	38	1. $S\text{-}P_1\text{-}P_2\text{-}P_3\text{-}P_3\text{-}E$ 2. $S\text{-}P_1\text{-}P_2\text{-}P_3\text{-}P_4\text{-}P_4\text{-}P_5\text{-}E$ 3. $S\text{-}P_1\text{-}P_2\text{-}P_3\text{-}P_4\text{-}P_4\text{-}E$ 4. $S\text{-}P_1\text{-}P_2\text{-}P_3\text{-}P_4\text{-}P_5\text{-}P_4\text{-}E$ 5. $S\text{-}P_1\text{-}P_2\text{-}P_3\text{-}P_4\text{-}P_5\text{-}P_5\text{-}E$ 6. $S\text{-}P_1\text{-}P_2\text{-}P_3\text{-}P_4\text{-}P_5\text{-}P_6\text{-}C_1\text{-}E$ 7. $S\text{-}P_1\text{-}P_2\text{-}P_3\text{-}P_4\text{-}P_5\text{-}P_6\text{-}P_7\text{-}E$ 8. $S\text{-}P_1\text{-}P_2\text{-}P_3\text{-}P_4\text{-}P_5\text{-}P_6\text{-}E$ 9. $S\text{-}P_1\text{-}P_2\text{-}P_3\text{-}P_4\text{-}P_5\text{-}E$ 10. $S\text{-}P_1\text{-}P_2\text{-}P_3\text{-}P_4\text{-}C_1\text{-}E$ 11. $S\text{-}P_1\text{-}P_2\text{-}P_3\text{-}P_4\text{-}E$ 12. $S\text{-}P_1\text{-}P_2\text{-}P_3\text{-}C_1\text{-}E$ 13. $S\text{-}P_1\text{-}P_2\text{-}P_3\text{-}E$ 14. $S\text{-}P_1\text{-}P_2\text{-}E$
3	13	0.3	3.0	6	1. $S\text{-}C_1\text{-}P_1\text{-}P_1\text{-}P_2\text{-}E$ 2. $S\text{-}C_1\text{-}P_1\text{-}P_1\text{-}E$ 3. $S\text{-}C_1\text{-}P_1\text{-}P_2\text{-}E$ 4. $S\text{-}C_1\text{-}P_1\text{-}E$ 5. $S\text{-}I_1\text{-}P_1\text{-}P_1\text{-}P_2\text{-}E$ 6. $S\text{-}I_1\text{-}P_1\text{-}P_1\text{-}E$ 7. $S\text{-}I_1\text{-}P_1\text{-}P_2\text{-}E$ 8. $S\text{-}I_1\text{-}P_1\text{-}E$

Based on the result shown in Table 3, we conclude that users in this group are more interested in gathering information of products in different categories. In cluster 2 users are interested in reviewing general pages (to gather general information), although some of them may also request some categories and products pages, as shown in the SUPs below ($\theta > 0.3$):

$$\text{S-P1-P2-P3-C1-I1-E}$$
$$\text{S-P1-P2-P3-P4-P5-P6-C1-C2-E}$$
$$\text{S-P1-P2-P3-P4-P5-C4-I6-I7-I8-E}$$

In cluster 3, the average session length is only 3. We conclude that users in this group are casual visitors. This is reflected in their behavior patterns that they leave the site and end the visit session after they come to the Web site for one category or product page and then a couple of general pages. Note that BNF notation proves to be a valuable tool to label the significant patterns from each cluster. The corresponding BNF expressions of the SUPs in these three clusters are given in Table 4. In the BNF representation, we ignore the subscript in corresponding P, D, C, and I.

Let us examine SUPs beginning at a specific page, P86806. In the three generated clusters in the non-purchase group, the form of patterns is similar to those starting from "Start" (S) page in the corresponding cluster. Their BNF expressions are given in Table 4.

The SUPs (in BNF notation) generated from the three clusters in purchase group are provided in Table 4 as well. Users in cluster 1 appears to be direct buyers, since the average session length in this cluster is relatively short (14.9) compared with the other two clusters in the purchase group. Customers in this cluster may come to the Web site, pick up the items(s) they want, and then fill out the required information and leave. The following are some sample SUPs from cluster 1:

$$\text{S-}C_1\text{-}I_1\text{-}P_1\text{-}P_2\text{-}P_3\text{-}P_4\text{-}P_5\text{-}P_6\text{-}P_7\text{-}P_8\text{-}P_9\text{-}P_{10}\text{-}P_{11}\text{-}P_{12}\text{-E}$$
$$\text{S-}P_1\text{-}P_2\text{-}P_3\text{-}P_4\text{-}P_5\text{-}P_6\text{-}P_7\text{-}P_8\text{-}P_9\text{-}P_{10}\text{-}P_{11}\text{-}P_{12}\text{-}P_{11}\text{-E}$$
$$\text{S-}I_1\text{-}P_1\text{-}P_2\text{-}P_3\text{-}P_4\text{-}P_5\text{-}P_6\text{-}P_7\text{-}P_8\text{-}P_9\text{-}P_{10}\text{-}P_{11}\text{-}P_{12}\text{-}P_{13}\text{-E}$$

SUPs in cluster 2 show that shoppers in this cluster may like to compare the product(s) of their interests, or have a long shopping list — they request many category pages before going to the general pages (possibly for checking out). An example SUP from this cluster is given below:

$$\text{S-}C_1\text{-}C_2\text{-}C_3\text{-}C_4\text{-}C_5\text{-}C_6\text{-}C_7\text{-}C_8\text{-}C_9\text{-}C_{10}\text{-}C_{11}\text{-}C_{12}\text{-}C_{13}\text{-}C_{14}\text{-}C_{15}\text{-}C_{16}\text{-}C_{17}\text{-}C_{18}\text{-}C_{19}\text{-}C_{20}\text{-}$$
$$C_{21}\text{-}C_{22}\text{-}C_{23}\text{-}P_4\text{-}P_5\text{-}P_6\text{-}P_7\text{-}P_8\text{-}P_9\text{-}P_{10}\text{-}P_{11}\text{-}P_{12}\text{-}P_{13}\text{-}P_{14}\text{-}P_{15}\text{-}P_{16}\text{-}P_{17}\text{-}P_{18}\text{-}P_{19}\text{-}P_{20}\text{-E}$$

Customers in cluster 3 are more like hedonic shoppers, since the usage patterns show that they first go through several general pages, and then suddenly go to the product pages (possibly for purchase) which may be stimulated by some information provided in general pages. The following is a sample SUP from this cluster:

$$\text{S-}P_1\text{-}P_2\text{-}P_3\text{-}P_4\text{-}P_5\text{-}P_6\text{-}P_7\text{-}P_8\text{-}P_9\text{-}P_{10}\text{-}I_{13}\text{-}I_{14}\text{-}I_{15}\text{-}P_{10}\text{-}P_{11}\text{-}P_{12}\text{-}P_{16}\text{-}P_{15}\text{-}P_{17}\text{-}P_{18}\text{-}P_{19}\text{-}C_1\text{-}$$
$$C_2\text{-}C_3\text{-}C_4\text{-}C_5\text{-}C_6\text{-E}$$

For SUPs starting from page P86806 in the purchase group, a similar pattern is shown to those that start from "Start" (S) page in the corresponding cluster. The BNF expressions of their SUPs are provided in Table 4.

When comparing SUPs in both purchase and non-purchase super-groups, we notice two main differences:

1. The average length of SUPs is longer in the purchase group than in the non-purchase group.
2. SUPs in the purchase cluster have a higher probability than those in the non-purchase cluster.

The first difference might be due to the fact that users proceed to review the information, compare among products, and fill out the payment and shipping information. A possible explanation for the second phenomenon is that users in the purchase group may already have some specific product(s) in mind to purchase when they visit the Web site. Therefore, they show similar search patterns, product comparison patterns, and purchase patterns. This causes the SUPs in the purchase group to have a higher probability. In contrast, users in the non-purchase group have a random browsing behavior, since they have no specific purchase purpose for visiting the Web site.

From the above result, we can see that SUPs associated with different clusters are different but meaningful. In addition, given the flexibility of specifying specific beginning and/or ending Web pages, practitioners can more freely investigate the patterns of their specific preferences.

Table 4. Clusters in non-purchase vs. purchase

Cluster	Cluster No.	No. of Sessions	Average Session Length	No. of States	Threshold (θ)	Beginning Web page	SUPs in BNF Notation
Non-Purchase	1	1746	9.6	98	0.3	S	S-{C}-E
					0.25	P86806	P86806-{C}-E
	2	241	6.6	38	0.37	S	S-{P}-[C]-E
					0.34	P86806	P86806-[I]-{P}-E
	3	13	3.0	6	0.3	S	S-<C I I>-{P}-E
					0.2	P86806	P86806-[{P}- [P86806]]-E
Purchase	1	1858	14.9	55	0.47	S	S-[C]-[I]-{P}-E
					0.51	P86806	P86806-[I]-{P}-E
	2	132	39.1	100	0.457	S	S -[{{C}I{I}}]-{P}-E
					0.434	P86806	P86806-[{C }]-{P}-E
	3	10	31.6	47	0.52	S	S-{P}-[{I}]-[{P}]-{C}-E
					0.43	P86806	P86806-[I]-[{P}]-{C}-E

5   Conclusion and Future Work

In this study the *Significant Usage Pattern (SUP)*, a variation of "user preferred navigational trail", is presented. This technique aims at analysis of dynamic websites. Compared with "user preferred navigational trail", SUPs are generated from clustered abstracted Web sessions, and characterized with a normalized probability of occurrence higher than a threshold. The beginning and/or ending Web page(s) may be included in the SUPs. SUPs can be used to find groups of users with similar motivations when they visit a specific website. By providing the flexibility to specify the beginning and/or ending Web page(s), practitioners can have more control in generating patterns based on their preferences. With the normalized probability for SUPs, it is easy for practitioners to specify a probability threshold to identify the corresponding patterns. The experiments conducted using J.C.Penney's Web data show that different SUPs associated with different clusters of Web sessions have different characteristics. SUPs help to reveal the preferences of users when visiting the J. C. Penney's Web site in the corresponding clusters.

To extend this study, other clustering algorithms can be examined to identify the optimal algorithm in terms of efficiency and effectiveness. In addition, patterns in different clusters can be explored in more detail. Studies of information of these types will be valuable for Web owners, especially for e-commerce Website owners, to design their Web pages in order to target different user groups. Furthermore, by separating users into predefined clusters based on their current navigation patterns, further navigation behaviors can be predicted. This prediction of Web page usage could be extremely useful for cross sell or up sell in the e-commence environment. Future work can also examine sampling techniques for data post-sessionized so as to reduce the overhead of the pattern generation process.

Acknowledgements

The authors would like to thank Dr. Saad Mneimneh at Southern Methodist University for many useful discussions on this study. In addition, we also would like to thank J.C. Penney for providing the dataset for this research.

References

1. R. Agrawal and R. Srikant, "Mining Sequential Patterns", In Proc. 11 Intl. Conf. On Data Engineering, Taipi, Taiwan, March 1995.
2. A. G. Buchner, M. Baumgarten, S. S. Anand, M. D. Mulvenna, and J. G. Hughes, "Navigation Pattern Discovery From Internet Data", In Workshop on Web Usage Analysis and User Profiling, August 1999.
3. P. Berkhin, "Survey Of Clustering Data Mining Techniques", Accrue Software, Technical Report, 2002.
4. A. Banerjee, and J. Ghosh, "Clickstream Clustering using Weighted Longest Common Subsequences", in Proc. of the Workshop on Web Mining, SIAM Conference on Data Mining (Chicago IL, April 2001), 33-40.
5. J. Borges and M. Levene, "Data Mining of User Navigation Patterns", In Proc. the Workshop on Web Usage Analysis and User Profiling (WEBKDD'99), 31-36, San Diego, August 15, 1999.
6. J. Borges and M. Levene, "An average linear time algorithm for web data mining", International Journal of Information Technology and Decision Making, 3, (2004), 307-320.
7. I. V. Cadez, D. Heckerman, C. Meek, P. Smyth, and S. White, "Visualization of Navigation Patterns on a Web Site Using Model Based Clustering", Proc. of 6th ACM SIGKDD Intl' Conf. on Knowledge Discovery and Data Mining, 2000.

8. R. Cooley, B. Mobasher, and J. Srivastava, "Data preparation for mining world wide web browsing patterns", Knowledge and Information Systems, 1(1):5-32, 1999.
9. M-S Chen, J. S. Park, and P. S. Yu, "Efficient Data Mining for Path Traversal Patterns", IEEE Transactions on Knowledge and Data Engineering, 10(2):209-221, March/April, 1998.
10. M. H. Dunham, "Data Mining Introductory and Advanced Topics", Prentice-Hall, 2003.
11. Y. Fu, K. Sandhu, and M. Shih, "Clustering of web users based on access patterns", Workshop on Web Usage Analysis and User Profiling (WEBKDD99), August 1999.
12. A. Foss, W. Wang, and O. R. Zaïane, "A non-parametric approach to web log analysis", In Proc. of Workshop on Web Mining in First International SIAM Conference on Data Mining, 41-50, Chicago, April 2001.
13. S. Guha, R. Rastogi, and K. Shim, "ROCK: a robust clustering algorithm for categorical attributes", In ICDE, 1999.
14. Ş. Gündüz, M. T. Özsu, "A Web page prediction model based on click-stream tree representation of user behavior", Proceedings of the ninth ACM SIGKDD international conference on Knowledge discovery and data mining, Washington, D.C, August 24-27, 2003.
15. J. F. Hair, R. E. Andersen, R. L. Tatham, and W. C. Black, "Multivariate Data Analysis", Prentice Hall, New Jersey, 1998.
16. B. Hay, G. Wets and K. Vanhoof, "Clustering Navigation Patterns on a Website Using a Sequence Alignment Method", IJCAI's Workshop on Intelligent Techniques for Web Personalization, 2001
17. G. Karypis, E-H. Han, and V. Kumar, "Chameleon: A hierarchical clustering algorithm using dynamic modeling", IEEE Computer, 32(8):68-75, August 1999.
18. W. W. Moe, "Buying, Searching, or Browsing: Differentiating between Online Shoppers Using In-Store Navigational Clickstream", Journal of Consumer Psychology, 13 (1&2), 29-40, 2003.
19. J. Pei, J. Han, B. Mortazavi-Asl, and H. Zhu, "Mining Access Patterns Efficiently From Web Logs", In Proc. of Pacific Asia Conf. on Knowledge Discovery and Data Mining, pp592, Kyoto, Japan, April 2000.
20. J. Srivastava, R. Cooley, M. Deshpande and P. Tan, "Web Usage Mining: Discovery and Applications of Usage Patterns from Web Data", SIGKDD Explorations, 1(2):12--23, 2000.
21. Setubal, Meidanis, "Introduction to Computational Molecular Biology", PWS Publishing Company, 1997.
22. M. Spiliopoulou and C. Pohle, M. Teltzrow, "Modelling Web Site Usage with Sequences of Goal-Oriented Tasks", Multi-Konferenz Wirtschaftsinformatik 2002 vom 9.-11. September 2002 in Nürnberg.
23. W. Wang and O. R. Zaïane, "Clustering Web Sessions by Sequence Alignment", Third International Workshop on Management of Information on the Web in conjunction with 13th International Conference on Database and Expert Systems Applications DEXA'2002, pp 394-398, Aix en Provence, France, September 2-6, 2002.
24. Y-Q Xiao and M. H. Dunham, "Efficient mining of traversal patterns", Data and Knowledge Engineering, 39(2):191-214, November, 2001.
25. O. Nasraoui, H. Frigui, A. Joshi and R. Krishnapuram, "Mining Web Access Logs Using Relational Competitive Fuzzy Clustering," Proceedings of the Eighth International Fuzzy Systems Association Congress, Hsinchu, Taiwan, August 1999.
26. O. Nasraoui, H. Frigui, R. Krishnapuram and A. Joshi, "Extracting Web User Profiles Using Relational Competitive Fuzzy Clustering", International Journal on Artificial Intelligence Tools, Vol. 9, No. 4, pp. 509-526, 2000.

Using and Learning Semantics in Frequent Subgraph Mining

Bettina Berendt

Institute of Information Systems, Humboldt University Berlin,
D-10178 Berlin, Germany
http://www.wiwi.hu-berlin.de/~berendt

Abstract. The search for frequent subgraphs is becoming increasingly important in many application areas including Web mining and bioinformatics. Any use of graph structures in mining, however, should also take into account that it is essential to integrate background knowledge into the analysis, and that patterns must be studied at different levels of abstraction. To capture these needs, we propose to use taxonomies in mining and to extend frequency / support measures by the notion of context-induced interestingness. The AP-IP mining problem is to find all frequent abstract patterns and the individual patterns that constitute them and are therefore interesting in this context (even though they may be infrequent). The paper presents the fAP-IP algorithm that uses a taxonomy to search for the abstract and individual patterns, and that supports graph clustering to discover further structure in the individual patterns. Semantics are used as well as learned in this process. fAP-IP is implemented as an extension of Gaston (Nijssen & Kok, 2004), and it is complemented by the AP-IP visualization tool that allows the user to navigate through detail-and-context views of taxonomy context, pattern context, and transaction context. A case study of a real-life Web site shows the advantages of the proposed solutions.

ACM categories and subject descriptors and keywords: H.2.8 [**Database Management**]: Database Applications—*data mining*; H.5.4 [**Information Interfaces and Presentation**]: Hypertext/Hypermedia —*navigation, user issues*; graph mining; Web mining; background knowledge and semantics in mining.

1 Introduction

Background knowledge is an invaluable help in knowledge discovery. Examples include the use of ontologies for text mining and the exploitation of anchor texts for crawling, indexing, and ranking. In Web usage mining, background knowledge is needed because the raw data consist of administration-oriented URLs, whereas site owners and analysts are interested in events in the application domain.

In the past years, various algorithms for including background knowledge in mining have been proposed. In particular, the use of taxonomies in association rule, sequence, and graph mining has been investigated.

O. Nasraoui et al. (Eds.): WebKDD 2005, LNAI 4198, pp. 18–38, 2006.

In the raw data, each individual set, sequence, or graph of items is generally very infrequent. Relying on statistical measures of interestingness like support and confidence, the analyst either finds no patterns or a huge and unmanageable number. Taxonomies solve this problem and generally produce a much smaller number of patterns with high values of the statistical measures. In addition, they allow the analyst to enhance mining by semantic measures of interestingness.

A number of powerful algorithms and tools exist that can mine patterns determined by a wide range of measures. However, they ignore an important source of interestingness: taxonomic context. What is behind a frequent pattern—what types of individual items/behaviour constitute it, and how are they distributed (e.g., equally distributed or obeying Zipf's law)? To make patterns and their abstractions/individualizations visible, mining algorithms and tools must support a "drill-down" into patterns, and tools should provide simultaneous detail-and-context views on patterns. This provides for a structured and fine-grained view of data, and a highly focussed and sensitive monitoring of changes occurring in streams of data. Context-and-detail views are particularly valuable when patterns reveal a lot of structure, as in sequence or in graph mining.

The contributions of this paper are as follows: (1) We present fAP-IP (fast Abstract Pattern – Individual Pattern mining). The algorithm identifies statistically frequent patterns at an abstract level, and it gives the possibility of "drilling down" into these patterns to get detailed information about their typical individual instances. fAP-IP works on undirected or directed, node- and edge-labelled graph transactions; patterns are connected subgraphs. (2) We propose two simplifications to speed up individual-subgraph pattern identification. The first is applicable when transaction data have a bijective individual-label function, the second uses a graph representation that aggregates slightly over graph structure, but retains semantic information. (3) We introduce two different approaches to defining and identifying individual patterns: one that relies only on the taxonomy and one that relies on graph clustering. An optional pre-processing step identifies the conceptual structure of transactions, which may differ from the raw data graph structure on which other miners operate. (4) We present a visualization tool that allows the user to interact with the solution space by navigating in different semantic detail-and-context dimensions: taxonomy context (abstract patterns and individual patterns), pattern context (subpatterns and superpatterns), and transaction context (patterns and their embeddings). (5) We demonstrate the usefulness of the proposals by a case study that investigated navigation in a large real-world Web information portal.

The paper is organized as follows: Section 2 gives a short overview of related work. Section 3 identifies the mining problem, and Section 4 describes the algorithm. Section 5 illustrates the problem of conceptual transaction structure and the pre-processing steps used to solve it. Section 6 introduces the visualization tool, and Section 7 describes selected results from the case study. Section 8 concludes the paper and gives an outlook on future research.

2 Related Work

Frequent subgraph mining. The problem of frequent subgraph mining has been studied intensively in the past years, with many applications in bioinformatics/chemistry, computer vision and image and object retrieval, and Web mining. Algorithms are based on the a priori principle stating that a graph pattern can only be frequent in a set of transactions if all its subgraphs are also frequent. The main problem of frequent subgraph mining is that two essential steps involve expensive isomorphism tests: First, the same pattern candidate may be generated repeatedly and has to be compared to already generated candidates; second, the candidates have to be embedded in the transactions to compute support.

Several algorithms have been developed to discover arbitrary connected subgraphs. One research direction has been to explore ways of computing canonical labels for candidate graphs to speed up duplicate-candidate detection [19,28]. Various schemes have been proposed to reduce the number of generated duplicates [28,11]. In particular, candidates that are not in canonical form need not be developed and investigated further. The Gaston approach that leverages the fact that many graph patterns are in fact not full cyclic graphs but trees or even paths (which have simpler canonical forms) has been shown to be fastest on a number of datasets [23,27]. For a detailed discussion of the canonical-form approach and of commonalities and differences between the different algorithms, see [6]. For a detailed analysis of algorithm performance, see [27].

Other algorithms constrain the form of the sought subgraphs: [13,14] search for induced subgraphs (a pattern can only be embedded in a transaction if its nodes are connected by the same topology in the transaction as in the pattern). [29] focus on "relational graphs" (graphs with a bijective label function, see Section 4.1) with constraints on node connectivity.

Going beyond exact matching, [10] pre-process their data to find rings which they treat as special features and introduce wildcards for node labels, and [21] find "fuzzy chains", sequences with wildcards. A general form of structural abstraction us used by [15], who identify shared topological minors as patterns.

Taxonomies in frequent subgraph mining. Taxonomies have been used to find patterns at different levels of abstraction for differently-structured data. In [25,26], frequent itemsets / association rules and frequent sequences are identified at the lowest possible levels of a taxonomy. Concepts are chosen dynamically, which may lead to patterns linking concepts at different levels of abstraction (e.g., "People who bought 'Harry Potter 2' also bought 'books by Tolkien' "). Building on these ideas, [12] proposed an algorithm for finding frequent induced subgraphs at different levels of a taxonomy. However, the restriction to induced subgraphs poses problems for a number of domains. For example, in Web usage mining transactions (sessions) are highly idiosyncratic (an example is presented in Fig. 4 below), such that there are often many transactions that share a common subgraph as pattern, but that each have a different topology overlaid on the nodes of this pattern. For example, a chain of items may be part of different transactions, but in many of them, there are also additional links between the constituents of that chain, because some users made backward moves at different positions of the chain. Frequent induced subgraph mining would miss that pattern. A second problem of [25,26,12] was already mentioned in Section 1: the loss of taxonomic context brought about by finding only the least abstract subgraph that still exceeds the frequency threshold.

Taxonomies / ontologies and graphs in Web usage mining. In Web usage mining, the use of concepts abstracting from URLs is common (see [3] for an overview). The general idea is to map a URL to the most significant contents and/or services that are delivered by this page, expressed as concepts [5]. One page may be mapped to one or to a set of concepts. For example, it may be mapped to the set of all concepts and relations that appear in its query string [24]. Alternatively, keywords from the page's text and from the pages linked with it may be mapped to a domain ontology, with a general-purpose ontology like WordNet serving as an intermediary between the keywords found in the text and the concepts of the ontology [9].

The subsumption hierarchy of an existing ontology can be employed for the simultaneous description of user interests at different levels of abstraction as in [22]. In [7], a scheme is presented for aggregating towards more general concepts when an explicit taxonomy is missing. Clustering of sets of sessions identifies related concepts at different levels of abstraction. Sophisticated forms of content extraction are made possible by latent semantic models [16], from which taxonomies can be derived [8]. In [9], association rules, taxonomies, and document clustering are combined to generate concept-based recommendation sets. Some approaches use multiple taxonomies related to OLAP: objects (in this case, requests or requested URLs) are described along a number of dimensions, and concept hierarchies or lattices are formulated along each dimension to allow more abstract views [30].

Graph structures in Web navigation have been studied in single user sessions (e.g., [20]), in frequent tree mining (e.g., [31]), and in extensions of sequence mining [1].

3   The AP-IP Frequent Subgraph Mining Problem

Based on the requirements described in the Introduction, we formulate the **AP-IP mining problem**: Given a dataset of labelled-graph transactions, a taxonomy of concepts, a mapping from labels to concepts, and a minimum support threshold, find all *frequent abstract subgraphs* (at the concept level, above the minimum-support threshold, also called APs or abstract patterns) and their corresponding *AP-frequent individual subgraphs* (at the individual-label level, may be below the threshold, also called IPs or individual patterns).

An example shows the role of abstract and individual patterns: If 10% of the transactions contain the path *(Harry Potter 1, Lord of the Rings)*, 5% contain *(Harry Potter 2, The Hobbit)*, and 7% contain *(Harry Potter 1, Lord of the Rings, The Hobbit, Harry*

Potter 2) (all sets disjoint), and the minimal support is 20%, then *(Rowlings book, Tolkien book)* has support 22% and is a frequent abstract pattern. Its AP-frequent individual patterns are *(Harry Potter 1, Lord of the Rings)* (17%) and *(Harry Potter 2, The Hobbit)* (12%).

Notation I: Mining input (a) a dataset $D = \{G^d\}$ of graph transactions $G^d = (V^d, E^d, l^d)$, where each G^d consists of a finite set of nodes V^d, a set of edges E^d, and labels from a set I given by $l^d : V^d \cup E^d \mapsto I$; (b) a taxonomy T consisting of concepts from a set C; (c) a mapping to abstract concepts $ac : I \mapsto C$; (d) $minsupp \in [0, 1]$.

Definition 1. *An abstract subgraph is a connected graph $G^a = (V, E, l^a)$ consisting of a finite set of nodes V, a set of edges E, and labels given by $l^a : V \cup E \mapsto C$. A **frequent abstract subgraph** is one that can be embedded in at least* minsupp $\times |D|$ *transactions.*

*An **AP-frequent individual subgraph** is defined as follows: (a) It is a graph $G^i = (V', E', l^i)$ with labels given by $l^i : V' \cup E' \mapsto I$. (b) There exists a frequent abstract subgraph G^a such that the graph $G'' = (V', E', ac \circ l^i)$ with labels given by $ac \circ l^i(v') = ac(l^i(v'))$ and $ac \circ l^i(e') = ac(l^i(e'))$, is an automorphism of G^a. G'' is also called the **abstraction** of G^i with respect to T and ac. (c) G^i can be embedded in at least one transaction of D.*

G^a can be embedded in a transaction $d \in D$ if there is an AP-frequent individual subgraph G^i whose abstraction is automorphic to G^a, and which can be embedded in d.

4   The fAP-IP Algorithm

fAP-IP ("fast AP-IP miner") consists of two graph-processing modules:

(1) A standard frequent-subgraph miner operates on the transaction data abstracted according to the taxonomy. Following the apriori principle, this miner extends frequent patterns of size $k - 1$ by frequent patterns of size 1 (frequent edges) in order to generate the candidates of size k. The miner relies on canonical forms to avoid (as much as possible) the generation of duplicate pattern candidates. The algorithm identifies and counts each unique candidate's embeddings in the data, and adds the candidate to the set of frequent patterns if the number of embeddings exceeds the required threshold.

Patterns can be grown in breadth-first or in depth-first order. Depth-first is more economical on space, which was an important consideration for handling the large numbers of patterns arising in AP-IP mining. From the set of existing depth-first miners, Gaston [23] was chosen because of the very good performance of this algorithm, in particular on datasets that have many path- or tree-shaped patterns (this is often the case in the application domain Web usage mining). Of Gaston's two forms, we chose the one in which embeddings are re-computed (instead of stored), because the alternative, while somewhat faster, required far too much memory to handle even small datasets in our domain.

The resulting algorithm *fAP-IP* is shown in the table below. Its lines 1–3 and 7–8 constitute the procedure *DFGraphMiner* of [23]. Lines 4–6 were added, and D is treated differently (signature and support constraint in line 7 of fAP-IP). For details of *DFGraphMiner*, including completeness proofs, the reader is referred to [23]. Mining starts by considering the frequent edges as graphs G.

(2) During the examination of the embeddings, each embedding is analyzed further in its individual-label form. In general, there is an n:1 mapping from embeddings to IP-frequent graphs. This is shown in the procedure *ip-gen*.

Notation II: Graphs. A graph G (simplified for G^a in Section 3) can be extended by adding a forward edge to a new node (node refinement), or by adding a backward edge that connects nodes that were already connected by a path (cycle-closing refinement). An operation to refine a graph is called a leg. A node refining leg for a graph $G = (V, E, l)$ consists of a node in V, an edge label, and a node label. A cycle closing refining leg consists of two different nodes in V and an edge label. The refinement operator $\rho(G, leg)$ refines a graph G by adding leg *leg*.

G.viCode denotes a code based on vertex invariants. We use a lexicographically sorted list of node labels and degrees; this list can also be enriched by edge labels.

leg (L) is a leg (set of legs). *cip* (candidate individual pattern) and *fip* (AP-frequent individual pattern, in the set FIP) are graphs (G^i in Section 3). t is a transaction ID. The set of transactions into which a pattern can be embedded is called its TID list.

$D^a(T, ac) = \{(V, E, l^a) | G = (V, E, l^i) \in D, \forall x \in V \cup E : l^a(x) = ac(l^i(x))\}$ is the set of abstracted transactions, i.e. all labels are coarsened according to the taxonomy T and the mapping function ac.

Graph codes and canonical graph codes are defined as in [23]: (a) for a path (a graph in which two nodes have degree 1, and all other nodes have degree 2): the sequence of node labels and edge labels, starting from one of the two nodes with degree 1. The canonical label is the lexicographically smaller of the two possible sequences. (b) for a free tree (a graph without cycles): a depth sequence obtained by a depth-first traversal, which is a sequence of (node depth, ingoing edge label, node label) tuples. The canonical label is the lexicographically largest of all possible depth sequences. (c) for a cyclic graph (all other graphs): the concatenation of (i) the code for the tree from which this graph was grown (this tree is a spanning tree of the graph) and (ii) a sequence of (v_i, v_j, label) tuples that defines two nodes $v_i < v_j$ connected by an edge through a cycle-closing refinement. The canonical label is the lexicographically smallest of all possible codes.

Algorithm. fAP-IP (G, leg, L, D, T, ac)

1: $G' \leftarrow \rho(G, leg)$
2: **if** G' is not canonical **then return**
3: output graph G'
4: $FIP \leftarrow \emptyset$
5: **for each** embedding *em* of G' in TID t **do** ip-gen(em, t, FIP)
6: **for each** $fip \in FIP$ **do** output *fip*
7: $L' \leftarrow \{leg' \mid leg'$ is a necessary leg of G', $support(\rho(G', leg'), D^a(T, ac)) \geq minsupp$,
       $leg' \in L$, or leg' is a node refinement$\}$
8: **for all** $leg' \in L'$ **do** fAP-IP(G', leg', L', D, T, ac)

Procedure. ip-gen(cip, t, FIP)

---

1.   **if** cip is a known automorphism of a graph G in FIP **then**
2. $G.TidList \leftarrow G.TidList \cup \{t\}$
3.   **return**
4.   **if** cip is automorphic to a graph G in FIP with $G.viCode = cip.viCode$ **then**
5. $G.TidList \leftarrow G.TidList \cup \{t\}$
6.   **return**
7. $cip.TidList \leftarrow \{t\}$
8. $FIP \leftarrow FIP \cup \{cip\}$

The general steps of frequent subgraph mining have to be performed both for APs and IPs. AP candidate generation, support counting, and duplicate pruning are performed in fAP-IP, steps 2., 7., and 8.

IP candidate generation happens in step 5. of the main algorithm, **IP duplicate pruning** in steps 1. and 4. of ip-gen (only new candidates are added to the list of AP-frequent IPs in line 8.). Some optimization steps are not applicable here. In particular, non-canonical APs can be pruned because the growing procedure guarantees that the canonical form of the same graph will also be found (fAP-IP, step 2). This is not possible for IPs—depending on the individual labels and topology, we might never encounter any embedding that is in canonical form. Instead, in principle each candidate must be mapped to its canonical form, and a list of all canonical forms (IPs) must be maintained while one AP is analyzed. Canonical form definition and computation relies on Gaston's basic logic and code, with chains, trees, and cyclic graphs each using their own canonical form (see [23] for details).

However, not every candidate's canonical form needs to be computed: If the inspected graph is a known automorphism, transformation has already been done. In that case, we simply increment counts (ip-gen, steps 1–3, see also [19]). If the graph has not been encountered before, but there are IPs that *could* match it (identical vertex invariants, see step 4.), it is transformed into its canonical form to check whether the two *do* match, and if this is the case, assigned as a newly found automorphism to the known IP (steps 4–6). If both tests fail, the candidate is indeed a new IP (steps 7–8).

IP support counting occurs by the addition of each transaction ID in which the candidate occurs in lines 2., 5., and 7. Each candidate is regarded as a subgraph/subset of a transaction and therefore only counted once. IP support pruning is not necessary, because only IPs with at least one occurrence in the data are found, and IPs' minimum frequency is by definition 1.

Size pruning. A maximal pattern size can be set; in that case, the recursion in step 8. of the main algorithm is only entered if that pattern size is not exceeded (not shown in the pseudocode).

fAP-IP is complete: Gaston finds all frequent APs (see [23]), and all AP-frequent IPs are found because each of them must, by definition, have at least one embedding, and all embeddings are inspected.

The main problem is situated in step 4. of ip-gen: the computation of a canonical form, i.e., an isomorphism check that in the general case cannot be performed efficiently. Two solutions are possible: a search for special classes of graphs or transactions that allow an efficient computation, or the relaxation of ip-gen's goal of partitioning the set of embeddings by the full information of graph structure and labels. Three strategies for doing this will be described next.

4.1   Simplification 1 for Data with Bijective Label Functions

In many domains, an individual (node) label either occurs in a transaction once, or not at all. For example, in Web usage mining, sessions are usually modelled as either including visit(s) to a particular page or not; so there is at most one node in the graph with that page's label. Such modelling gives rise to a special class of graph transactions: The mapping from nodes to labels is bijective. For simplicity, if several edges join one node to another, they are treated as one.

In this case, a canonical code can be used for all graphs that, in the general case, is simpler and cheaper to compute than the forms explained above: a lexicographically sorted list of edges described by the two node labels and the edge label. Sorting can be done efficiently, speeding up step 4. of ip-gen.

4.2   Simplification 2: Grouping Based on Vertex Invariants

As outline above, several IPs may have the same set of node and edge labels and degrees. To take a simple example, the two distinct graphs $a - b - a - a - a$ and $a - a - b - a - a$ can both be described as $[(a,1),(a,1),(a,2),(a,2),(b,2)]$. If both a and b map to the same concept c, the common AP is a path involving 5 instances of this concept c.

Depending on the domain and analysis question, this coarsened form may already bear enough information to describe commonalities and differences between different AP instances. In particular, node label and degree illustrate what is present (or not), and the role of items or concepts (an endpoint of a pattern if the degree is 1, or a hub if the degree is high).

This leads to a second simplification, a graph code applicable for all types of label functions: the lexicographically sorted pairs of (node label,node degree), plus optionally edge labels. In step 4. of ip-gen, the simplification implies that only the vertex invariants for $cip.viCode$ need to be computed, there is no test for automorphism. Again, sorting can be done efficiently.

4.3   Graph Clustering for Finding Individual Patterns

The notion of AP-frequent subgraphs rests on differentiating between all possible individual-level instances of an abstract pattern. However, this can lead to a large variety of patterns. Even for undirected, not-edge-labelled graphs, an AP with n nodes that are concepts with an average branching factor of b can give rise to up to b^n IPs. As the case study below demonstrates, there are indeed very many IPs even for comparatively sparse transaction data, if the branching factor is high (as for example in Web usage mining on requests to database-fed Web sites). While the APs already define a structure on these many patterns, the question arises whether it is possible to identify more structure within one AP.

One answer is to carry simplification 2 further by treating each graph *cip* as a bag of items. This bag is available in all forms of ip-gen (it is simply the set of labels of the embedding's nodes V). By clustering these bags, we can obtain a high-level grouping of the graphs based on their content (and, if desired, salient structural properties). The clusters are an alternative form of IPs.

To enable this form of graph clustering, the basic representation (a set of graphs, each described by a bag of items) must be enriched with further information. For example, an item-item distance matrix may be derived from the taxonomy or from other information sources. An alternative is to decompose each item into a feature vector of information tokens, and to treat each graph as the sum of all its item feature vectors. Alternatively or in addition, each item may be enriched by further information. Examples of such decompositions and enrichments in Web usage mining on whole sessions are given in Section 2. Clustering may be partition-based or hierarchical to reveal further structure.

All three forms *use* background knowledge / semantics to enable the clustering algorithm to form groups, but also in all three forms semantics are *learned* in the sense that actually existing instantiations of a particular template (here defined by the graph structure) are discovered. In Web usage mining, this learning identifies composite application events—behavioural patterns in the data [3].

4.4 Time and Space Requirements

Theoretical evaluation. fAP-IP's time and space worst-case requirements are determined by (a) the size of the dataset, and (b) the number, (c) diversity, and (d) size of patterns. Other factors have indirect influences on these magnitudes; in particular, a lower support threshold or a larger concept branching factor generally lead to more, more diverse, and/or longer patterns. However, more data also often lead to more patterns, and more patterns are often longer patterns.

Described very briefly, the following influences are expected on time (over and above the requirements of Gaston, which are described in [23]):

Each embedding of an AP causes one call of ip-gen. The test in line 1. is a hashtable lookup taking constant time. The mapping to a canonical form in line 4. only occurs for some of the embeddings; its worst-case complexity is exponential in pattern size in the general case, but $O(n \, log \, n)$, with n being pattern size, for either of the simplifications (Sections 4.1–4.3). The set updates (remaining lines) take constant time. This determines the expected effect of (d) pattern size. It also shows that the time needed for processing an embedding depends neither on data set size nor on the number of patterns.

If (a) only the number of transactions increases and all other factors remain equal, the number of embeddings to be considered grows proportional to the number of transactions; therefore, a linear dependence is expected. The same reasoning holds if (b) only the number of patterns increases and the number of embeddings increases proportional to them, or (c) the diversity of patterns (= the number of IPs per AP, or the number of ways in which the same pattern is embedded in the data) increases.

Space requirements include an overhead determined by the size of the dataset. Of the APs, only the current one is held in main memory. In addition, all IPs associated with the current AP, and all their encountered automorphisms, are stored. Space requirements for each IP are linear in the number of nodes if only node labels are abstracted, or linear in the number of nodes + number of edges if edge labels are also abstracted.

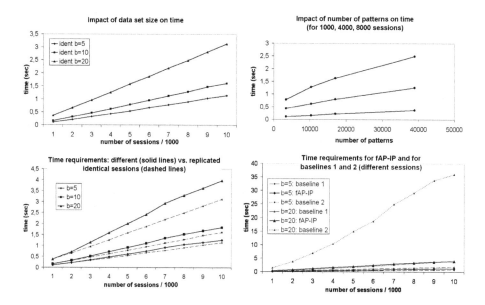

Fig. 1. Simulated navigation data. *Top (a), (b):* Impact of data set size and number of patterns in isolation; $pS = 0.8$; $pL = 0.05$; $minsupp = 0.05$; *Bottom (c):* Combined impact of data set size and number of patterns; same parameters. *(d):* The cost of context-induced interestingness (see text for details).

Experiments. To investigate actual performance, simulated and real data were analyzed. For reasons of space, this section focusses on performance of simplification 1 on simulated data tailored to the domain Web usage mining, and on performance of the base form and simplification 2 on a standard chemical-compounds dataset. In Section 7, application-oriented results with respect to real data are described. (Main performance results were similar.) All experiments focussed on the semantic abstraction of node labels (i.e., the edge label abstraction mapping was the identity function).

fAP-IP was implemented in C++ using the STL and compiled with the -o3 compilation flag, extending the code of Gaston 1.1 RE (obtained from http://-hms.liacs.nl). It was run on a Pentium 4 3GHz processor, 1GB main memory PC under Debian Linux. For simplicity, the simulated data were generated by

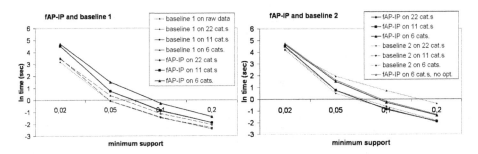

Fig. 2. PTE dataset: the cost of context-induced interestingness (see text for details)

first-order Markov models (see e.g. [16]), under variation of the number of trans-
actions/sessions, the branching factor b of the concepts in a one-level taxonomy
(and thus the number of patterns found in a total of 100 "URLs"), the diversity of patterns (each node had a parameterized transition probability pS to one
other, randomly chosen node and an equal distribution of transition probabilities
to all other nodes), and the length of patterns (the transition probability pL to
"exit"—average session length becomes $1/pL$, and pattern length increases with
it). Parameter values reflected the properties of real Web usage data. To obtain
sufficient numbers and diversity of patterns, data were modelled as undirected
graphs with constant edge labels.

First, the influence of data set size and number of patterns were studied in
isolation: 1000 sessions were duplicated to generate 2000 sessions with the same
number of patterns, concatenated 3 times to generate 3000 sessions, etc. Figure
1 (a) shows that time is linear in data set size, and that the slope increases with
the number of patterns (induced by increasing the concept branching factor).
Figure 1 (b) plots the same data (plus one run with an intermediate branching
factor) by the number of patterns, keeping the number of sessions constant
along each line. It shows that in this setting, time is sublinear in the number of
patterns. Figure 1 (c) shows the combined effects. It compares the mere addition
of new transactions (data from (a)) with the addition of transactions with more
patterns, and it shows that the algorithm still scales linearly with data set size.

Similar graphs were obtained for a wide variety of parameter settings and
for real data. Runtime increased with average pattern size (slightly more than
linearly), but remained linear in dataset size. This is essential for most domains,
in which average pattern size is stable, but datasets are huge and growing.

Performance costs of context-induced interestingness. The performance of fAP-
IP cannot be directly compared to that of existing frequent subgraph mining
(FSG) algorithms, because the algorithms do something different. However, it is
possible to measure the cost of mining at different semantic levels by comparing
fAP-IP to its underlying FSG miner in a number of baseline settings.

The cost measure consists of two parts: (i) the cost of additional interesting
patterns: the time needed by fAP-IP for finding all n_1 frequent APs and all
n_2 AP-frequent IPs, minus the time needed by the underlying FSG miner for

finding the same n_1 frequent APs ("baseline 1"). (ii) the cost of finding patterns with semantic structure: the time needed by fAP-IP as in (i), compared to the time needed by the underlying FSG miner for finding $(n_1 + n_2)$ frequent patterns (APs) ("baseline 2"). Baseline 1 is a lower bound on fAP-IP because the involved operations are a strict subset of the operations involved in fAP-IP. Baseline 2 must take longer than baseline 1, but there is no definitional upper-bound or lower-bound relation to fAP-IP.

Since the underlying miner is Gaston, the two baselines were computed in Gaston, using $D^a(T, ac)$ as data input. Baseline 1 used the same support threshold as the fAP-IP run. Baseline 2 used a lower support threshold determined as follows: If fAP-IP returned x patterns at the chosen support threshold, support in Gaston was lowered to a value s that returned $x' \leq x$ patterns, with the next-lowest value $s - incr(s)$ returning $x'' > x$ patterns. (This procedure often led to x' that were considerably smaller than x; we therefore regard it as a "conservative" version of baseline 2.)

Figure 1 (d) shows the comparison for two of the settings (branching factor 5 or 20) in (c). Comparing fAP-IP with baselines 1 and 2, one sees that while fAP-IP does need more time, and the difference increases with the number of IPs, the additional time needed is very small compared to the additional time needed to find the same number of interesting patterns in the conventional way. Expressed differently, there is a (positive) cost of additional interesting patterns, but the cost of finding patterns with semantic structure is actually negative.

Figure 2 (a) shows the performance of fAP-IP on a standard dataset, the 340 PTE chemical compounds (http://web.comlab.ox.ac.uk/oucl/research/-areas/machlearn/PTE), for the commonly investigated support values, see e.g., [23,12]. To strike a balance between comparability with the artificial data described above and previous research (the PTE data were used in [12] with a taxonomy not described in that paper), we formulated 3 taxonomies that do not reflect domain knowledge, but take into account the frequency distribution of the 66 atoms in the dataset. The 66 atoms were grouped into 22, 11, and 6 categories, with the category given by the atom's number (in the PTE representation available in the Gaston distribution) modulo the total number of categories.

fAP-IP was compared to the same two baselines as before. It cannot be directly compared to [12] because the latter finds only least-abstract frequent patterns, and because it is restricted to induced subgraphs. Figure 2 (a) shows the time requirements of baseline 1, and (b) shows the time requirements of baseline 2. The solid lines are equal in both figures, they show the performance of fAP-IP with simplification 2. In addition, (a) shows baseline 1 performance on the raw dataset D (i.e., all frequent IPs are found, not all frequent APs), and (b) shows the performance of fAP-IP for 6 categories without the optimization by simplification 2. Times were equal for 22 and 11 categories because in these cases, there was little more than 1 IP per AP. For the same reason, times were also equal for fAP-IP on 22 and 11 categories without the optimization by simplification 2; to increase clarity, the lines were removed from the figures. The general observation is similar as in Fig. 1: for most settings, the cost of additional interesting patterns is positive, but the cost of semantic structure on interesting patterns is negative. However, in these experiments with a small dataset and large pattern sizes, performance relative to baseline 2 deteriorates as support decreases and the number of patterns increases.

In all examined settings, the program required 2-2.5MB main memory.

A performance analysis of fAP-IP with graph clustering was not performed because at present, clustering is done by an external system call to the WEKA package (http://www.cs.waikato.ac.nz/ml/weka). Consequently, requirements depend on the WEKA algorithm and parameters chosen.

5   Pre-processing: Graph Partitioning for Finding Conceptual Transaction Structure

In a number of domains, differently-named nodes at the individual level can be synonymous for the purposes of an analysis. For example, in Web navigation data, the raw data give rise a graph that has one node per distinct URL in the access log. However, this graph may not be an adequate representation of the conceptual structure of navigation in the following sense:

Consider a visitor who visited the following medical Web pages: *[text for diagnosis A, text for diagnosis B, text for diagnosis C, picture for diagnosis A]*. Viewed as a structure on concepts, did this visitor request (a) a chain of four different instances of the general "diagnosis" concept, or (b) a ring involving three distinct instances of the general "diagnosis" concept, with the visitor returning to the first concept? We found that for many applications, (b) is a more adequate model of the original sequence.

To allow for mining according to interpretation (b), the following steps are applied: (i) For each node in the raw data, the concept in the taxonomy is identified which makes the distinctions necessary for the analysis at hand (but no further distinctions). We call these *base concepts*. (ii) The original raw-data graph is partitioned by collapsing all nodes that map to the same base concept to one node, and collapsing the edges in turn.

Formally, we add to the concept-mapping function $ac : I \mapsto C$ (see Section 3) the base concept function $bc : I \mapsto C$.[1] $bc(l^i(v))$ can be identical to $ac(l^i(v))$ for a node v, or any child of $ac(l^i(v))$ in T. This gives rise to

Definition 2. *Given a graph $G^d = (V^d, E^d, l^d)$ from the raw dataset D and the concept-mapping function bc, the* **conceptual transaction structure** *$G^p(G^d) = (V^p, E^p, l^p)$ is defined as follows:*

(1) $V^p = \{v^p | \exists v^d \in V^d \text{ with } bc(l^i(v))) = l^p(v^p)\}$,
(2) $E^p = \{(v_1^p, v_2^p) | \exists (v_1^d, v_2^d) \in E^d \text{ with } bc(l^i(v_1^d)) = l^p(v_1^p), bc(l^i(v_2^d)) = l^p(v_2^p)\}$.
If self-loops are excluded, all edges $e' = (v', v')$ are removed.

---

[1] To make the formalism more portable across datasets, one could instead use a function that maps an item label to to its finest-level concept $lc : I \mapsto C$, and define both ac and bc as mapping this element to a concept. The present shortcut was used to simplify notation. For the same reason, abstractions of edge labels were disregarded.

For mining, each graph in the dataset of transactions D is replaced by its conceptual transaction structure. Frequent subgraphs are defined as in Def. 1, with I replaced by C and l^i by l^p.

This preprocessing step may alter the graph topology of the input data and thus determines which subgraphs *can* be (AP-)frequent. It uses semantics to describe which base concept graphs exist. In contrast, AP-IP mining does not alter graph topology: It groups (individual) subgraphs that are isomorphic and that map to the same abstract and frequent subgraph. It uses semantics to identify which graphs are (AP-)frequent and therefore interesting. Both steps may be necessary to understand patterns at a conceptual level.

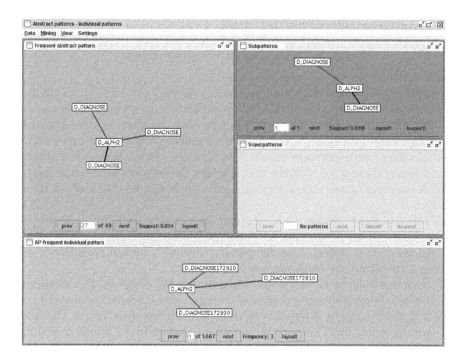

Fig. 3. Visualization of taxonomy context and pattern context

6   AP-IP Visualization

The AP-IP visualization tool is a front end for fAP-IP. It is implemented in Java and allows the user to navigate along the different dimensions of different semantic detail-and-context dimensions: taxonomy context (abstract patterns and individual patterns), pattern context (subpatterns and superpatterns), and transaction context (patterns and their embeddings).

Figure 3 shows a screenshot of the pattern part when transactions and subgraphs are modelled as undirected graphs: When a dataset has been loaded, the mining parameters have been specified, and the result has been computed,

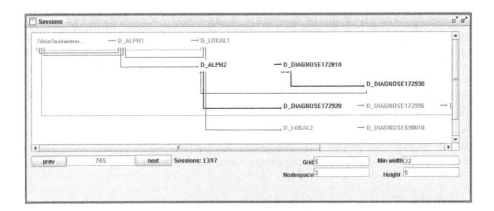

Fig. 4. Visualization of transaction context

the first frequent abstract pattern appears in the top left window. In the bottom window, the first associated AP-frequent individual pattern is shown, and all other IPs can be browsed or searched by their number. IPs are sorted by frequency; user tests showed that absolute frequency values were easier to understand than relative support values. The "Cluster" option below the "Mining" main-menu entry starts a dialogue that specifies the preprocessing script and the WEKA command line. The clustering results appear in textual form in the IP window.

In the top right windows, the abstract subpatterns and superpatterns are shown (only a part of the full AP lattice is shown: the spanning tree of the pattern generation order). The rightmost, "Inspect!" button transfers a sub- / superpattern into the main window.

Transaction context is shown in a separate window (Fig. 4). This shows the full context, allowing a representation of transactions as directed multigraphs (as shown in the figure), or alternatively as their spanning trees, and it highlights the embedded pattern. This part of the tool is based on ISM (Individualised Site Maps [2,4]) which was created specifically to visualize single sessions for Web usage mining. Depending on the requirements of the domain, other visualization options may be more adequate; this will be explored in future work.

7   Case Study

7.1   Data

Navigation data from a large and heavily frequented eHealth information site were investigated. The site offers different searching and browsing options to access a database of diagnoses (roughly corresponding to products in an eCommerce product catalog). Each diagnosis has a number of different information modes (textual description, pictures, and further links), and diagnoses are hyperlinked via a medical ontology (links go to differential diagnoses). The interface is

identical for each diagnosis, and it is identical in each language that the site offers
(at the time of data collection: English, Spanish, Portuguese, and German).

The initial data set consisted of close to 4 million requests collected in the
site's server log between November 2001 and November 2002. In order to investigate the impact of language and culture on (sequential) search and navigation
behaviour, the log was partitioned into accesses by country, and the usual data
preprocessing steps were applied [18]. For the present study, the log partition
containing accesses from France was chosen as the sample log; the other country
logs of the same size exhibited the same patterns, differing only in the support
values. The sample log consisted of 20333 requests in 1397 sessions. The concept
hierarchy and mappings ac and bc developed for [18] were used.

Mining was performed on a base concept graph: All types of information on
a diagnosis X were mapped to the base concept "information on X", and the
search functions were mapped to their abstract values ("LOKAL1" = first step of
location search, etc.). The remaining URLs were mapped to their corresponding
leaf concepts in the taxonomy.[2]

7.2   Results

Basic statistics. The log is an example of concepts corresponding to a high
number of individual URLs (84 concepts with, on average, 82 individual URLs),
and highly diverse behaviour at the individual level. This is reflected in a high
ratio of the number of IPs to APs (compared to the simulated data above):
At a support value of 0.2, there were 7 frequent APs of sizes 1–5 with 55603
AP-frequent IPs, at 0.1, the values were: sizes 1–8, 34 APs, 414685 IPs; at 0.05,
the values for $K = 6$ were: 104 APs, 297466 IPs. This search was not extended
because no further (semantically) interesting patterns were found.

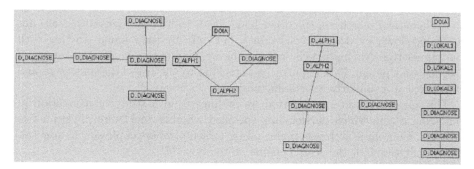

Fig. 5. Selected frequent abstract patterns

Chains of diagnoses were the most frequent patterns: a chain of 6 diagnoses
had support 7.2% (5: 9.2%, 4: 13%, 3: 18.9%). In addition, patterns with 3 or

---

[2] Graph partitioning is simple for log data: The raw data are scanned, and each label
l^i is replaced by $bc(l^i)$. The routine that establishes the graph structure of D works
on this transformed log.

more other diagnoses branching off the "hub" diagnosis as shown at the left of Fig. 5 (support 5.3%) were frequent. Rings also occurred at slightly lower support thresholds (see Fig. 5, second from left).

Search options: linear vs. hub-and-spoke. Patterns illustrated the use of different search options.

The internal search engine appeared only in very few patterns (only in 2-node patterns: 4.2% for search-engine and a diagnosis, 3.5% for search-engine and alphabetical search—probably a subsequent switch to the second, more popular search option). This was because the search engine was less popular than the other search options (used about 1/10 as often), but far more efficient in the sense that searches generally ended after the first diagnosis found (assuming that finding a diagnosis was the goal of all search sessions). This is consistent with results from our other studies of search behaviour [1].

The alphabetical search option generally prompted a "hub-and-spoke naviga-tion", as shown on the right of Fig. 5 (support 6.4%) or in Fig. 3. In contrast, location search generally proceeded in a linear or depth-first fashion, as shown on the far right of Fig. 5 (support 5%; with one diagnosis less: 6.9%).

This may be interpreted as follows: Location search prompts the user to spec-ify, on a clickable map, the body parts that contain the sought disease. This is in itself a search that can be refined (LOKAL1 – LOKAL2 in the figure; a similar pattern of LOKAL1 – LOKAL2 – LOKAL3, followed by 2 diagnoses, had a support of 5.1%). This narrowing-down of the medical problem by an as-pect of its surface symptoms (location on the body) helps the user to identify one approximately correct diagnosis and to find the correct one, or further ones, by retaining the focus on symptoms and finding further diagnoses by following the differential-diagnosis links. Thus, non-expert users in particular can focus on surface features that have meaning in the domain, and they can acquire some medical knowledge in the process.

Alphabetical search, on the other hand, leads to lists of diseases that are not narrowed down by domain constraints, but only by their name starting with the same letter. Navigation choices may be wrong due to a mistaken memory of the disease's name. This requires backtracking to the list-of-diseases page and the choice of a similarly-named diagnosis.

This interpretation is supported by findings from a study of navigation in the same site in which participants specified whether they were physicians or patients. Content search was preferred by patients, whereas physicians used al-phabetical search or the search engine more often [17].

Investigation of the most frequent individual patterns in alphabetical search showed a possible effect of layout: the top-level page of diagnoses starting with "A" was the most frequent entrypoint. This pattern can help to filter out accesses of "people just browsing" in order to focus further search for patterns on more directed information search.

Investigation of the most frequent individual patterns in location-based search showed that the combination of the human head as the location of the illness and a diagnosis which is visually prominently placed on the result page was most frequent. This possible effect of layout on navigation is one example of patterns that can be detected by fAP-IP but would have gone unnoticed otherwise because the individual pattern itself was below the statistical threshold.

Transaction context may give further insights into individual users', or user groups', behaviour. An example is the resumption of alphabetical search after an apparently fruitless location-based search in Fig. 4.

The temporal interpretation, as shown in the top-to-bottom ordering in Fig. 5, is justified by site topology (one cannot go from a diagnosis to coarser and coarser search options, unless by backtracking). The temporal interpretation of "backtracking and going to another diagnosis" is likewise justified by site topology, but the left-to-right ordering of diagnoses in the figure is arbitrary.

Note also that there may be an arbitrary number of steps between the transition from the ALPH node in Fig. 5 to the first diagnosis and the transition from the ALPH node to the second (or third) diagnosis. This intentional abstraction from time serves to better underline the "hub" nature of the ALPH page as a conceptual centre of navigation.

Results of graph clustering. Figure 3 reveals a very high number of individual patterns, an observation that was commonly made in these data: Individual patterns with frequency = 1 constituted 99% of all patterns. The reasons are the very large database behind the Web site and the highly idiosyncratic information needs of its users; they make the request for each data record (and for each set of data records) very infrequent.

To obtain coarser and more meaningful groupings of the data, each URL was enriched by the ICD-9 (International Classification of Diseases, http://icd9cm.-chrisendres.com) top-level group it referred to. Query mining that based the feature-space representation of patterns on URLs was used for two reasons that also apply in many other Web-server log analyses: First, to understand what visitors were looking for rather than what they obtained (often, empty result sets), and second, because URLs were much more amenable to semantic analysis than their corresponding Web pages, which often consisted of pictorial material with very heterogeneous characteristics. A domain-specific ontology (ICD-9) was chosen instead of a general-purpose ontology like WordNet to support domain-relevant interpretations and avoid spurious similarities based on linguistic choices unrelated to medical information content.

Clustering used the EM algorithm, the number of clusters was not specified ex ante. Across APs, 2–7 clusters were returned, a much more manageable result set size. For example, the AP shown in Fig. 3 gave rise to 1667 graph IPs with a maximal frequency of 3, and 6 clusters with a minimum probability of 12%.

Regardless of search option (= across all APs like the rightmost two in Fig. 5), a small but distinct subgroup of patterns emerged that involved 'socially embarrassing' diseases and nothing else (cluster probability < 10%), indicating a high social value of the site as an anonymous first point of information.

Another result concerned diseases from the ICD-9 category "injury and poisoning"—these were associated much more often with alphabetic search than with location-based search (mean values AS: 0.57 in a cluster representing 17%

of patterns vs. LBS: 0.06 or 0.09 in all clusters). In addition, they characterized important clusters within longer chains of diagnoses (e.g., 5 diagnoses: mean 0.89 in a cluster with probability 51%). These findings indicate that these diagnoses could not be retrieved otherwise because poisoning often has no circumscribed symptomatic location on the body, and that it causes longer search histories towards the desired information. Combined with the result that alphabetic search is less suitable for patients, this suggests that alternative search options such as Q+A dialogues should be developed for location-unspecific diseases.

8   Conclusions and Outlook

We have described a new mining problem, the AP-IP mining problem, and the fAP-IP algorithm that solves it. fAP-IP uses a taxonomy and searches for frequent patterns at an abstract level, but also returns the individual subgraphs constituting them. This is motivated by the context-induced interestingness of these individual subgraphs: While they generally occur far more seldom than a chosen support threshold, they are interesting as instantiations of the frequent abstract patterns.

We have proposed the use of graph partitioning and graph clustering as semantic pre- or postprocessing steps that help to focus on fewer and more interesting patterns.

The clustering approach has the advantage that it can refer to different taxonomies simultaneously, that it can take into account further semantic information, that different distance measures and partition-based and hierarchical clustering schemes can be employed, and that grouping within an AP can be as coarse or as fine as required. While the use of the full taxonomy (and thus a hierarchical structure within an AP) is in principle also possible when analyzing IPs with their graph structure, clustering affords greater flexibility and may avoid some problems of search space explosion. However, further research is needed to explore adequate measures of cluster interestingness.

Another very promising approach for further abstraction was suggested by an inspection of single transactions. Rings of diagnoses in our log often contained "other" contents such as navigation/search pages in between. This calls for wildcards as in [10] or topological abstraction as in [15].

For an adequate interpretation of results, one has to deal with pattern overlap. fAP-IP focusses—like other pattern discovery algorithms—on finding all patterns that are present in a data set. Each AP is counted only once for each transaction in which it can be embedded (also if it can be embedded in different ways), and likewise each IP is counted at most once per transaction. However, for one AP and one transaction, different IPs may occur in that transaction. This is in line with the idea of finding all IPs, i.e. of doing complete pattern discovery at the IP level: Each search episode (etc.) that can be abstracted to an AP is potentially interesting. If two patterns share a common subgraph, the occurrences of these patterns (their embeddings into a transaction) can overlap or be disjoint. Different APs can overlap, and so can different IPs.

The possibility of pattern overlap is common to most frequent-structure miners including the frequent subgraph miners described in Section 2. It has the consequence that certain inferential statistics cannot be applied [1], and that patterns cannot be combined in a modular way to simulate typical transactions. Overlapping patterns can only be avoided by modifying mining algorithms so they count each dataset item (e.g., the request for a URL) only once. Methods for doing this in the case of frequent sequences are described in [1]; they could be adapted to FSG mining.

Last but not least, Web dynamics pose interesting challenges for AP-IP mining: when content changes, it suffices to extend the URL-concept mapping, but what is to be done when semantics evolve? One approach would be to use ontology mapping to make graph patterns comparable and to store more and more abstracted representation of patterns as they move further into the past.

References

1. Berendt, B. (2002). Using site semantics to analyze, visualize and support navigation. *Data Mining and Knowledge Discovery*, 6(1):37–59.
2. Berendt, B., & Brenstein, E. (2001). Visualizing Individual Differences in Web Navigation: STRATDYN, a Tool for Analyzing Navigation Patterns. *BRMIC, 33*, 243–257.
3. Berendt, B., Hotho, A., & Stumme, G. (2004). Usage mining for and on the semantic web. In H. Kargupta et al. (Eds.), *Data Mining: Next Generation Challenges and Future Directions* (pp. 461–480). Menlo Park, CA: AAAI/MIT Press.
4. Berendt, B., & Kralisch, A. (2005). Analysing and visualising logfiles: the Individualised SiteMap tool ISM. In *Proc. GOR05*.
5. Berendt, B., & Spiliopoulou, M. (2000). Analysis of navigation behaviour in web sites integrating multiple information systems. *The VLDB Journal*, 9(1):56–75.
6. Borgelt, C. (2005). On Canonical Forms for Frequent Graph Mining. In *Proc. of Workshop on Mining Graphs, Trees, and Sequences (MGTS'05 at PKDD'05)* (pp. 1–12).
7. Dai, H., & Mobasher, B. (2001). Using ontologies to discover domain-level web usage profiles. In *Proc. 2nd Semantic Web Mining Workshop at PKDD'01*.
8. Dupret, G., & Piwowarski, B. (2005). Deducing a term taxonomy from term similarities. In *Proc. Knowledge Discovery and Ontologies Workshop at PKDD'05* (pp. 11–22).
9. Eirinaki, M., Vazirgiannis, M., & Varlamis, I. (2003). Sewep: Using site semantics and a taxonomy to enhance the web personalization process. In *Proc. SIGKDD'03* (pp. 99–108).
10. Hofer, H., Borgelt, C., & Berthold, M.R. (2003). Large scale mining of molecular fragments with wildcards. In *Advances in Intelligent Data Analysis V.* (pp. 380–389).
11. Huan, J., Wang, W., & Prins, J. (2003). Efficient mining of frequent subgraphs in the presence of isomorphisms. In *Proc. ICDM* (pp. 549–552).
12. Inokuchi, A. (2004). Mining generalized substructures from a set of labeled graphs. In *Proc. ICDM'04* (pp. 414–418).
13. Inokuchi, I., Washio, T., & Motoda, H. (2000). An apriori-based algorithm for mining frequent substructures from graph data. In *Proc. PKDD'00* (pp. 13–23).

14. Inokuchi, I., Washio, T., Nishimura, K., & Motoda, H. (2002). *A fast algorithm for mining frequent connected subgraphs.* Research Report, IBM Research, Tokyo.
15. Jin, R., Wang, C., Polshakov, D., Parthasarathy, S., & Agrawal, G. (2005). Discovering frequent topological structures from graph datasets. In *Proc. SIGKDD'05* (pp. 606–611).
16. Jin, X., Zhou, Y., & Mobasher, B. (2005). A maximum entropy web recommendation system: Combining collaborative and content features. In *Proc. SIGKDD'05* (pp. 612–617).
17. Kralisch, A., & Berendt, B. (2005). Language sensitive search behaviour and the role of domain knowledge. *New Review of Hypermedia and Multimedia, 11,* 221–246.
18. Kralisch, A., Eisend, M., & Berendt, B. (2005). Impact of culture on website navigation behaviour. In *Proc. HCI-International 2005.*
19. Kuramochi, M., & Karypis, G. (2001). Frequent subgraph discovery. In *Proc. ICDM* (pp. 313–320).
20. McEneaney, J.E. (2001). Graphic and numerical methods to assess navigation in hypertext. *Int. J. of Human-Computer Studies, 55,* 761–786.
21. Meinl, Th., Borgelt, Ch., & Berthold, M.R. (2004). Mining fragments with fuzzy chains in molecular databases. *Proc. Worksh. Mining Graphs, Trees&Sequences at PKDD'04* (pp.49–60).
22. Meo, R., Lanzi, P.L., Matera, M., & Esposito, R. (2004). Integrating web conceptual modeling and web usage mining. In *Proc. WebKDD'04 Workshop at SIGKDD'04* (pp. 105–115).
23. Nijssen, S. & Kok, J.N. (2004). A quickstart in frequent structure mining can make a difference. In *Proc. SIGKDD'04* (pp. 647–652); extended version: LIACS, Leiden Univ., Leiden, The Netherlands, Tech. Report April 2004, http://hms.liacs.nl.
24. Oberle, D., Berendt, B., Hotho, A., & Gonzalez, J. (2003). Conceptual user tracking. In *Proc. AWIC'03* (pp. 155–164).
25. Srikant, R. & Agrawal, R. (1995). Mining generalized association rules. In *Proc. 21st VLDB Conference* (pp. 407–419).
26. Srikant, R. & Agrawal, R. (1996). Mining sequential patterns: Generalizations and performance improvements. In *Proc. EDBT* (pp. 3–17).
27. Wörlein, M., Meinl, T., Fischer, I., & Philippsen, M. (2005). A quantitative comparison of the subgraph miners MoFa, gSpan, FFSM, and Gaston. In *Proc. PKDD'05* (pp. 392–403).
28. Yan, X., & Han, J. (2002). gSpan: Graph-based substructure pattern mining. In *Proc. ICDM* (pp. 51–58).
29. Yan, X., Zhou, X.J., & Han, J. (2005). Mining closed relational graphs with connectivity constraints. In *Proc. SIGKDD'05* (pp. 324–333).
30. Zaïane, O.R. & Han, J. (1998). Discovering web access patterns and trends by applying OLAP and data mining technology on web logs. In *Proc. ADL'98* (pp. 19–29).
31. Zaki, M.J. (2002). Efficiently mining trees in a forest. In *Proc. SIGKDD'02* (pp. 71–80).

Overcoming Incomplete User Models in Recommendation Systems Via an Ontology

Vincent Schickel-Zuber and Boi Faltings

School of Computer and Communication Sciences – IC
Swiss Federal Institute of Technology (EPFL)
Lausanne, Switzerland
{vincent.schickel-zuber, boi.faltings}@epfl.ch

Abstract. To make accurate recommendations, recommendation systems currently require more data about a customer than is usually available. We conjecture that the weaknesses are due to a lack of inductive bias in the learning methods used to build the prediction models. We propose a new method that extends the utility model and assumes that the structure of user preferences follows an ontology of product attributes. Using the data of the MovieLens system, we show experimentally that real user preferences indeed closely follow an ontology based on movie attributes. Furthermore, a recommender based just on a single individual's preferences and this ontology performs better than collaborative filtering, with the greatest differences when little data about the user is available. This points the way to how proper inductive bias can be used for significantly more powerful recommender systems in the future.

1 Introduction

Consider a situation where you find yourself with an evening alone and would like to rent a DVD to watch. There are hundreds of movies to choose from. For several reasons, this is a difficult problem. First, most people have limited knowledge about the alternatives. Second, the set of alternatives changes frequently. Third, this is an example of a low user involvement decision process, where the user is not prepared to spend hours expressing his preferences. Recommender systems, RS, have been devised as tools to help people in such situations. Two kinds of techniques are widely used in e-commerce sites today.

The first technique is item-to-item collaborative filtering (CF, [11]), which recommends products to users based on other users' experience. Amazon.com[1], with over 29 million customers and several million catalog items [11], uses this technique which is more commonly known to end-user as "Customers who bought this item also bought these items:". CF generates recommendations based on the experience of like-minded groups of users, based on the assumption that similar users like similar objects. Therefore, CF's ability to recommend items depends on the ability to successfully identify

---

[1] http://www.amazon.com

O. Nasraoui et al. (Eds.): WebKDD 2005, LNAI 4198, pp. 39–57, 2006.

the set of similar users, known as the target user's neighbourhood. CF does not build an explicit model of the users preferences. Instead, preferences remain implicit in the ratings that the user gives to some subset of products, either explicitly or by buying them. In practice, CF is the most popular recommendation technique and this is due to three main reasons. First, studies have shown it to have satisfactory performance when sufficient data is available. Second, it can compare items without modeling them, as long as they have been previously rated. Finally, the cognitive requirements on the user are low. However, as argued by many authors [12][13][18] [19][21], CF suffers from profound problems such as:

- *Sparsity*. This is CF's major problem and occurs when the number of items far exceeds what an individual can rate.
- *Cold start*: When a new user enters the system, he is usually not willing to make the effort to rate a sufficient number of items.
- *Latency problem:* Product catalogs evolve over time; however, the collaborative approach cannot deal with new products as they have not been previously rated.
- *Scalability*. The computation of the neighborhood requires looking at all the items and users in the systems. Thus, the complexity grows with the number of users.
- *Privacy*. In most systems, the similarity matrix is located on a server and is accessible to a third party, thus raising privacy concerns.
- *Shilling attacks*: malicious users can alter user ratings in order to influence the recommendations.

The other widely used technique is preference-based recommendation. Here, a user is asked to express explicit preferences for certain attributes of the product. If preferences are accurately stated, multi-attribute utility theory (MAUT, 10) provides methods to find the most preferred product even when the set of alternatives is extremely large and/or volatile, and thus has no problems of sparsity, cold starts, latency or scalability. Furthermore, since recommendations are based only on an individual user's data, there are no problems with privacy or shilling. However, the big drawback of preference-based methods is that the user needs to express a potentially quite complex preference model. This may require a large number of interactions, and places a higher cognitive load on the user since he has to reason about the attributes that model the product.

However, attribute-based preference models can also be learned from user's choices or ratings, just as in collaborative filtering. In our experiments, this by itself can already result in recommendations that are almost as good as those of collaborative filtering. The main novelty of this paper, however, is to use an ontology of product attributes to provide an inductive bias that allows learning of this individual preference model to succeed even with very few ratings. This leads us to a technique for recommender systems that outperform the best known collaborative filtering techniques on the MovieLens data that we have been using for our experiments. Furthermore, very few ratings, just 5 movies, suffice to get recommendations that are almost as good as what can be reached with many, 30 or more, ratings. At the same time, the user effort required by this technique is not significantly different from collaborative filtering system. Thus, we can effectively get the best of both techniques.

This paper is organized as follows: Section 2 provides fundamental background in Collaborative Filtering, Multi—Attribute Utility Theory, and Ontology Reasoning, while our novel approach with its algorithm is explained in Section 3. Section 4 contains experimental results with comparison to existing techniques. Finally, Section 5 provides the conclusions.

2   Existing Techniques

Our approach uses the cognitive simplicity of Collaborative Filtering whilst maintaining the advantages of the Multi-Attribute Utility Theory. This is achieved by employing the knowledge of an ontology and reasoning over its concepts instead of the item's content itself. Before defining our model, we start by introducing fundamental background.

2.1   Collaborative Filtering

In pure collaborative filtering systems, users state their preferences by rating a set of items, which are then stored in a user-item matrix called S. This matrix contains all the users' profiles, where the rows represents the users $U = \{u_1,...,u_m\}$, the columns the set of items $I = \{i_1,...,i_q\}$, and $S_{k,l}$ the normalized rating assigned to item l by the user k. Given the matrix S and a target user u_i, a user-based CF predicts the rating of one or more target items by looking at the rated items of the k nearest neighbors to the target user. On the other hand, an item-based CF algorithm looks at the k most similar items that have been co-rated by different users. Due to the complexity of the user-based CF, we will not consider it and focus on item-based CF.

The first step of item-based collaborative filtering is to compute the similarity between two co-rated items. Many similarity measures exist, but the most common one is the *cosine metric*, which measures the angle between two vectors of size m. When 2 items are similar, then the angle between them will be small and consequently give a cosine value close to 1; conversely, when items are very different then the value is close to 0. Over the years, the cosine metric has been updated in order to take into account the variance in the ratings of each user. For example, the *adjusted cosine similarity* subtracts from each user rating $S_{j,a}$, the user's average rating. Once all the similarities have been computed, CF estimates the rating of an item a by selecting the k most similar items to a, and computes the weighted average of the neighbor's rating based on the similarity the neighbors have with a.

Unfortunately, as the number of items and/or users grows so will the data sparsity in the matrix. This is CF's fundamental problem and explains why numerous authors [12][13][21] have focused their work to try to overcome it. Data-mining [21] or the Two-way Aspect Model [19] are now used to extract the item similarity knowledge by using association between the user's profile [21] and the object's content [19] in order to augment a standard similarity matrix. To overcome the latency problem, the content of the object has also been used to try to predict its rating. This is achieved by filling up the similarity matrix [4] or simply by using a weighted combination [12] of the content and collaborative prediction.

2.2 Multi-attribute Utility Theory

Formally, each item is defined by a set of n attributes $\mathbf{X} = \{X_1,...,X_n\}$. Each X_i can take any value d_i from a domain $D_i = \{d_1,...,d_k\}$. The Cartesian product $\mathbf{D} = D_1 x D_2 x... x D_n$ forms the space of all the possible items $\mathbf{I}$. The user expresses his preferences by defining the utility function and weight of each attribute. The simplified form of the Von Neumann and Morgenstern [23] theorem states that, if item x is considered better or equivalent to item y, then there exists a utility function u such that u(x) is bigger or equal than u(y). In this paper, we do not consider uncertainty, therefore the utility function becomes equivalent to a value function, but later we consider expected values of similarity.

Furthermore, if we assume Mutual Preferential Independence (MPI, [10]), then the theorem of Additive Value Function[10] can be used , and we can define the utility V of an item o_k as the sum of the sub-utility functions v_i of item o_k on each attribute multiplied by its weight w_i. This is commonly called the Weighted Additive Strategy (WADD, [10]), and the item with then highest overall evaluation value is chosen as the optimal solution.

$$V(o_k) = \sum_{i=1}^{n} w_i v_i(o_k) \qquad (1)$$

Theoretically, when the MPI assumption holds, this strategy can achieve 100% accuracy if all the parameters can be precisely elicited. Unfortunately, the elicitation of the parameters is expensive and various authors have tried to simplify this elicitation process in order to make it usable in real systems. Stolze et al. [20] for example, exploit the idea of a scoring tree where a user expresses his preferences by modifying an existing tree via the use of rules. Once the preferences have been elicited, the system translates the scoring tree into a MAUT additive value function and then searches in the catalog for the most suitable products. Incremental Utility Elicitation [7], IUE, is another approach that eases the elicitation by an incremental process that interleaves utility elicitation and filtering of the items based on the elicited information. A major contribution in that domain is the work done by Ha et al [7][8], where polyhedral cones and pair wise comparison are used to estimate the user's true weights. Also, [8] makes the assumption that the utility function has a multi-linear form, and that all the sub-utility functions are known. Regrettably, computing the cone is a hard problem that makes it unsuitable for real life scenarios. More recently, Blythe in [2] has simplified the process by assuming MAUT additive value functions and used a linear programming formulation and pair wise comparison of alternatives to estimate the user's true utility. Nevertheless, all of the mentioned approaches work only for a small number of attributes. This makes them difficult to apply to real life scenarios where alternatives are modeled by many features.

2.3 Ontology Reasoning

With the emergence of the Semantic Web, it has been widely accepted that ontologies can be used to model the world we live in. In its general form, an ontology is a lattice, where a node represents a concept (i.e.: an object of the world we want to model) whilst the edges between concepts correspond to their semantic relations.

One of the simplest forms of an ontology is the concept tree (CT); A graph where the topology is a tree with only *is-a* relations. The tree structure makes the reasoning computationally efficient and the modeling of the domain easy. Despite its simplicity, a CT can greatly enhance modeling the domain and the filtering process. In [3], Bradley et al. have successfully used a concept tree to model the job domain and shown through experimentation that it is very useful for personalization.

Concept similarity is the predominant form of ontology reasoning. Most techniques use the distance between the concepts in a concept tree or similar graphical ontology to estimate their similarities; the smaller the distance between two concepts the more similar they are. In [3], for example, distance was simply the number of edges between the concepts, while Yang and al. in [24] used the depth of the lowest common ancestor. In [16], Resnik defined similarity based on the information content shared by the concepts rather than its distance. Resnik's metric postulates higher similarity among rare concepts. While this makes sense for concepts themselves, there is no reason why this would also hold for preferences.

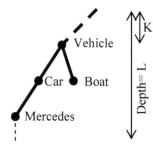

Fig. 1. A CT on transports

The metrics in [3][16][24] assume that the similarity between two concepts is symmetric, i.e.: the similarity between concepts A and B is identical to the similarity between concepts B and A. However, in real life situations, the distance should be considered asymmetric. Consider for example the concept tree in Fig. 1. If a user liked any kind of vehicle, then he will probably like Mercedes cars to a similar degree. On the other hand, liking Mercedes cars does not necessarily mean liking any vehicle as some people become sick on boats.

Formally, and assuming that $P(X)$ corresponds to the probability of X occurring [16], and $P(V \cap M)$ is equal to α, then the probability $P(V \mid M)$ is equal to $\alpha \times (L/(K+2))$ while $P(M \mid V)$ is equal to $\alpha \times (L / K)$. This implies that $P(V \mid M) < P(M \mid V)$, which means that the similarity function is asymmetric.

Andreason et al. in [1] defined an asymmetric metric based on the principle of upward reachable nodes. Their metric can be applied to any graph structure, and differentiates between the cost of traveling upward or downward the ontology. Three important postulates that reflect common sense intuitions are defined in [1]:

1. *Generalization cost property.* The cost of generalization should be significantly higher than the cost of specialization.
2. *Specificity cost property.* The cost of traversing edges should be lower when nodes are more specific.
3. *Specialization cost property.* Further specialization reduces similarity.

The generalization cost property models the asymmetry of the similarity function, which implies that the similarity function is not a metric. The specificity cost property represents the fact that sub-concepts are more meaningful to the user than super-concepts, whilst the specialization property reflects the fact that the further away two concepts are, then the more dissimilar they become. As a consequence, the specificity property reduces the cost of traversing edges as we go deeper in the ontology and the specialization property increases the cost between two concepts if other concepts are found on the path between these concepts.

3   Heterogeneous Attribute Preference Propagation Model

The utility model defined in section 2 is a powerful tool as long as we have a complete user model, and all the items are defined by the same set of attributes. However, in volatile environments such as the web, products continuously change, yet the utility model can only compare outcomes if they have the same attributes. In this section, we introduce the *heterogeneous attribute preference propagation model*, HAPPL, which is capable of building an accurate user model from implicit preferences. HAPPL relaxes the previous two conditions and uses two key components to evaluate the user's parameters:

- *Ontologies* to model and propagate utility values.
- *Multiple regression* to estimate the weights.

The ontology is the key ingredient of our model and we assume that the one required for modeling our attribute is already existing and available. [14][15] were first to propose the idea of using a concept hierarchy directly inferred from the website structure to enhance web usage mining. Major e-commerce sites such as Amazon and Yahoo also uses concept tree to model the item they sale, and to the best of our knowledge, these ontology were hand crafted. This work does not consider how such an ontology was constructed as this is way beyond the scope of this paper. Currently, most ontologies are hand crafted by experts as no fully automated tools are yet available. However, the clustering community has promising result with non-supervised incremental hierarchical conceptual algorithm such as COBWEB [6].

For our experiments, we built a movie recommender system and the ontology modeling a movie. The concept tree was built from scratch based on our common sense as there is none modeling the movie domain. We did not learn it on the data set, but instead we used term definitions found in various dictionaries. To give an idea of the resources require to build the ontology, it took the author about one working day to conceive it.

3.1   Basic Idea

To illustrate the principle that ontology can be used to model and estimate user preferences, take the following problem, where items are defined by a set of 3 attributes X_1, X_2, and X_3. For our DVD example, X_1 could be the theme, X_2 the duration of the

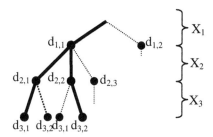

Fig. 2. Representation of the Attributes

movie, and X_3 its MPPA rating. Fig. 2 illustrates a possible representation of the domain as a concept tree, where each level represents an attribute and the different concepts at depth i the possible domain values of the attribute i. Let item o be defined by the domain values $\{d_{1,1}; d_{2,1}; d_{3,1}\}$ and item p by $\{d_{1,1}; d_{2,2}; d_{3,2}\}$.

Again, Fig. 2 shows clearly that the 2 items have some similarity as they both share the node $d_{1,1}$, which means that they both have this domain value in common.

We define a simple similarity function (isim) between 2 items o and p as the number of attributes they share over the total number of possible attributes. This normalization guarantees that the item similarity value lies in the interval [0..1].

$$isim(o, p) = |\{x \mid x(o) = x(p)\}| / |\{X\}| \qquad (2)$$

where x(o) is the set of attributes defining item o, and $\{X\}$ is the set of all attributes. Furthermore, this equation assumes that each attribute is equally likely to contribute to whether one likes an item, and that each item is defined by the same number of attributes. In our example and using equation (2), we can deduce that items p and q have a similarity equal to 1/3. Informally, this means that if the user liked item p, then there is one chance out of three that he will like outcome q. Notice that the additive utility model makes the assumption that if a user has liked features A and B, then he/she will like items containing A+B. This assumption is not made in probabilistic models, where the features and their combination are considered to be completely independent. This introduces an inductive bias that we think is realistic in most real life situations; and this is supported by our experimental results.

In volatile environments, items do not always have the same number of attributes. For example, suppose that item o is defined by the values $\{d_{1,1}; d_{2,1}\}$, q by $\{d_{1,1}; d_{2,2}\}$ and p by $\{d_{1,1}; d_{2,2}; d_{3,2}\}$. Following equation (2), the similarity between o and q is equal to 1/3, which is also equal to the similarity between o and p. Furthermore, the similarity between o and q is equal to the similarity q and o. However, both situations are incorrect as the former violates the specialization property, while the latter violates the generalization cost property.

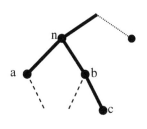

Fig. 3. A simple tree

According to ontology theory, if two concepts are closely related in terms of distance in the graph, then we can assume that they are very similar in terms of meaning. Furthermore, the similarity between two concepts is equal to one minus the distance between those concepts, where the distance is defined as a metric. Consider for example the simple generic graph of Fig. 3. The distance between nodes a and b can be given as the distance between node a and its ancestor n plus the distance between node n and b. However, due to the generalization property, the distance from a to its ancestor should be higher than the distance from the ancestor to b. This property implies that the distance is in fact asymmetric; taking into account that the transitivity property of the distance, we can define the asymmetric distance between two nodes as:

$$adist(a,b) = \rho \times dist(a,lca_{a,b}) + (1-\rho) \times dist(lca_{a,b},b) \qquad (3)$$

where ρ is a generalization coefficient, and $lca_{a,b}$ is the lowest common ancestor to node a and b. Notice that this coefficient implements the generalization property stated in section 0, which means that it must be included in the interval (0.5, 1]. In practice, ρ is learnt by trial and error on a subset of data. In our experiment, we have found that the optimal value lies close to ¾. However, this coefficient is task dependent and will be greatly influenced by the ontology, which is also task dependent.

After substituting the distance by one minus the similarity and simplifying equation (3), the asymmetric similarity can be decomposed between two nodes a and b as:

$$asim(a,b) = \rho \times sim(a,lca_{a,b}) + (1-\rho) \times sim(lca_{a,b},b) \qquad (4)$$

Furthermore, and by considering equation (2), we can define the similarity between a node a and the closest common ancestor of node a and b as the number of nodes on the path from the root to the common ancestor over the number of nodes on the path from the root to node a.

$$sim(a,lca(a,b)) = |URN(lca_{a,b})|/|URN(a)| \qquad (5)$$

In this equation, URN(a) is the set of upward reachable nodes from node a to the root of the tree, which corresponds to the path of a to the tree root. Subsequently, URN($lca_{a,b}$) is the set of nodes from the closest common ancestor of both nodes a and b to the root. Note that in our model, the root node is not contained in the path.

By considering equations (4) and (5), we improve equation (2) to measure the similarity between heterogeneous items o and p, which are respectively modeled by concept c and d as:

$$asim(c,d) = \rho \times \frac{|URN(lca_{c,d})|}{|URN(c)|} + (1-\rho) \times \frac{|URN(lca_{c,d})|}{|URN(d)|} \qquad (6)$$

Following this, if we know that a user has liked concept c with a score equal to x, then we can estimate that he or she will also like concept d by a score equal to x×asim(c, d). Consequently, if we know that a user has liked the domain value $d_{2,1}$ by a value y, then we can estimate that they will like $d_{2,2}$ by a value equal to y×asim($d_{2,1}$, $d_{2,2}$). Hence, we can make use of concept tree as user model to store the user's utility values and also estimate missing ones by looking at the similarity between the concept representing the missing value and the nearest concept on which the user has expressed a preference.

Once all the utility values are known, we propose a novel way of estimating the weights. Rather than eliciting the weights from the user, we suggest to estimate them by multiple regression. This is made possible by the fact that each user has rated a given number of items, and thus we can obtain a system of n equations with n unknowns.

3.2 Definitions

Section 0 introduced the idea that attributes could be modeled by a concept tree, and that a concept tree could be used to estimate missing values. We can extend this idea on domain values, as they usually also have some kind of relationship between them. For example, if you like *action* movies then you will probably also like *adventure* movies, as action and adventure are closely related. We represent this information by an *attribute concept tree*, where the domain values are modeled by concepts, the value of the concept represents the user's utility value, and the relationships between them are is-a relations.

Definition 1. *An attribute concept tree, ACT, is defined by the 8-tuple: <X, D, T, ≤ DCT, f, sim, comb >, where*

- X is a concept representing the attribute X, and linked to *DCT* with the binary relations *hasDom*.
- D is the domain of the attribute X.
- T defines the type of all the elements in D.
- ≤ is an ordering relation on all the element of D.
- DCT is a concept tree modeling D, with the *null* concept as the root.
- f is function f:d →c, where d ∈ D, c ∈ DCT.
- sim is a function that computes the similarity between any two concepts in DCT.
- comb is a function that estimates the value of a concept in DCT.

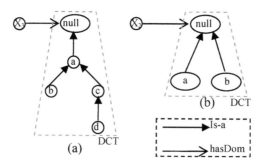

(a) DCT
(b) DCT

Fig. 4. (a) ACT with is-a relationship between domain values, and (b) without

Depending on the nature of the domain D, the DCT is built differently. When the domain D is discrete, the HAPPL technique exploits the *is-a* relationships in the domain D by building a hierarchy (Fig. 4.a). On the other hand, if a domain value is without any relationship, then it will be directly attached to the null concept (Fig 4.b). The null concept represents the null domain value, and is used if an object does not contain that attribute. However, if D is continuous, we tend to use the classic ordering (i.e. ≤), and each element of D is directly connected to the root concept as before.

Hence, if we know that two concepts are linked to the root concept, then we can deduce that they have nothing in common, and the similarity function will return zero.

In many situations, different attributes represent the same concept or have similar meaning. In the computer domain, for example, the attributes processor speed and RAM are related because large memory usually implies a fast processor. Our model exploits this pattern by grouping similar attributes together in a set called a *compound attribute*.

Definition 2. *A compound attribute concept tree CACT is defined by the 7-tuple: <CA, Z, ≤, AsCT, f, sim, comb >, where*

- CA is a compound attribute concept representing the compound attribute CA, and linked to AsCT with the binary relations *hasDom*.
- Z is the set of attributes in CA.
- ≤ is an ordering relation on all the element of Z
- AsCT is a concept tree ontology modeling all the elements in Z and with the *root* concept as the root.
- f is function f:d→c, where d ∈ Z, c ∈ AsCT.
- sim is a function that computes the similarity between any two concepts in AsCT
- comb is a function that estimates the value of a concept in AsCT.

Note that the concepts of a compound attribute concept tree are in fact attribute concept trees. Informally, a CACT can be seen as a bi-dimensional ontology, where one dimension represents the attributes, while the other represents their corresponding domain values. Similarly to an ACT, if 2 attributes have no relation between them, then they will be attached to the root concept.

Given an ontology λ made of CACTs, we see the heterogeneous attribute preference propagation model (HAPPL) as a possible extension of the multi-attribute utility theory (MAUT), where all the outcomes are modeled by λ, and where the mutual preferential independence hypothesis holds on all the attributes. By generalizing the MAUT, we need to generalize equation (1). Thus given a problem where items are defined using the HAPPL model, the optimal solution is the item that maximizes the utility in equation (7).

$$V(o_k) = \sum_{i=1}^{m} w_i' v_i'(o_k) \quad , where \quad v_i'(o_k) = \sum_{j=0}^{n_i} w_j v_j(o_k) \tag{7}$$

In this equation, m is the number of compound attributes defining the class modeling the items, and n_i is the number of attributes in the compound attribute i. The sub-utility functions v_j and v'_i, and the weights w'_i of the compound attributes are defined on the interval [-1, 1] and $\sum |w_i'|=1$. However, the weights w_j are defined on the interval [0,1] and $\sum w_j=1$. Notice that this slightly differs from utility theory where utilities and weights are defined on the interval [0, 1]. This distinction was necessary to reflect the fact that in our model, a negative utility implies disliking by the user while a positive value implies liking.

In our model, we apply the Equal Weight Policy [24] to compute the value of each w_j, and use multiple regression to compute the weights w'_i. The EWP consists of assigning the same value ($w_j=1/n_i$) to each weight, while making sure that $\sum w_j=1$. We have preferred this strategy as it has a very high relative accuracy compared to more complex one [24], while requiring no cognitive effort from the user. The computation of the w_i is explained in more details in section 3.4.2.

Finally, HAPPL estimates the missing utility value of concept c by propagating the average weighted utility value of the closest concepts on which we have preferences, {CCP}. Formally, the estimated utility value of a concept c is computed as follows:

$$utility(c) = \frac{\sum_{i=0}^{|\{CCP\}|} \left(utility(CCP_i) \times asim(CCP_i, c) \right)}{\sum_{i=0}^{|\{CCP\}|} asim(CCP_i, c)} \tag{8}$$

where CCP_i is the ith closest concept on which we have a utility value, and asim is the similarity metric of the concept tree from which the concept c is instanced . The size of the CCP set plays a crucial role, and must be build in order to represent the domain we are modeling. Obviously and in general, the bigger the set, the more accurate will be the utility estimation. By definition of our problem, only a few values can be elicited from the user, which means that a tradeoff as to be done.

3.3 HAPPL Process

The HAPPL algorithm is a four step iterative process as shown in Figure 5.

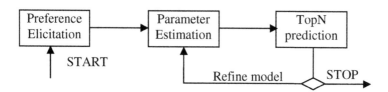

Fig. 5. Illustration of the HAPPL Process

3.3.1 Preference Elicitation
The preference elicitation process is designed to be very simple and similar to collaborative filtering. Each user is asked to define a learning set (LS) composed of at least m outcomes with their associated ratings. The number m corresponds to the number of compound attributes, whilst the rating is usually an integer ranging from one to five.

3.3.2 Parameter Estimation
Once the elicitation is completed, we apply a simple algorithm, *utilityEstimation*, on the learning set in order to estimate as many utility values as possible.

The algorithm works as follows. First we convert the rating of each movie in LS into a score, ranging in the interval [-1, 1].

```
Algorithm utilityEstimation(LS, λ)return CCP:
  CCP ← {};
  for x ∈ LS loop
      score ← rating2score(x);
      for d ∈ x loop
          λ.f(d).utility ← λ.f(d).utility + score;
          λ.f(d).isCCP ← true;
  for c ∈ λ loop
      if λ.f(d).isCCP then
          λ.c.utility ← λ.c.utility / |LS|;
          CCP ← CCP ∪ λ.c;
  return CCP;
```

Then, and for each features of the movie x, d ∈ x, we add the score of the movie to the utility of the representative concept in the ontology λ, λ.f(d).utility + score. Remember that the representative concept of a domain value d is extracted from λ by using the function f defined in section 3.2. Once all the movies in the learning set have been processed, and for all the concepts with a utility value, we normalize their utility values, λ.c.utility / |LS|, and add the concept to the set CCP. Notice that the algorithm assumes the independence of the attributes, and does not look at any combination what so ever. Note that our model is built on the additive utility model that makes such hypothesis.

Unfortunately, the algorithm utilityEstimation is very unlikely to have computed the utility of each possible domain value. Consequently, we use another algorithm called *utilityPropagtion* that will estimate the missing utilities by propagating the utility values already known. This propagation is achieved by calling the function *estimate MissingUtility* that will take the set of known values, CCP, and apply equation (8).

```
Algorithm utilityPropagation(λ, CCP):
  for c ∈ λ ∧ c ∉ CCP loop
      λ.c.utility ← estimateMissingUtility(c,CCP);
```

Once all the sub-utility functions have been computed, we have to estimate the weights of the compound attributes. After that, the utiliyPropagation algorithm has been applied, we are left with a system with at least m equations, m unknowns, and m grades. Thus, we use classical multiple regression (MR) to estimate the weights of the compound attributes. Finally, the weights are normalized to satisfy to the properties defined in section 3.2.

3.3.3 Top-N Selection

Once all the user parameters have been estimated, we can compute the utility of each outcome by applying equation (7). Then, we rank the outcomes in decreasing order of the computed utility and select the first N one; this is called the *top-N items recommendation* strategy where N is a parameter set by the system (usually ∈ [3, 10]).

3.3.4 Refinement Process

Finally, the user has the opportunity to add or remove outcomes from the learning set in order to refine his model. Furthermore, he can directly modify the utility value or weights assigned to each attribute. This allows building a dynamic user model using both implicit and explicit preferences.

3.3.5 Complexity Analysis

To simplify the complexity analysis, we will suppose that our model has m compound attributes, each consisting of r attributes and with n attributes in total. Among those r attributes, we have q attributes with known utility functions, and thus r-q without. The worst case complexity for the different component of our model is as follows:

1. *Elicitation Process*: ask m questions to the user. Thus, the complexity is $O(m)$.
2. *Utility Estimation*: looks at the attributes of the m outcomes in LS. In the worst case scenario, all the outcomes have values on all the attributes which implies a complexity of $O(mn)$.
3. *Utility Propagation*: estimate the r-q missing values of each m compound attributes by looking at the similarities with its neighbors. If we assume that each concept in the ontology knows its depth, and knowing that $n \geq r$, then our similarity function (6) will have a complexity of $O(n)$. Thus, to estimate the missing values, equation (8) will look at the q neighbors. Thus, the complexity is $O(qn)$.
4. *Weight Estimation*: Villard has shown in [22] that the complexity for solving a linear system of m equations with m unknown is $O(m^w)$, with w~2.38.
5. *Top-N Selection*: must compute the utility of all p items and then select the N best ones. The utility computation of an item can requires up to n operations. Thus, the top-N estimation requires $p \times n$ + plogp operations, if the MergeSort algorithm is being used. In most problems n>logp, which implies a complexity $O(pn)$.

In today's system with millions of outcomes with tens of attributes, this implies that $p \gg n^{2.38}$. Thus, we can estimate the overall complexity of the HAPPL as $O(pn)$.

4 Experimental Results

In this section, we explain the experimental methodology and the metric used to validate the hypothesis of our model. We ran our model on the MovieLens[2] data set. We used this data set as it is widely being used through out the research community [13][18][19], and it contains the data requires to solve our example given in the introduction. MovieLens is a data set containing the rating of 943 users on at least 20 movies. There are 1682 movies in the database described by 19 themes (drama, action, and so forth). To increase the description of the movies, we wrote a wrapper that extracted the year, MPPA rating, duration, actors and directors (due to the high sparsity of the actors and directors, it was decided to ignore those attributes in our experiments) from the IMDB[3] website, given the movie's URL.

---

[2] http://www.cs.umm.edu/Research/GroupLens/data/ml-data.zip
[3] http://www.imdb.com

Unfortunately and to the best of our knowledge, there is no ontology modeling the movie domain. Thus, we created the concept trees from scratch based on our common sense, and from definitions found in various dictionaries.

4.1 Overall Performance Analysis

To benchmark our approach, we tested the accuracy of the HAPPL technique against existing recommendation techniques, and studied how many ratings were required by the parameters estimation algorithm in order to obtain an accurate model.

The experiment was as follows. First, users with less than 115 ratings were removed from the data set and for each remaining user, 15 ratings were inserted into a test set, while the rest was inserted into a temporary set. From the temporary set, 11 learning sets of varying size were created in order to test the accuracy of the model. The size of the sets varied incrementally from 4 to 100 ratings, and with learning_set$_{i+1}$ = learning_set$_i$ ∩ ratings_from_temporary_set. Various techniques were used to estimate the weights and the utility functions from the learning set: the model defined in the previous section with a ρ set to 0.75 – HAPPL, random utility values for all the missing utility value but compound attributes' weights estimated by multiple regression– *randFunc*, and random compound attributes' weights but with the utility values estimated by the ontology – randWeights. HAPPL was benchmarked on the users' test set against two popular strategies:

– random policy (*RAND*) which assigns a random rating to each movie in the test set.
– the adjusted cosine collaborative filtering with 90 neighbors (CF). We did not implement the CF algorithm; instead, we used the freely available MultiLens[4] package with the filter ZScore which will allow us to perform adjusted cosine similarity. We set the neighbors to 90 as authors [13][18] have shown that the optimal for the MovieLens data set is very close to this value.

Collaborative Filtering algorithm was chosen as benchmark over classical content based filtering as it is known that it is today's best performing filtering, and the most widely used recommendation system. Moreover, experimental results by Melvielle et al [12] have shown that CF performs better than pure content based filtering in the movie domain. Furthermore, content-based approach requires many ratings to train the user mode, which is not available in our situation.

The top-5 policy was used to select the best movies to show to the user. For each strategy, all the movies in the test sets are sorted based on their predicted ratings, and the first five movies are returned as the recommended items.. In order to compare HAPPL with existing work, the accuracy of the recommendations was measured using the Mean Absolute Error (MAE), which measures the mean average deviation between the predicted rating and the user's true ratings. Herlocker et al. in [9] have argued that MAE may be less appropriate measure when the granularity of the preference is small. However, the problem we are solving has very sparse data, which leads to significant differences between the predicted ratings and the real user's ratings. On the other hand, it was argued in [8] that the MAE has two main advantages:

---

[4] http://knuth.luther.edu/~bmiller/multilens.html

simple to understand and has well studied statistical properties when comparing two approaches.

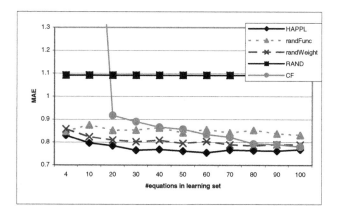

Fig. 6. Accuracy measure of various recommendation techniques bases on the number of known ratings in the learning set

The experiment was run 5 times, and the averaged results are illustrated in Fig. 6. The graph shows that HAPPL can be used to build robust recommendation systems as it has the lowest MAE, whatever the size of the learning set. Our approach is sensitive on the quality of the preference value of the CCP set, which is shown by an in increase in accuracy with increasing size of the learning set as However, after 60 ratings, the accuracy slightly decreases, which is due to the over fitting of the user's true preference value As expected, collaborative filtering performs poorly when the number of ratings in the learning set is very low. It rapidly improves until it reaches the 20 ratings threshold, and then the improvement slows down. This is a well known effect that is due to the high data sparsity (sparsity>0.99), it also reflects the behavior of the systems when new items are added and need to be evaluated. These results clearly show that CF is unsuitable for volatile environments and low involvement users. On the other hand, the HAPPL approach performs well even with high data sparsity, with a mean average error of up to 76.4% lower. The student test reinforces this statement with a t-obs=-39.99 and p -value<< 0.01. The random policy was also plotted to see if our HAPPL approach does actually improve something; and with an MAE of ~1.09, it is clear that it does.

An interesting aspect to consider is whether or not our utility propagation and estimation algorithm is better than just using random values? The graph clearly illustrates that HAPPL performs better than random values (randFunc) and statistical analysis showed that the improvement is significant when we had at least 10 ratings in the learning set (t-test: t-obs= 2.99, p-value=0.0016). This behavior makes sense and implies that a minimum of knowledge on some of the values must be known in order to estimate the rest of the utility values. Concerning the utility of the multiple regression to estimate the weights, we cannot assert anything as we obtained a p-value~0.1. However, the graph shows that HAPPL performs slightly better than randWeights, whatever the size of the learning set. Finally, it is worth pointing out that with only 4 ratings in the learning set, the HAPPL model is able to perform reasonable well. The optimal accuracy is obtained with 60 ratings in the learning set, which is 10% better that CF. Moreover, this experiment shows that HAPPL is quite robust as the accuracy hardly changes with varying size of the learning set.

4.2 Ontology Influence

Finally, we tested the influence of the ontology on the recommendation with the HAPPL technique defined in the previous section. For this experiment, HAPPL used the ontology made up from our common sense and from definitions found in various dictionaries (*DictOntology*). We also created a second ontology with a topology similar to the previous one, but rearranged randomly the concepts (*RandOntology*).

We ran the experiment 5 times on users who had at least 65 ratings. From each user's ratings, 10 were used in the learning set, and 15 others were inserted in the test. From those 10 ratings, we extracted using our utility estimation algorithm the preference on a set of 5 representative attributes (RCset) and estimated the other utilities using HAPPL with: the optimized ontology (*DictOntology*), the random ontology (*RandOntology*), and randomly generated values as utilities (*RandFunctions*).

Table 1. Accuracy measure of the HAPPL based on various apprach to estimate the utilities

	DictOntology	RandOntology	RandFunction
MAE	0.809	0.873	0.887

Table 1 shows the results obtained when applying the top-5 policy. As expected, DictOntology performed much better than RandOntology. As a matter of fact, the improvement is statistically very significant with an average $t_{obs}=-2.6$ and p-value<0.005. Furthermore, the HAPPL with the random ontology performed nearly as bad as when the utility functions where randomly generated.

These results tend to prove two things. First, the ontology plays an important role in predicting the user's preference. Second, the choice of the ontology is crucial as a bad one will perform badly. As mentioned in section 3, this paper does not focus on the construction of the ontology, but the results shows that our model could be used to evaluate the quality of the ontology, with respect to the user's true ratings.

4.3 Discussion

Many researchers have tried to boost the accuracy of Collaborative Filtering. Mel-vielle et al. [12] is probably the most famous work in this domain. They use a content-based approach to try to fill up the CF's matrix in order to avoid the sparsity problem and new-item problem. They performed experiments on the EachMovie data set, and obtained an improvement of 4% over classical CF when they have 25% of the ratings in the test set. With this configuration, HAPPL generates an improvement of over 10%. However, MovieLens is a subset of the EachMovie data so we cannot draw any clear conclusion. Mobasher et al. in [13] improved CF by adding semantic context to the problem. They extracted the attribute values of each movie and from it created a semantic matrix. This matrix is exploited in order to compute the similarity between two movies. Finally, they predicted the rating using a weighted combination of the semantic matrix result and CF. Their method shows very good performance, with up to 22% improvement on the MAE metric when data sparsity is high. The best improvement is achieved when the ratio of the learning / test set is around 0.3. At very low ratio, their improvement is around 15%, which is still 60% worse than our HAPPL technique.

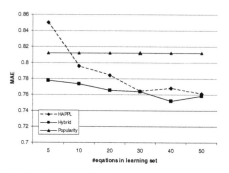 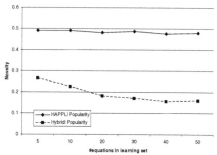

Fig. 7. Accuracy of HAPPL, Hybrid, and Popularity techniques

Fig. 8. Novelty of HAPPL and Hybrid compared to the Popularity technique

Those results tend to show that we could improve our HAPPL technique by combining it with CF. By doing that, we could improve the accuracy but we would then violate the user's privacy, make it vulnerable to schilling attacks, and decrease the novelty. We tested this observation on users who had at least 65 ratings and implemented three approaches:

- *HAPPL*: our model defined in section 4.1
- *Popularity*: select the most popular movies (learnt over users who had <65 ratings).
- *Hybrid*: that combines HAPPL and Popularity by averaging the predicted grades.

First, it is amazing to see (Fig. 7) that a simple popularity approach has a MAE of nearly 0.81, which performs even better than our model when we have just 5 ratings in the learning set. However, HAPPL quickly outperforms the popularity approach when the number of equations in the learning set increases. Notice that the popularity approach is a very basic collaborative strategy as it uses other people ratings to predict a movie's rating. One major difference with CF is the fact that it does not use the actual user's data, which explains why it performs so much better than CF when there is few ratings in the learning set. Our hybrid approach that combines the two previous techniques clearly improves the recommendation, especially when the number of learning equations is less than 30. This can be explained by the inaccuracy of our utility estimation algorithm when high data sparsity occurs.

Finally, we tested the novelty of the HAPPL technique and the hybrid approach against the popularity approaches, and display the result in Fig. 8. In this paper, we define the novelty between two approaches a and b as the number of correct predictions in the recommendations made by algorithm a that is not present in b over the total number of correct prediction made by algorithm a. The results are very interesting and show that our method has about 50% novelty in the prediction over classical popularity strategy, which tends to prove that HAPPL recommends more personalized results. Furthermore, and as with the MAE, HAPPL's novelty remains constant whatever the size of the learning set. This tends to show that our method is robust, and that the propagation method works well even with very few data.

As expected, the hybrid approach has low novelty score, around 20%, but higher accuracy than all the other approaches. This confirms our hypothesis that by trading off the privacy and novelty, we can improve overall recommendation accuracy.

5   Conclusion

As shown in our experiment, most of the existing recommendation techniques include insufficient inductive bias to obtain an accurate user model from the amount of data that is typically available. We have shown how ontologies can provide the right inductive bias so that accurate recommendations are possible even with very little data about the user's preferences. On experiments using the MovieLens data, they consistently outperform collaborative filtering even when very little data is available.

Note that our HAPPL technique does not use any information about other users' preferences as in collaborative filtering. Instead, knowledge of what is common behavior is brought in through the ontology. The next step is now to apply ontology learning techniques to automatically construct reasonable ontologies for a given attribute model of the items. This should allow to better fine-tune the ontology to actual user's preferences, and achieve further significant performance gains. We also consider using a collaborative approach, as well as a learning technique, to better estimate the generalization coefficient rather than using a fixed value. Finally, we would like to perform live experiments to test whether or not the refinement process allows the user to build more dynamic user model.

References

1. Andreasen, T., Bulskov, H., Knappe, R.: From Ontology over Similarity to Query Evaluation. 2nd Int. Conf. ODBASE'03, Italy (2003)
2. Blythe, J.: Visual Exploration and Incremental Utility Elicitation. 18th national conference on Artificial Intelligence, Canada (2002) 526 - 532
3. Bradley, K., Rafter, R., Smyth, B.: Cased-Based User Profiling for Content Personalization. Int. Conf. on AH'00, (2000)
4. Claypool, M., Gokhale, A., Miranda, T.: Combining Content-Based and Collaborative Filters in an Online Newspaper. ACM SIGIR Workshop on Recommender Systems (1999)
5. Debreu, G.: Topological Methods in Cardinal Utility theory. Mathematical Methods in the Social Siences, Standford University Press, California (1960).
6. Fisher, D.H.: Knowledge Acquisition Via Incremental Conceptual Clustering. Machine Learning 2, (1987) 139 – 172.
7. Ha, V., Haddawys, P.: Problem-focused incremental elicitation of multi-attribute utility model. 13th Conf. UAI'97, (1997) 215 - 222

8. Ha, V., Haddawys, P.: A Hybrid Approach to Reasoning with Partially Elicited Preference Models. 15th Conf. Conf. UAI'99, (1999) 263 - 270
9. Herlocker, J.L., Konstan, J.A., Terven, L.G., Riedl, J.T.: Evaluating Collaborative Filtering Recommender Systems. ACM Transactions on Information Systems, Vol. 22, Issue 1, (2004) 5-53
10. Keeney, R., Raiffa, H.: Decisions with Multiple Objectives: Preference and Value Trade-offs. Cambridge University Press (1993)
11. Linden, G., Smith, B., York, J.: Amazon.com Item-to-Item Collaborative Filtering. IEEE Internet Computing (2003)
12. Melville, P., Mooney, R.J., Nagarajan, R.: Content-Boosted Collaborative Filtering. ACM SIGIR Workshop on Recommender Systems, (2001)
13. Mobasher, B., Jin, X., Zhou, Y.: Semantically Enhanced Collaborative Filtering on the Web. EWMF04, LNAI Vol. 3209, Springer, (2004)
14. Nasraoui O., Frigui H., Joshi A., and Krishnapuram R., Mining Web Access Logs Using Relational Competitive Fuzzy Clustering. Proc. of the Eighth Int. Fuzzy Systems Association Congress, Hsinchu, Taiwan (1999)
15. Nasraoui O., Frigui H., Krishnapuram R., Joshi A.: Extracting Web User Profiles Using Relational Competitive Fuzzy Clustering. International Journal on Artificial Intelligence Tools, Vol. 9, No. 4, (2000) 509 – 526
16. Resnik, P.: Semantic Similarity in a Taxonomy: An Information-Based Measure and its Application to Problems of Ambiguity in Natural Language. J. of Artificial Intelligence Research (1999) 95 - 130
17. Salzberg, S. L.: On Comparing Classifiers: Pitfalls to Avoid and a Recommended Approach. Data Mining and Knowledge Discovery, Vol. 1, Issue 3, (1997) 317 - 327
18. Sarwar, B., Karypis, G., Konstan, J. , Riedl, J.: Analysis of Recommendation Algorithms for E-Commerce. ACM Conf. EC'00, (2000)
19. Schein, A.L., Popesucl, A., Ungar, L.H., Pennock, D.M.: Methods and Metrics for Cold-Start Recommendations. 25th Int. ACM SIGIR'02 (2002)
20. Stolze, M: Soft navigation in electronic product catalogs. Int. J. on Digit. Libr., Vol. 3, Issue 1 (2000)
21. Sullivan, D.O., Smyth, B., Wilson, D.C., McDonald, K., Smeaton, A.: Improving the Quality of the Personalized Electronic Program Guide. User Modeling and User-Adapted Interaction, Vol. 14, Issue 1 (2004)
22. Villard, G.: Computation of the Inverse and Determinant of a Matrix. Algorithms Seminar INRIA (2003) 29 - 32.
23. Von Neumann, J., Morgenstern, O.: The Theory of Games and Economic Behavior. Princeton University Press, Princeton (1944)
24. Yang, J., Wenyin, L., Zhang, H., Zhuang, Y.: Thesaurus-Aided Approach For Image Browsing and Retrieval. IEEE Int. Conf. on Multimedia and Expo (2001)
25. Zhang, J., Pu, P.: Effort and Accuracy Analysis of Choice Strategies for Electronic Product Catalogs. ACM Sym. Applied Computing, (2005) 808- 814

Data Sparsity Issues in the Collaborative Filtering Framework

Miha Grčar, Dunja Mladenič, Blaž Fortuna, and Marko Grobelnik

Jožef Stefan Institute, Jamova 39, SI-1000 Ljubljana, Slovenia
miha.grcar@ijs.si

Abstract. With the amount of available information on the Web growing rapidly with each day, the need to automatically filter the information
in order to ensure greater user efficiency has emerged. Within the fields
of user profiling and Web personalization several popular content filtering techniques have been developed. In this chapter we present one of
such techniques – collaborative filtering. Apart from giving an overview
of collaborative filtering approaches, we present the experimental results
of confronting the k-Nearest Neighbor (kNN) algorithm with Support
Vector Machine (SVM) in the collaborative filtering framework using
datasets with different properties. While the k-Nearest Neighbor algorithm is usually used for collaborative filtering tasks, Support Vector Machine is considered a state-of-the-art classification algorithm. Since collaborative filtering can also be interpreted as a classification/regression
task, virtually any supervised learning algorithm (such as SVM) can also
be applied. Experiments were performed on two standard, publicly available datasets and, on the other hand, on a real-life corporate dataset that
does not fit the profile of ideal data for collaborative filtering. We conclude that the quality of collaborative filtering recommendations is highly
dependent on the sparsity of available data. Furthermore, we show that
kNN is dominant on datasets with relatively low sparsity while SVM-
based approaches may perform better on highly sparse data.

1 Introduction

Collaborative filtering is based on the assumption that "similar users have similar
preferences". In other words, by finding users that are similar to the active user
and by examining their preferences, the recommender system can (i) predict the
active user's preferences for certain items and (ii) provide a ranked list of items
which the active user will most probably like. Collaborative filtering generally
ignores the form and the content of the items and can therefore also be applied to
non-textual items. Furthermore, collaborative filtering can detect relationships
between items that have no content similarities but are linked implicitly through
the groups of users accessing them.

This chapter is arranged as follows. In Sect. 2 we first give an overview of
collaborative filtering approaches. Later on, we discuss different characteristics
of collaborative filtering datasets and present major issues concerning dataset

O. Nasraoui et al. (Eds.): WebKDD 2005, LNAI 4198, pp. 58–76, 2006.

properties in the context of collaborative filtering (Sect. 3). To understand the influence that highly sparse server-side collected data has on the accuracy of collaborative filtering, we ran a series of experiments in which we used two publicly available datasets and, on the other hand, a real-life corporate dataset that does not fit the profile of ideal data for collaborative filtering. In Sect. 4 we present our evaluation platform and in Sect. 5 we describe the datasets that we used for our experiments. In Sect. 6 and 7 we present the experimental results of confronting the k-Nearest Neighbor (kNN) algorithm with Support Vector Machine (SVM) in the collaborative filtering framework using datasets with different properties. The chapter concludes with a discussion and a short presentation of some ideas for future work (Sect. 8).

2   About Collaborative Filtering

Collaborative filtering compares users according to their preferences. Therefore, a database of users' preferences must be available. The preferences can be collected either explicitly (explicit ratings) or implicitly (implicit preferences). In the first case, the user's participation is required. The user explicitly submits his/her rating of the given item. Such rating can, for example, be given as a value on a rating scale from 1 to 5. The implicit preferences, on the other hand, are derived from monitoring the user's behavior. In the context of the Web, access logs can be examined to determine such implicit preferences. For example, if the user accessed the document, he/she implicitly rated it 1. Otherwise the document is assumed to be rated 0 by the user (i.e. "did not visit"). The collaborative filtering process can be divided into two phases: (i) the model generation phase and (ii) the recommendation phase. Algorithms which tend to skip the first phase are the so called memory-based approaches (also referred to as lazy learning approaches or the nearest neighbors algorithms) (see Sect. 2.1). The preferences database is a huge user-item matrix, $R = [r_{i,j}]$, constructed from the data at hand. A matrix element $r_{i,j}$ represents user i's rating of item j. Memory-based approaches search the matrix to find relationships between users and/or items. Model-based approaches, on the other hand, use the data from R to build a model that enables faster and more accurate recommendations (see Sect. 2.2). The model generation is usually performed offline over several hours or days.

When dealing with collaborative filtering, two fundamental problems of collaborative filtering have to be taken into account: (i) the sparsity of the data and (ii) the scalability problem. The first problem, which we encounter when R is missing many values, can be partially solved by incorporating other data sources (such as the contents of the items) [14], by clustering users and/or items [4,19], or by reducing the dimensionality of the initial matrix. The last two techniques also counter the scalability problem. This problem arises from the fact that with the growth of the number of users and the number of items, the basic nearest neighbors algorithm fails to scale up its computation. Some of the approaches for countering the two problems are described in Sect. 2.2 (Dimensionality Reduction Techniques).

2.1 Memory-Based Approach to Collaborative Filtering

A straightforward algorithmic approach to collaborative filtering involves finding k nearest neighbors (i.e. the most similar users) of the active user and averaging their ratings of the item in question. Even more, we can calculate the weighted average of the ratings – weights being similarity, correlation or distance factors (later on in the text, the term "similarity" is used to denote any of the three measures) between a neighbor user and the active user (e.g. [4]). We can look at a user as being a feature vector. In this aspect, items that are being rated are features and ratings given by the user to these items are feature values. The following formula can be applied to predict user u's rating of item i:

$$p_{u,i} = \overline{v_u} + \kappa \sum_{j \in Users} w(u,j) \left(v_{j,i} - \overline{v_j} \right) \ , \tag{1}$$

where $w(u_1, u_2)$ is the weight which is higher for more similar, less distant or more correlated users (feature vectors), $\overline{v_u}$ is the mean rating given by user u, $v_{j,i}$ is the rating of item i given by user j, and κ is merely a normalization factor which depends on our choice of weighting.

When representing a user as a feature vector, many of the features have missing values since not every item was explicitly rated by the user. This fact introduces the sparsity problem which implies that measuring similarity between two feature vectors is not a trivial task. Many times two feature vectors have only a few or no overlapping values at all. When computing similarity over only a few values, the similarity measure is unreliable. Furthermore, when there is no overlapping between two vectors, the degree of similarity can not be determined.

Equation 1 was introduced by [15]. If no ratings of item i are available, the prediction is equal to the average rating given by user u. This is an evident improvement to the equation that simply calculates the weighted average.

Weight Computation. The weights can be defined in many different ways. Some of the possibilities are summarized in the following paragraphs.

Cosine Similarity. The similarity measure can be defined as the cosine of the angle between two feature vectors. This technique is primarily used in information retrieval for calculating similarity between two documents, where documents are usually represented as vectors of word frequencies. In this context, the weights can be defined as:

$$w(u_1, u_2) = \sum_{i \in Items} \frac{v_{u_1,i} \, v_{u_2,i}}{\sqrt{\sum_{k \in I_1} v_{u_1,k}^2} \sqrt{\sum_{k \in I_2} v_{u_2,k}^2}} \ . \tag{2}$$

Pearson Correlation. The weights can be defined in terms of the Pearson correlation coefficient [15]. Pearson correlation is primarily used in statistics to evaluate the degree of linear relationship between two random variables. It ranges from -1 (a perfect negative relationship) to $+1$ (a perfect positive relationship), with 0 stating that there is no relationship whatsoever. The formula is as follows:

$$w(u_1, u_2) = \frac{\sum_{j \in Items} (v_{u_1,j} - \overline{v_{u_1}})(v_{u_2,j} - \overline{v_{u_2}})}{\sqrt{\sum_{j \in Items} (v_{u_1,j} - \overline{v_{u_1}})^2 \sum_{j \in Items} (v_{u_2,j} - \overline{v_{u_2}})^2}} . \qquad (3)$$

2.2 Model-Based Approaches to Collaborative Filtering

In contrast to a memory-based method, a model-based method first builds a model out of the user-item matrix. The model enables faster and more accurate recommendations. In the following paragraphs we present two different approaches to model-based collaborative filtering. In the first one, we perceive collaborative filtering as a classification task. We employ a supervised learning algorithm to build a model. In the second one, we are concerned with reducing the dimensionality of the initial user-item matrix and thus build a model that is a lower-dimensional representation of the initial user-item database.

Collaborative Filtering as a Classification Task. The collaborative filtering task can also be interpreted as a classification task, classes being different rating values [3]. Virtually any supervised learning algorithm can be applied to perform classification (i.e. prediction). For each user we train a separate classifier. A training set consists of feature vectors representing items the user already rated, labels being ratings from the user. Clearly the problem occurs if our training algorithm cannot handle the missing values in the sparse feature vectors. It is suggested by [3] to represent each user by several instances (optimally, one instance for each possible rating value). On a 1–5 rating scale, user A would be represented with 5 instances, namely A-rates-1, A-rates-2, ..., A-rates-5. The instance A-rates-3, for example, would hold ones ("1") for each item that user A rated 3 and zeros ("0") for all other items. This way, we fill in the missing values. We can now use such binary feature vectors for training. To predict a rating, we need to classify the item into one of the classes representing rating values. If we wanted to predict ratings on a continuous scale, we would have to use a regression approach instead of classification.

Dimensionality Reduction Techniques. We are initially dealing with a huge user-item matrix. Since there can be millions of users and millions of items, the need to reduce the dimensionality of the matrix emerges. The reduction can be carried out by selecting only relevant users (instance selection) and/or by selecting only relevant items (feature selection). Other forms of dimensionality reduction can also be employed, as described later on in this section.

It is shown by some researchers that feature selection, instance selection and other dimensionality reduction techniques not only counter the scalability problem but also result in more accurate recommendations [19,12,18]. Furthermore, the sparsity of the data is consequentially decreased.

When reducing the dimensionality, the first possibility that comes to mind is removing the users that did not rate enough items to participate in collaborative filtering. From the remaining users, we can randomly choose n users to limit our search for the neighborhood of the active user. This method is usually referred to as random sampling. Also, rarely rated items can be removed for better performance. Still, these relatively simple approaches are usually not sufficient for achieving high scalability and maintaining the recommendation accuracy.

Latent Semantic Analysis (LSA). A more sophisticated dimensionality reduction approach is called Latent Semantic Analysis (LSA) [8]. It is based on Singular Value Decomposition (SVD) of the user-item matrix. By using linear algebra, we can decompose a matrix into a triplet, namely $M = U\Sigma V^T$. The diagonal matrix Σ holds the singular values of M. If we set all but K largest singular values to zero and thus obtain Σ', we can approximate M as $M' = U\Sigma'V^T$. By doing so, we transform our initial high-dimensional matrix into a K-dimensional (low-dimensional) space. The neighborhood of the active user can now be determined by transforming the user vector into the low-dimensional space of the approximated matrix and finding k nearest points representing other users. Searching through a low-dimensional space clearly demands less time. Furthermore, dimensionality reduction reduces sparsity and captures transitive relationships among users. This results in higher accuracy.

Probabilistic Latent Semantic Analysis (pLSA). On the basis of LSA, Probabilistic Latent Semantic Analysis (pLSA) was developed [11]. pLSA has its roots in information retrieval but can also be employed for collaborative filtering [12]. In a statistical model, an event like "person u 'clicked on' item i" is presented as an observation pair (u, i) (note that in such case we are dealing with implicit ratings). User u and item i "occur" paired with a certain probability: $P(u, i)$. We are in fact interested in the conditional probability of item i occurring given user u: $P(i|u)$. This conditional form is more suitable for collaborative filtering since we are interested in the active user's interests.

The main idea of an aspect model (such as pLSA) is to introduce a latent variable z, with a state for every possible occurrence of (u, i). User and item are rendered independent, conditioned on z: $P(u, i) = P(z)P(u|z)P(i|z)$. $P(i|u)$ can be written in the following form:

$$P(i|u) = \sum_z P(i|z)P(z|u) \ . \tag{4}$$

Note that we limit the number of different states of z so that it is much smaller than the number of (u, i) pairs. Let us denote the number of users with N_u, the number of items with N_i, and the number of different states of z with N_z, where $N_z << N_u, N_i$. We can describe the probabilities $P(i|u)$ with $S_1 = N_i \times N_u$ independent parameters. On the other hand, we can summarize the probabilities $P(i|z)$ and $P(z|u)$ with $S_2 = N_i \times N_z + N_u \times N_z$ independent parameters. The dimensionality reduction is evident from the fact that $S_2 < S_1$ (if N_z is small enough). Such latent class models tend to combine items into groups of similar items, and users into groups of similar users. In contrast to clustering techniques (see Sect. 2.4), pLSA allows partial memberships in clusters (clusters being different states of z).

In (4), the probabilities $P(z|u)$ and $P(i|z)$ can be determined by the Expectation Minimization (EM) algorithm using various mixture models. To support explicit ratings, we extend pLSA by incorporating ratings to our observation pairs and thus observing triplets of the form (u, i, r), where r represents a rating value.

The relation of this method to LSA and SVD can be explained by representing the probabilities $P(u, i)$ in the form of a matrix $\boldsymbol{M_p}$ which can be decomposed into three matrices, namely $\boldsymbol{M_p} = \boldsymbol{U_p \Sigma_p V_p}^T$. The elements of these matrices are $u_{i,k} = P(u_i|z_k)$, $\sigma_{k,k} = P(z_k)$, $v_{j,k} = P(i_j|z_k)$ ([2], Chap. 7).

2.3   Item-Based Collaborative Filtering

All collaborative filtering approaches that we have discussed so far, are user-centric in the way that they concentrate on determining the user's neighborhood. Some researchers also considered item-based collaborative filtering [17]. The main idea is to compute item-item similarities (according to the users' ratings) offline and make use of them in the online phase. To predict user u's rating of item i, the online algorithm computes a weighted sum of the user u's ratings over k items that are most similar to item i. The main question in this approach is how to evaluate item-item similarities to compute a weighted sum of the ratings. Item-item similarities can be computed by using the techniques for computing user-user similarities, described in Sect. 2.1. The winning technique, according to [17], is the so called adjusted cosine similarity measure. This is a variant of cosine similarity which incorporates the fact that different users may have different rating scales. The similarity measures are then used as weights for calculating a weighted sum of k nearest items.

2.4   Some Other Approaches

Let us briefly summarize some other techniques. Interested reader should consider the appropriate additional reading.

Horting. Horting is a graph-theoretic approach to collaborative filtering [1]. It involves building a directed graph in which vertices represent users and edges denote the degree of similarity between them. If we want to predict user u's rating of item i, we need to find a directed path from user u to a user who rated item i. By using linear transformations assigned to edges along the path, we can predict user u's rating of item i. One characteristic of horting graph is that item i is not rated by any other user along this path. This means that Horting also explores transitive relationships between users.

Clustering Techniques. Bayesian and non-Bayesian clustering techniques can be used to build clusters (or neighborhoods) of similar users [4,19,12]. The active user is a member of a certain cluster. To predict his/her rating of item i, we compute the average rating for item i within the cluster that the user belongs to. Some such methods allow partial membership of the user in more than one cluster. In such case, the predicted rating is summed over several clusters, weighted by the user's participation degree. Clustering techniques can also be used as instance selection techniques (instances being users) that are used to reduce the candidate set for the k-Nearest Neighbors algorithm.

Bayesian Networks. Bayesian networks with a decision tree at each node have also been applied to collaborative filtering [4,6]. Nodes correspond to items, and states of each node correspond to possible rating values. Conditional probabilities at each node are represented as decision trees in which nodes again are items, edges represent preferences, and leaves represent the possible states (i.e. rating values). Bayesian networks are built offline over several hours or even days. This approach is not suitable in systems that need to update rapidly and frequently.

3 Collaborative Filtering Data Characteristics

As already mentioned, the data in the user-item interaction database can be collected either explicitly (explicit ratings) or implicitly (implicit preferences). In the first case, the user's participation is required. The user is asked to explicitly submit his/her rating for the given item. In contrast to this, implicit preferences are inferred from the user's actions in the context of an item (that is why the term "user-item interaction" is used instead of the word "rating" when referring to users' preferences in the following sections). Data can be collected implicitly either on the client side or on the server side. In the first case, the user is bound to use modified client-side software that logs his/her actions. Since we do not want to enforce modified client-side software, this possibility is usually omitted. In the second case, the logging is done by a server. In the context of the Web, implicit preferences can be determined from access logs that are automatically maintained by Web servers.

Collected data is first preprocessed and arranged into a user-item matrix. Rows represent users and columns represent items. Each matrix element is in general a set of actions that a specific user took in the context of a specific item. In most cases a matrix element is a single number representing either an explicit rating or a rating that was inferred from the user's actions.

Since a user usually does not access every item in the repository, the vector (i.e. the matrix row) representing the user is missing some/many values. To emphasize this, we use the terms "sparse vector" and "sparse matrix".

The fact that we are dealing with a sparse matrix can result in the most concerning problem of collaborative filtering – the so called sparsity problem. In order to be able to compare two sparse vectors, similarity measures require some values to overlap. What is more, the lower the amount of overlapping values, the lower the reliability of these measures. If we are dealing with a high level of sparsity, we are unable to form reliable neighborhoods. Furthermore, in highly sparse data there might be many unrated (unseen) items and many inactive users. Those items/users, unfortunately, cannot participate in the collaborative filtering process.

Sparsity is not the only reason for the inaccuracy of recommendations provided by collaborative filtering. If we are dealing with implicit preferences, the ratings are usually inferred from the user-item interactions, as already mentioned earlier in the text. Mapping implicit preferences into explicit ratings is a non-trivial task and can result in false mappings. The latter is even more true for server-side collected data in the context of the Web since Web logs contain very limited information. To determine how much time a user was reading a document, we need to compute the difference in time-stamps of two consecutive requests from that user. This, however, does not tell us weather the user was actually reading the document or he/she, for example, went out to lunch, leaving the browser opened. What is more, the user may be accessing cached information (either from a local cache or from an intermediate proxy server cache) and it is not possible to detect these events on the server side.

Also, if a user is not logged in and he/she does not accept cookies, we are unable to track him/her. In such cases, the only available information that could potentially help us to track the user is his/her IP address. However, many users can share the same IP and, what is more, one user can have many IP addresses even in the same session. The only reliable tracking mechanisms are cookies and requiring users to log in in order to access relevant contents [16].

From this brief description of data problems we can conclude that for applying collaborative filtering, explicitly given data with low sparsity are preferred to implicitly collected data with high sparsity. The worst case scenario is having highly sparse data derived from Web logs. When so, why would we want to apply collaborative filtering to Web logs? The answer is that collecting data in such manner requires no effort from the users and also, the users are not obliged to use any kind of specialized Web browsing software. This "conflict of interests" is illustrated in Fig. 1.

4   Evaluation Platform

To understand the influence of highly sparse server-side collected data on the accuracy of collaborative filtering, we built an evaluation platform. This platform is a set of modules arranged into a pipeline. The pipeline consists of the following four consecutive steps: (i) importing a user-item matrix (in the case of implicit preferences, data needs to be processed prior to entering the pipeline), (ii) splitting the data according to an evaluation protocol, (iii) setting a collaborative filtering algorithm (in the case of the kNN algorithm we also need to specify a similarity measure), (iv) making predictions about users' ratings and collecting evaluation results. The platform is illustrated in Fig. 2.

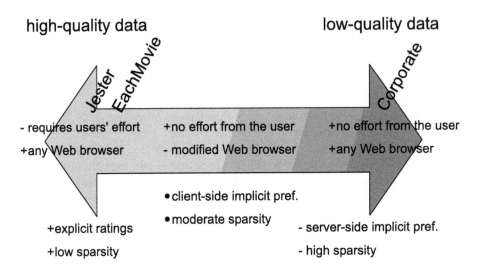

Fig. 1. Data characteristics that influence the data quality and the positioning of the three datasets used in our experiments according to their properties

Let us briefly discuss some of these stages. Ratings from each user in the test set are further partitioned into "given" and "hidden" ratings, according to the evaluation protocol. For example, 30% of randomly selected ratings from a particular user are hidden, the rest are treated as our sole knowledge about the user (i.e. given ratings). Given ratings are used to form neighborhoods or to build models, while hidden ratings are used to evaluate the accuracy of the selected collaborative filtering algorithm. The algorithm predicts the hidden ratings and since we know their actual values, we can compute the mean absolute error (MAE) or apply some other evaluation metric.

5   Data Description

For our experiments we used three distinct datasets. The first dataset was EachMovie (provided by Digital Equipment Corporation) which contains explicit ratings for movies. The service was available for 18 months. The second dataset with explicit ratings was Jester (provided by [9]) which contains ratings for jokes, collected over a 4-year period. Users were using a scrollbar to express their ratings – they had no notion of actual values. The third dataset was derived from real-life corporate Web logs containing accesses to an internal digital library of a fairly large company. The time-span of acquired Web logs is 920 days. In this third case the users' preferences are implicit and collected on the server side, which implies the lowest data quality for collaborative filtering.

In contrast to EachMovie and Jester, real-life corporate Web logs first needed to be extensively preprocessed. Raw logs contained over 9.3 million requests.

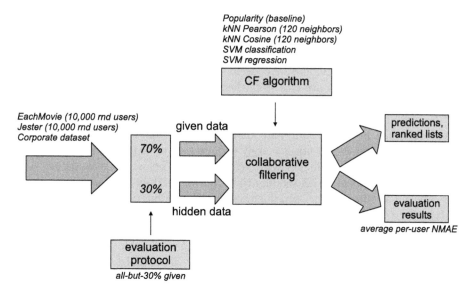

Fig. 2. The evaluation platform. The notes in *italics* illustrate our experimental setting (see Sect. 6).

First, failed requests, redirections, posts, and requests by anonymous users were removed. We were left with slightly over 1.2 million requests (14% of all the requests). These requests, however, still contained images, non-content pages (such as index pages), and other irrelevant pages. What is more, there were several different collections of documents in the corporate digital library. It turned out that only one of the collections was suitable for the application of collaborative filtering. Thus, the amount of potentially relevant requests dropped drastically. At the end we were left with only slightly over 20,500 useful requests, which represents 0.22% of the initial database size.

The next problem emerged from the fact that we needed to map implicit preferences contained in log files into explicit ratings. As already explained, this is not a trivial task. The easiest way to do this is to label items as 1 (accessed) or 0 (not accessed) as also discussed in [4]. The downside of this kind of mapping is that it does not give any notion of likes and dislikes. [7] have shown linear correlations between the time spent reading a document and the explicit rating given to that same document by the same user (this was already published by [13]). However, their test-users were using specialized client-side software, which made the collected data more reliable (hence, in their case, we talk about client-side implicit preferences). Despite this fact we decided to take reading times into account when preprocessing Web logs.

We plotted reading times inferred from consecutive requests onto a scatter plot shown in Fig. 3. The x-axis shows requests ordered by their time-stamps, and the y-axis shows the inferred reading time on a logarithmic scale. We can see that the area around 24 hours is very dense. These are the last accesses of a day. People went home and logged in again the next day, which resulted in an approximately 24-hour "reading" time. Below the 24-hour line, at an approximately 10-hour reading time, a gap is evident. We decided to use this gap to define outliers – accesses above the gap are clearly outliers. We decided to map reading times onto a discrete 3-value scale (ratings being 1= "not interesting", 2= "interesting", and 3= "very interesting"). Somewhat ad-hoc (intuitively) we defined two more boundaries: one at 20 seconds and another at 10 minutes. Since items were research papers and 20 seconds is merely enough to browse through the abstract, we decided to label documents with reading times below 20 seconds as "not interesting". Documents with reading times between 20 seconds and 10 minutes were labelled as "interesting" and documents with reading times from 10 minutes to 10 hours were labelled as "very interesting". We decided to keep the outliers due to the lack of data. They were labelled as "interesting" which is the most "neutral" value on our rating scale. Since we had no reliable knowledge about the outliers, this should have minimized the error we made by taking them into account.

Table 1 shows the comparison between the three datasets. It is evident that a low number of requests and somewhat ad-hoc mapping onto a discrete scale are not the biggest issues with our corporate dataset. The concerning fact is that the average number of ratings per item is only 1.22, which indicates extremely poor overlapping. Sparsity is consequently very high (99.93%). The other two datasets are much more promising. The most appropriate is the Jester dataset with very low sparsity, followed by EachMovie with higher sparsity but still relatively high average number of ratings per item. Also, the latter two contain explicit ratings, which means that they are more reliable than the corporate dataset (see also Fig. 1).

Table 1. The comparison between the three datasets

	Ratings		Size			Sparsity		
	Explicit/ implicit	Scale	Num of users	Num of items	Num of ratings	%**	Avg # of r'tings/usr	Avg # of ratings/item
EachMovie	Explicit	Discrete 0–5	61,131	1,622	2,558,871	97.42	41.86	1,577.60
Jester	Explicit	Continuous −10 − +10	73,421	100	4,136,360	43.66	56.34	41,363.60
Corporate	Implicit	Discrete 1–3*	1,850	16,941	20,669	99.93	11.17	1.22

*after preprocessing
**computed as the number of missing values divided by the user-item matrix size (i.e. the number of rows times the number of columns)

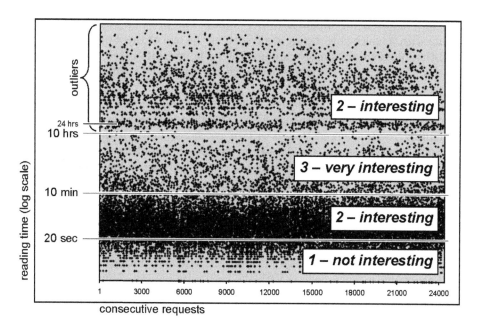

Fig. 3. Mapping implicit preferences contained in the corporate Web logs onto a discrete 3-value scale

6   Experimental Setting

We ran a series of experiments to see how the accuracy of collaborative filtering recommendations differs between several different approaches and the three different datasets (from EachMovie and Jester we considered only 10,000 randomly selected users to speed up the evaluation process). Ratings from each user were partitioned into "given" and "hidden" according to the "all-but-30%" evaluation protocol. The name of the protocol implies that 30% of all the ratings were hidden and the remaining 70% were used to form neighborhoods.

We applied three variants of memory-based collaborative filtering algorithms: (i) k-Nearest Neighbor using the Pearson correlation coefficient (kNN Pearson), (ii) k-Nearest Neighbor using the cosine similarity measure (kNN Cosine), and (iii) the popularity predictor (Popularity). The latter predicts the user's ratings by simply averaging all the available ratings for the given item. It does not form neighborhoods or build models and it provides each user with the same recommendations. It serves merely as a baseline when evaluating collaborative filtering algorithms (termed "POP" in [4]). For the kNN variants we used a neighborhood of 120 users (i.e. k=120), as suggested in [9].

In addition to the variants of a memory-based approach we also applied two variants of a model-based approach: SVM classifier and SVM regression. In general, SVM classifier can classify a new example into one of two classes: positive or negative. If we want to predict ratings, we need a multi-class variant of SVM classifier, classes being different rating values. The problem also occurs when dealing with a continuous rating scale such as the one of the Jester dataset. To avoid this problem, we simply sampled the scale interval and thus transformed the continuous scale into a discrete one (in our setting we used $0.\overline{3}$ precision to sample the Jester's rating scale).

Although the work of [3] suggests using items as examples, the task of collaborative filtering can equivalently be redefined to view users as examples. Our preliminary results showed that it is best to choose between these two representations with respect to the dataset properties. If the dataset is more sparse "horizontally" (i.e. the average number of ratings per user is lower than the average number of ratings per item), it is best to take users as examples. Otherwise it is best to take items as examples. Intuitively, this gives more training examples for building models which are consequently more reliable. With respect to the latter, we used users as examples when dealing with EachMovie (having on average 41.86 ratings per user vs. 1,577.60 ratings per item) and Jester datasets (having on average 56.34 ratings per user vs. 41,363.60 ratings per item) and items as examples when dealing with the corporate dataset (having on average 11.17 ratings per user vs. 1.22 ratings per item).

We combined several binary SVM classifiers in order to perform multi-class classification. Let us explain the method that was used on an example. We first transform the problem into a typical machine learning scenario with ordered class values as explained earlier in the text. Now, let us consider a discrete rating scale with values from 1 to 5. We need to train 4 SVMs to be able to classify examples into 5 different classes (one SVM can only decide between positive and negative examples). We train the first SVM to be able to decide weather an example belongs to class 1 (positive) or to any of the classes 2–5 (negative). The second SVM is trained to distinguish between classes 1–2 (positive) and classes 3–5 (negative). The third SVM distinguishes between classes 1–3 (positive) and classes 4–5 (negative), and the last SVM distinguishes between classes 1–4 (positive) and class 5 (negative). In order to classify an example into one of the 5 classes, we query these SVMs in the given order. If the first one proves positive, we increase the number of votes for class 1 otherwise for classes 2–5, if the second one proves positive, we increase the number of votes for classes 1 and 2 otherwise for classes 3–5, and so on in that same manner. The class with the maximal number of votes is the final outcome of our multi-class SVM classifier. If there are several classes with the same number of votes, the average class value is computed (in the case of a discrete scale, the average value is rounded to the nearest integer value). We refer to this multi-class classifier as "head vs. tail voting". We used binary SVM classifier as implemented in TextGarden (http://www.textmining.net) with a linear kernel and $cost = 0.1$. We built a model only if there were at least 7 positive and at least 7 negative examples available (because our preliminary experiments showed that this is a reasonable value to avoid building unreliable models).

Another variant of a model-based approach is SVM regression which is much more suitable for the application to collaborative filtering than SVM classifier.

It can directly handle continuous and thus also ordered discrete class values. This means we only need to train one model as opposed to SVM classifier where several models need to be trained. We used SVM regression as implemented in LibSvm [5] with a linear kernel and $cost = 0.1$, $\epsilon = 0.1$. As in the case of SVM classifier, we built a model only if there were at least 14 examples available.

Altogether we ran 5 experiments for each dataset-algorithm pair, each time with a different random seed (each time we also selected a different set of 10,000 users from EachMovie and Jester). When applying collaborative filtering to the corporate dataset, we made 10 repetitions (instead of 5) since this dataset is smaller and highly sparse, which resulted in less reliable evaluation results. Thus, we ran 100 experiments altogether.

We decided to use normalized mean absolute error (NMAE) as the accuracy evaluation metric. We first computed NMAE for each user, then we averaged it over all the users (termed "per-user NMAE") [10]. MAE is extensively used for evaluating collaborative filtering accuracy and was normalized in our experiments to enable us to compare evaluation results over different datasets.

7   Evaluation Results

We present the results of experiments performed on the three datasets using the described experimental setting (see Sect. 6). We used two-tailed paired Student's t-Test with significance level $\alpha = 0.005$ to determine if the differences in results are statistically significant.

We need to point out that in some cases the algorithms are unable to predict the ratings as the given ratings do not provide enough information for the prediction. For instance, Popularity is not able to predict the rating for a particular item if there are no ratings in the given data for that item. When calculating the overall performance we exclude such cases from the evaluation as we are mainly interested in the quality of prediction when possible, even if the percentage of available predictions is low. We prefer the system to provide no recommendation if there is not enough data for a reasonably reliable prediction.

As mentioned earlier in Sect. 3, the three datasets we used have different characteristics that influence the accuracy of predictions. Jester is the dataset with the lowest sparsity and is thus in our case the most suitable for the application of collaborative filtering. We see that the kNN methods significantly outperform the other three methods. kNN Pearson slightly yet significantly outperforms kNN Cosine. Both SVM approaches clearly outperform Popularity. Of the two, SVM regression performs better, significantly outperforming SVM classifier.

EachMovie is sparser than Jester yet much more suitable for the application of collaborative filtering than the corporate dataset. As in the previous case, the kNN approaches perform best (of the two, kNN Cosine performs significantly better than kNN Pearson). However, kNN Pearson does not outperform SVM classifier significantly (it does, however, significantly outperform SVM regression and Popularity). Interestingly, SVM regression is outperformed by all other four algorithms (including Popularity).

The corporate dataset is the worst of the three – it is extremely sparse and collected implicitly on the server side. It reveals the weakness of the kNN approach – lack of overlapping values results in unreliable neighborhoods. Popularity significantly outperforms the two kNN approaches and it also significantly outperforms SVM classifier. SVM classifier significantly outperforms kNN Pearson while the difference between SVM classifier and kNN Cosine, on the other hand, is insignificant. The winning approach on this dataset is by far SVM regression – not only it outperforms the other four approaches, it is also more stable (this is evident from the error bars in Fig. 4) and is able to predict the highest number of ratings. In this paper we are not concerned with the inability to predict but it is still worth mentioning that SVM regression can predict 73% of the hidden ratings, Popularity 24%, and the kNN approaches only around 8% of the hidden ratings.

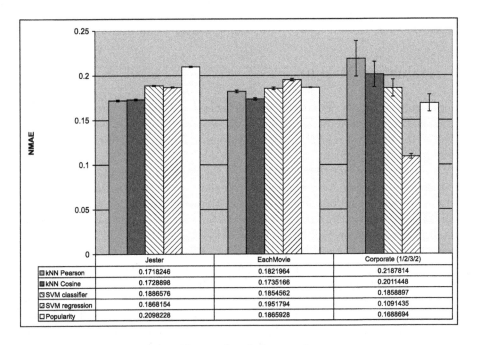

	Jester	EachMovie	Corporate (1/2/3/2)
▣ kNN Pearson	0.1718246	0.1821964	0.2187814
▨ kNN Cosine	0.1728898	0.1735166	0.2011448
▨ SVM classifier	0.1886576	0.1854562	0.1858897
▨ SVM regression	0.1868154	0.1951794	0.1091435
▢ Popularity	0.2098228	0.1865928	0.1688694

Fig. 4. The results of the experiments

To gain a better understanding of how the sparsity level (computed as the number of missing values in the user-item matrix divided by the matrix size, i.e. the number of rows times the number of columns) influences the prediction accuracy of the evaluated algorithms, we performed an additional experiment in which we gradually increased sparsity of a subset of the Jester dataset (1000 randomly selected users). We confronted the two SVM approaches with kNN Cosine ($k = 120$) and Popularity at 50%, 60%, 70%, 80%, 90%, 95%, and 98%

sparsity. This time, we did not impose any example count restrictions when building SVM models. The results are depicted in Fig. 5. We used two-tailed paired t-Test with significance level $\alpha = 0.05$ to determine if the differences in results are statistically significant. At 98% sparsity, kNN is significantly outperformed by the other three algorithms. Popularity significantly outperforms SVM classifier while the difference between Popularity and SVM regression is statistically insignificant. Also, the difference between the two SVM approaches is statistically insignificant.

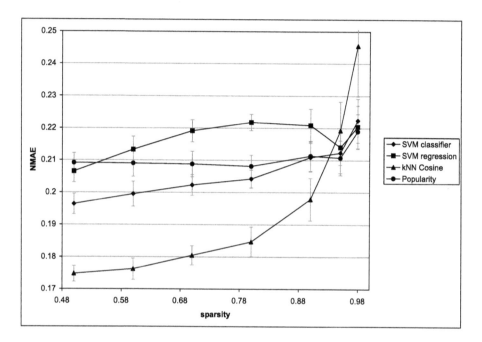

Fig. 5. The results of the additional experiment in which we gradually increased sparsity of the Jester dataset to gain a better understanding of how the sparsity level influences the prediction accuracy of the evaluated algorithms

8   Conclusions and Future Work

In our experimental setting we confronted the k-Nearest Neighbor algorithm with Support Vector Machine in the collaborative filtering framework. Our main experiment showed that kNN is dominant on the datasets with relatively low sparsity (i.e. EachMovie and Jester) and that it fails on the corporate dataset as it is unable to form reliable neighborhoods (see Fig. 4). On the corporate dataset, SVM regression is by far the best performing algorithm. We cannot conclude that SVM regression performs best on *any* highly sparse dataset as we would also need to take other data characteristics (such as distribution of rating values) into account in order to perform more complete analyses. We can, however, say that SVM regression handles sparsity and also uneven distribution of rating values in our corporate dataset better than the other four algorithms.

We believe that in general kNN is dominant on datasets with relatively low sparsity. As the sparsity increases, kNN starts failing as it is unable to form reliable neighborhoods. Our second experiment shows that kNN fails (in comparison to Popularity and the SVM approaches) at around 95% sparsity (see Fig. 5). In the case of such highly sparse data it is therefore better to use another approach. We propose the use of SVM regression as it has several advantages over SVM classifier and Popularity: (i) only one model needs to be built for each item (in contrast to building several binary models in the case of SVM classifier), (ii) the prediction is faster than with SVM classifier as only one model needs to be queried, (iii) SVM regression is able to predict more ratings than Popularity (as already explained, in this work we are not concerned with the inability to predict, nevertheless, this is still one of the strong points of SVM regression), and last but not least, (iv) SVM regression works better with eccentric users than Popularity (the analyses with eccentric users are beyond the scope of this work; intuitively Popularity only satisfies the "average" user while SVM regression is more sophisticated and gives good recommendations also to eccentric users).

What is also evident from the evaluation results is that an inadequate number of values in the corporate dataset represents our biggest problem. We will not be able to evaluate collaborative filtering algorithms on the given corporate dataset properly, until we reduce its sparsity. One idea is to apply LSI (Latent Semantic Indexing) [8] or to use pLSI (Probabilistic Latent Semantic Indexing) [11] to reduce the dimensionality of the user-item matrix, which consequently reduces sparsity. Another idea, which we believe is even more promising in this context, is to incorporate textual contents of the items. There were already some researches done on how to use textual contents to reduce sparsity and improve the accuracy of collaborative filtering [14]. Luckily, we are able to obtain textual contents for the given corporate dataset.

Also evident is the fact that the cosine similarity measure works just as well (or even better) as the Pearson correlation measure on EachMovie and Jester. Early researches show much poorer performance of the cosine similarity measure [4].

As a side-product we noticed that the true value of collaborative filtering (in general) is shown yet when computing NMAE over some top percentage of eccentric users. We defined eccentricity intuitively as MAE (Mean Absolute Error) over the overlapping ratings between "the average user" and the user in question (greater MAE represents greater eccentricity). The average user was defined by averaging ratings for each particular item. This is based on the intuition that the ideal average user would rate every item with the item's average rating. The incorporation of the notion of eccentricity can give the more sophisticated algorithms a fairer trial. We computed average per-user NMAE only over the top 5% of eccentric users. The supremacy of the kNN algorithms over Popularity became even more evident. In near future, we will define an accuracy measure that will weight per-user NMAE according to the user's eccentricity, and include it into our evaluation platform.

Acknowledgements

This work was supported by the Slovenian Research Agency and the IST Programme of the European Community under SEKT, Semantically Enabled Knowledge Technologies (IST-1-506826-IP) and PASCAL Network of Excellence (IST-2002-506778). (This publication only reflects the authors' views.) The authors would also like to thank Tanja Brajnik for her help.

References

1. C. C. Aggarwal, J. L. Wolf, K.-L. Wu, and P. S. Yu. Horting hatches an egg: A new graph-theoretic approach to collaborative filtering. In *Proceedings of the 5th ACM SIGKDD International Conference on Knowledge Discovery and Data Mining*, 1999.
2. P. Baldi, P. Frasconi, and P. Smyth. *Modeling the Internet and the Web: Probabilistic Methods and Algorithms*. Wiley, New York, 2003.
3. D. Billsus and M. J. Pazzani. Learning collaborative information filers. In *Proceedings of the 15th International Conference on Machine Learning*, 1998.
4. J. S. Breese, D. Heckerman, and C. Kadie. Empirical analysis of predictive algorithms for collaborative filtering. In *Proceedings of the 14th Conference on Uncertainty in Artificial Intelligence*, 1998.
5. C.-C. Chang and C.-J. Lin. *LibSvm: A Library for Support Vector Machines*, 2001. Software available at http://www.csie.ntu.edu.tw/~cjlin/libsvm.
6. D. M. Chickering, D. Heckerman, and C. Meek. A bayesian approach to learning bayesian networks with local structure. In *Proceedings of the 13th Conference on Uncertainty in Artificial Intelligence*, 1997.
7. M. Claypool, P. Le, M. Wased, and D. Brown. Implicit interest indicators. In *Proceedings of ACM 2001 Intelligent User Interfaces Conference*, 2001.
8. S. Deerwester, S. T. Dumais, and R. Harshman. Indexing by latent semantic analysis. *Journal of the Society for Information Science*, 41(6):391–407, 1990.
9. K. Goldberg, T. Roeder, D. Gupta, and C. Perkins. Eigentaste: A constant time collaborative filtering algorithm. *Information Retrieval*, (4):133–151, 2001.
10. J. L. Herlocker, J. A. Konstan, L. G. Terveen, and J. T. Riedl. Evaluating collaborative filtering recommender systems. *ACM Transactions on Information Systems*, 22(1):5–53, 2004.
11. T. Hofmann. Probabilistic latent semantic analysis. In *Proceedings of the 15th Conference on Uncertainty in Artificial Intelligence*, 1999.
12. T. Hofmann. Latent semantic models for collaborative filtering. *ACM Transactions on Information Systems*, 22(1):89–115, 2004.
13. J. A. Konstan, B. N. Miller, D. Maltz, J. L. Herlocker, L. R. Gordon, and J. Riedl. Grouplens: Applying collaborative filtering to usenet news. *Communications of the ACM*, 40(3):77–87, 1997.
14. P. Melville, R. J. Mooney, and R. Nagarajan. Content-boosted collaborative filtering for improved recommendations. In *Proceedings of the 18th National Conference on Artificial Intelligence*, 2002.
15. P. Resnick, N. Iaocvou, M. Suchak, P. Bergstrom, and J. Riedl. Grouplens: An open architecture for collaborative filtering for netnews. In *Proceedings of ACM 1994 Conference on Computer Supported Cooperative Work*, pages 175–186, 1994.

16. M. Rosenstein and C. Lochbaum. What is actually taking place on web sites: E-commerce lessons from web server logs. In *Proceedings of ACM 2000 Conference on Electronic Commerce*, 2000.

17. B. Sarwar, G. Karypis, J. Konstan, and J. Reidl. Item-based collaborative filtering recommendation algorithms. In *Proceedings of the 10th International Conference on World Wide Web*, 2001.

18. K. Yu, X. Xu, M. Ester, and H.-P. Kriegel. Selecting relevant instances for efficient and accurate collaborative filtering. In *Proceedings of the 10th International Conference on Information and Knowledge Management*, 2001.

19. C. Zeng, C.-X. Xing, and L.-Z. Zhou. Similarity measure and instance selection for collaborative filtering. In *Proceedings of the 12th International World Wide Web Conference*, 2003.

USER: User-Sensitive Expert Recommendations for Knowledge-Dense Environments

Colin DeLong[1], Prasanna Desikan[2], and Jaideep Srivastava[2]

[1] College of Liberal Arts, University of Minnesota, 101 Pleasant St. SE,
55455 Minneapolis, MN, United States of America
delo0041@umn.edu
[2] Department of Computer Science, University of Minnesota, 200 Union Street SE,
55455 Minneapolis, MN, United States of America
{desikan, srivasta}@cs.umn.edu

Abstract. Traditional recommender systems tend to focus on e-commerce applications, recommending products to users from a large catalog of available items. The goal has been to increase sales by tapping into the user's interests by utilizing information from various data sources to make relevant recommendations. Education, government, and policy websites face parallel challenges, except the product is information and their users may not be aware of what is relevant and what isn't. Given a large, knowledge-dense website and a non-expert user searching for information, making relevant recommendations becomes a significant challenge. This paper addresses the problem of providing recommendations to non-experts, helping them understand what they *need* to know, as opposed to what is popular among other users. The approach is *user-sensitive* in that it adopts a 'model of learning' whereby the user's context is dynamically interpreted as they browse and then leveraging that information to improve our recommendations.

1 Introduction

Current recommender systems typically ask the question "What does the user or groups of similar users find interesting?" and make recommendations, usually in the form of products or Web documents, on that basis. In some domains, however, the question of what is a relevant recommendation becomes a function of user interest *and* expert opinion, a need recommender systems haven't traditionally dealt with. This paper is meant to address this very issue: providing expert-driven recommendations. To our knowledge, this topic has been little-explored outside of a few tangentially-related recommender systems [24]. Essentially, the goal of an expert-driven recommendation system is to determine the user's context and provide recommendations by incorporating a mapping of expert knowledge. The idea is to direct users to what they need to know versus what is popular, as the two are not always in perfect alignment with each other. For instance, an important human resources policy affecting some subset of people in an organization may not receive much traffic online, but that in and of itself does not mean the policy is irrelevant or unimportant. Additionally, with more and more organizations putting more and more expert-oriented

O. Nasraoui et al. (Eds.): WebKDD 2005, LNAI 4198, pp. 77–95, 2006.

content online, user navigational issues can be exacerbated to the point where such websites are essentially unusable for non-experts. Other examples would include any Web sites that have dense policy information, such as those created for academic advising, tax law, and human resources.

This paper, which is an extension and update of a previous paper of ours [25], is a step towards providing a generalized framework for expert-driven recommendations. Our starting point is the "Model of Learning"; the philosophical basis our system and its components are constructed from. "User Intent" is modeled through usage data analysis, producing sets of sequential association rules, and "Expert Knowledge" through the structure and hypertext of the website itself, an expansion over our previous work, resulting in a concept graph mapped to individual URLs. Three separate rankings – UsageRank, ExpertRank, and GraphRank – produced and incorporated into an overall USER Rank, which produces the final list of recommendations. To the best of our knowledge, this approach of providing expert-driven recommendations is novel.

Section 2 talks briefly about the related work in this area. In Section 3 we discuss the key problems addressed by this paper. Section 4 describes our method from a philosophical and technical perspective. In Section 5 we give an overview of the architecture for the recommendation system that has been created for testing and evaluation purposes. We present our experiments and results in Section 6. Finally, we provide conclusions and some future research directions in Section 7.

2 Related Work

Research of recommendation systems started in early 90's, when these systems were meant to aggregate past preferences of all users to provide recommendations to users with similar interests [18], [21], [8], [17]. Various possible classifications of recommendation techniques have been proposed [6], [21], [22]. There have also been various survey papers with focus on particular aspects of recommender systems, such as rating-based recommendations [4], hybrid recommendations [5], and e-commerce applications [22]. In general, recommendation systems can be categorized, based on their approach, into four categories, an extension of the initial categorization (noted by earlier work [6], [4]):

- **Content-Based Approach:** These recommendations are derived from the similarity of a product the user is interested in with other products that the user has bought/referred to in the past and preference level to those products as expressed by the user.
- **Collaborative Approach:** In such an approach, similarity is measured with respect to the end products purchased by other users. For instance, a shared subset of previously-purchased items between the user and other customers would be a driving factor for recommendations.
- **Usage-Behavior Recommendations:** Similarity based on usage behavior of users is used as a criterion for recommendations. These recommendations are mapped to correlations in browsing behavior and mined from logs such as those generated by Web servers.
- **Hybrid Approach:** Any combination of the above three approaches.

Content-Based and Collaborative Filtering [6], [10] approaches require the avail-ability of user profiles and their explicitly-solicited opinion for a set of targeted prod-ucts. Collaborative approaches also suffer from well known problems such as *'Identi-fication Requirement, the "Pump Priming" problem, Scalability, Sparseness, and Rating Bias'* [7]. Web mining techniques such as Web Usage Mining overcome some of these problems through the use of the implicitly-influenced opinion of the user by extracting information from Web usage logs for ranking relevant Web pages [11], [20], [14]. The goal of most existing recommendation systems that follow collabora-tive approaches [13] or hybrid approaches [1],[2], [3] is to recommend products in order to boost sales, as opposed to recommending 'products' - Web documents in this paper - *necessary* to the user.

Web page recommendations and personalization techniques in which a user's pref-erences are automatically learned from Web usage mining techniques became popular in late 90s [14], [19]. Li and Zaiane have illustrated an approach to combine content, structure, and usage for Web page recommendations [11]. Huang et al make use of transitive associations and a bipartite graph to address the sparsity issue [27] and have conducted thorough research on other graph-based models as well [28]. An extensive study of Web personalization based on Web usage mining can be found in [12]. Ishi-kawa et al [9] have studied the effectiveness of Web usage mining as a recommenda-tion system empirically. Most of these recommendation systems have been developed through the use of data obtained from the explicit link structure of the Web and Web usage logs. For this extended paper, we use these same sets of data in our efforts to generalize the expert-recommendation problem and its potential solutions. Our previ-ous work in this area [25] focused on a richer data set, whereby each Web document was assigned one or more concepts by an expert via a custom content management system (CMS) called Crimson. For this paper, a similar mapping of concepts for Web pages has been assembled using the link structure and link text, but the construction of this mapping is automated, a departure from traditional knowledge-based methods. In our approach, the web graph itself can be thought of as an unprocessed representation of domain knowledge. This information is then leveraged to generate a set of recommen-dations relevant to the user's context in a knowledge-dense Web environment.

3   The Problem

The primary reason for the creation of an expert-driven recommender system is to facilitate the navigation of non-expert surfers through websites containing expert-defined content, the numbers of which are increasing rapidly. Parallel with the growth of the World Wide Web, user demands for complete content availability have also increased. To keep up with expectations of constituent users, expert-defined websites, such as those found in higher education, medicine, and government, are making available vast amounts of technically-oriented content, including policies, procedures, and other knowledge-dense information. Generally, this trend is good for users in that more information can be easily accessed by visiting websites, but diffi-culties arise when attempting to connect users to the "right" content. Here, two key problems arise.

First, the surfer is often unable to "ask the right question". Even if expert-defined websites are well-organized, the content language is often not intuitive to non-experts. Non-experts browsing such a website may quickly find themselves lost or uninterested because of this. Additionally, a site search using Google, for instance, will not always return relevant links if the surfer's query is inconsistent with the website's language. As such, surfer navigation can become a formidable task. This is further complicated when legal concerns must take precedence over the simplification of content wording, which might otherwise leave out important clauses or restrictions that could be applicable to the surfer.

The second problem, related to the first, is how expert-defined websites can meet educational goals by connecting surfers to content relevant to their questions. The determination of relevance is at the core of all recommender systems. However, for expert-defined websites, such recommendations must depend not only on the surfer's definition of relevance, but also on the expert's opinion. Higher education websites face this issue in particular, where a student's context must be brought into alignment with certain academic outcomes, such as timely graduation. As such, a set of relevant recommendations might include links that Web usage mining alone would have never produced. Relevance in an expert recommender system is, therefore, a function of both surfer intent and expert knowledge. This lays the foundation for the model of learning on which our initial system is built.

4 Method

The philosophical groundwork of learning in general had to be examined prior to the implementation of our candidate expert recommender system. This gave us an intuitive base to work from, presenting a clear picture of what pieces would be necessary in order to build a prototype, and what future work could be done to improve upon it.

4.1 Philosophical

Here, we introduce a model of learning which is ultimately recursive in nature, and represents the core philosophy at the foundation of our recommender system. This model is constructed from interactions typically found in a conversation between an expert and a learner, such as those between a student and their academic advisor.

First, a question is formulated by the learner and asked of the expert, who then leverages their accumulated knowledge in order to answer the question and/or ask other questions which try to discern the intent of the learner. Next, the expert must align the question's language with the language the answer or answers are defined in. As a result, the learner is able to more properly formulate additional questions and the expert can be more helpful – and detailed – in their replies. Using the student/advisor interaction as an example, an advisor may be asked about a policy the student does not understand (such as the 13-credit policy, where students must file a petition in order to take less than 13 credits of coursework in a semester). The student's question might not be worded consistently with name or content of the policy they are seeking to know more about, especially if it is technically-worded for legal reasons. The advisor must then bridge this knowledge gap by trying to discover the intent of the question and connect it to appropriate answers. Through conversation, the gap is further narrowed as the student's questions become more consistent with the language the policy is defined in.

Often, the advisor may have questions about the reason for the student's question ("Why do you want to file a petition?"), which may uncover additional information that can help the advisor in recommending the best course of action for the student. A student may not want to be asked about why they want to take less than 13-credits, but it is advisor's job to encourage a student's academic success, even if it means telling them to take a full credit load. This is a vital piece of our model: an expert is teaching the learner what they *need* to know, versus telling them what they *want* to know. This is the primary difference between the model presented in this work and those of other recommender systems.

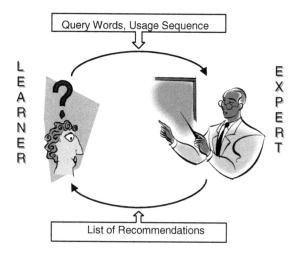

Fig. 1. Philosophical Model of Learning

Figure 1 is a visual representation of this model as demonstrated through the dynamic of an expert and a learner. Similar to the conversation between the student and their advisor, the model is recursive, a representation of learning at the meta level. We use this model as the foundation for our recommender system, which incorporates both learner intent and expert knowledge in order to generate a list of recommendations.

4.2 Technical

The different perspectives of the expert and user are captured using different models from the available data (described in more detail below). The problem then reduces to applying the set of ranking methods to the data representing expert and user opinions and finally merging them. The data contains the following descriptive elements:

- A set of concepts C = {C_1, C_2, C_3,....}, where each document D_i can be labeled by a subset of concepts from C
- A set of Web pages, S, generated by the content management system, which have a one-to-one mapping with each document D
- Web server usage logs

The views of an **expert** are captured explicitly by building a graph of Web pages connected by concepts that are derived from a Web graph generated by a set of experts using a content management system. While our earlier work [25] concentrated on deriving expert knowledge from the content management system itself, in our current work, we present a more generally-applicable case of dealing with a Web graph, thus removing the dependence on the content management system. The expert views are captured using this graph and the expert opinion of the relative importance of any given Web page is captured using an *ExpertRank*. The navigational importance is captured from the Web graph by the *StructureRank*. The queries of the **learner** are captured from the *UsageRank*. By defining these three different kinds of rank we are able to capture what the learner is intending to learn and what the expert thinks the learner needs to know.

The most popular kind of information infrastructure for representing documents and their interconnections is a link graph. Such an information infrastructure can be modeled as a graph, G (V, E) – where V is a set of vertices of that represents units of information and E is a set of edges that represents the interaction between them. For the scope of this paper, a vertex represents a single Web page and an edge represents a hyperlink between pages or a relation between two pages. As can be seen in Figure 2, two different graphs are constructed: each corresponding to a different type of edge relationship. In order to generate relevance ranks of nodes on these graphs, Google's PageRank [15] is used as a foundation due to its stability and success in the Web search domain. However, it should be noted that the best way to capture an experts advice on the whole set of documents automatically without an expert involved is an open issue of research.

ExpertRank: A concept graph is constructed from the Web graph. In this graph, a vertex is a single Web page and its edges correspond to its conceptual links with other Web pages. In the prototype recommender system, the concepts of a Web page are derived from the anchor text of the Web pages pointing to it. The concepts are represented by individual anchor text words and the information-retaining phrases that can be grown out of them. If two Web pages share a concept, but are not already explicitly-linked, then an implicit link is introduced between them. Two pages are determined to share a concept if the intersection of the set of concepts each represents is not empty. The set of concepts by themselves are determined by the anchor text of the pages pointing to them. On this constructed graph, PageRank is applied to obtain the importance ranking of these documents. Thus the rank of a document d is defined as:

$$ER(d) = \frac{\alpha}{N_D} + (1-\alpha) \cdot \sum_{d',d \in G} \frac{ER(d')}{OutDeg(d')} \qquad (1)$$

Where d is a given Web page and d' is a set of all Web pages that point to d, either by an explicit or an implicit link, N_D is the number of documents in the Web graph, and α is the dampening factor.

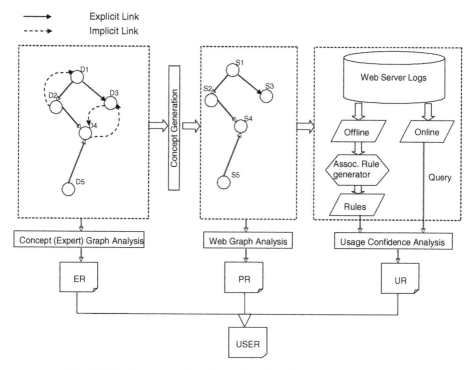

Fig. 2. Technical approach to obtain User Sensitive Expert Rank (USER)

GraphRank: The graph of the Web site is generated by the content management system. Here, the vertices represent individual Web pages and the edges represent the hyperlinks connecting them. Though the Web pages can be mapped to the document set, the edge set is different primarily due to the difference in purpose and method of creating the edges. The Structure graph contains *explicit* links that can are created mainly for easy navigation. Applying PageRank to this graph gives a set of rankings for which Web pages are important, in a very general sense. However, since the edges shared by two linked pages in the Web graph do not take context into account, this is not the optimal representation of relationships between documents/pages defined by experts. This graph contains information about certain Web pages that are important, such as good hubs, but the edge sets are vastly different from that of the concept graph and, hence, will not be reflected in the document rank in the same way. The PageRank of a page, S is computed using the PageRank metric:

$$PR(s) = \frac{\alpha}{N_s} + (1-\alpha) \cdot \sum_{s',s \in G} PR(s') \Big/ OutDeg(s') \qquad (2)$$

Where s is a given Web page and s' is a set of all Web pages that point to s, either by an explicit or an implicit link, N_S is the number of documents in the Web graph, and α is the dampening factor.

UsageRank: User interests are modeled based on user browsing patterns. User browsing patterns are mined and association rules are generated offline. For an online user browsing session, the current sequence of Web pages navigated by the user is considered as a 'Query' the user is interested in. Given this sequence and using association rules, the set of pages the user would likely be interested in navigating to in the next step is generated. The generated list of Web pages is ranked according to the confidence metric of each sequential association rule. The Usage Rank of a page is, however, dependant on the current browsing sequence of the user, and hence may have different values for different queries. Let us define a question, q to be sequence of pages that a user has browsed in the current session. Let A be the set of sequences, $\{q \rightarrow s_i\}$ that have been logged from previous user sessions, where s_i is an URL that a previous user has traversed to, after browsing a sequence of pages defined by, q. Thus the Usage Rank for the page s_i for a particular question q can be defined as:

$$UR(s_i) = \textbf{confidence}(q \rightarrow s_i) = \textbf{support}(q \rightarrow s_i)/\textbf{support}(q) \qquad (3)$$

Thus the output is a set of Web pages, S whose confidence metric is higher than a pre-defined threshold.

USER Rank: Once the sets of ranks are obtained, the task of obtaining an integrated score by a combination of the scores obtained from each ranking metric, intuitively translates into integration of user interest with expert advice. These sets are merged to produce the final list of recommendations using the following function:

$$USER(s) = (p*(n_1*UR(s)) + q*(n_2*ER(s)) + r*(n_3*PR(s))) / (p + q + r) \qquad (4)$$

p, q and r are floating point numbers between 0 and 1 used to weight their corresponding ranks. The weights p, q and r can be varied, giving more (or less) preference to one set of rankings over another. n_1, n_2, and n_3 are normalization values for each of the corresponding ranks. Since each of the ranking types has a different distribution of values, their results must be normalized prior to the application of p, q, and r. These values are pre-computed floating point numbers between 0 and 1, and can be thought of as a distribution normalizing share percentage. From the distribution of returned UR, ER, and PR scores, the average score value for each ranking type is calculated. These scores are used to compute each rank type's average "share" of the average total score (the sum of the average scores). Using these scores as "sample" values for each rank type and assuming each rank type contributes an equal proportion of the average total score, n_1, n_2, and n_3 are computed. It should be noted that while a linear method of combining the rank scores is adopted, it is not claimed to be the best approach. The area of optimal combination of ranks obtained from different dimensions is open for research, especially in this domain. Whether it is better to combine the ranks obtained from different models or use a single combination model to obtain a unique rank is still to be examined. It is better to avoid a single weight that overpowers the other parameters unduly, and it seems unlikely that there is a perfect weight for each rank for all usage sequences. Thus, more elegant methods of weight balancing, such as dynamic weighting, are an important part of our future work. However, the simple approach of linear combination of these ranks helps to begin the process of providing the user with recommendations reflecting what they *need* to know.

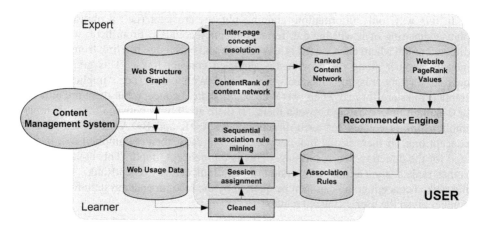

Fig. 3. System architecture of the CLASS Website Recommendation System

5 System Architecture

The recommender system architecture was designed to closely reflect a philosophical model of learning. In its initial implementation, the recommender system incorporates both the expert and learner portions of the learning model as shown in Figure 3. However, analysis of queries by an expert to a learner is left for future work. The recommender system works by integrating the output of three offline analysis - the expert knowledge and learner queries, and the PageRank of our Web graph – into a set of online recommendations determined by the user's current context.

Expert: As an introduction, the website data used to build and test the prototype recommender system was from the University of Minnesota's College of Liberal Arts Student Services (CLASS) website (*http://www.class.umn.edu*). The site is deployed and maintained through the use of an in-house content management system (CMS) called Crimson. Crimson distributes the workload of creating and maintaining websites to CLASS domain experts; the academic advisors. In this paper, conceptual information is derived from the Web graph and anchor tag text. For every Web page, we construct a term frequency vector using the anchor text from incoming links. Each term in this vector is then used as a seed for phrase growth, which builds an array of all possible left-to-right phrase candidates. These candidates are then pruned according to the following criteria:

- If a phrase occurs only once in the corpus, delete it.
- If a phrase is a stop word (using the MySQL 4.1 stop word list [26]), has a string length of 1, or is numeric, delete it.
- If a candidate phrase is a left-side perfect substring of a phrase one word longer than the candidate **and** their frequencies are equal, delete the candidate.
- If a candidate phrase is a right-side perfect substring of a phrase one word longer than the candidate **and** their frequencies are equal, delete the candidate.

In this way, only information-retaining phrases are kept (i.e.: a phrase and any phrase substring of it will have different frequency counts). From here, we create a directed graph where each vertex is a Web page and each edge is a link from one Web page to another along the previously-calculated concept links. This graph is then queried for any missing links between related Web pages (i.e.: "implicit" links). Implicit links are formed when two Web pages share a concept, but there are either 1 or 0 explicit links existing between them. If there are 0 links between them, then one implicit link is created for each direction (i.e.: A→B and B→A) along the shared concept link. If there is one link between them already, then one implicit link is created for the direction that is missing. This is our concept graph. This concept graph is then ranked using a modified version of PageRank called ContentRank. The resulting ranked concept graph can then be queried by the recommender system for relevant content given the user's concept context.

Learner: The Learner portion begins by retrieving usage data from the CMS. This usage data is then cleaned to remove bad addresses (the CMS records all visit attempts, even if the Web addresses are invalid), server visits resulting from periodic refreshing of RSS newsfeed content, and spider bot visits. For the remaining usage data, session id information is assigned using the IP address of the user and their visit timestamp. An integer indicating the numerical order in which the Web page was visited for each session is assigned as well, easing sequential association rule generation. Single-page user sessions are also deleted (i.e.: user visits one Web page on the site and then leaves). Finally, sequential association rules are generated with the cleaned, session-defined usage data according to the confidence metric. The resulting rules are stored as tuples in a rule database, easing rule recall for the recommender system.

USER System: The set of recommendations made to the learner while he/she browses the website is accomplished by determining the user's current context, creating a list of candidate recommendations, and merging their corresponding UsageRanks, ExpertRanks, and GraphRanks obtained from Web structure (the PageRank of a URL in the Web graph) to create a final list of recommendations.

To determine the learner's context, browsing history is used to query for all sequential association rules meeting the following conditions:

- The premise portion of the rule matches some ordered subset of the learner's browsing history
- The last URL in the premise portion of the rule is equal to the URL of the learner's current location

The rules returned from this query form the "usage recommendation set", the set of URLs retrieved from usage data. If we were making recommendations based on usage data alone, this is the set of URLs we would draw from – a set of predicted 'next' URLs for the learner to visit. These URLs are then resolved to each their conceptual components, such as 'advising' and '13-credit policy'. We then query our concept graph using these concepts to return a set of URLs conceptually related to the set of 'next' URLs, including the set of 'next' URLs themselves (as they are obviously related to the learner's context). For each URL in this set, the URL's rank (from the concept graph) is normalized using its corresponding rule confidence. In this way, individual URLs with high concept ranks in low confidence rules do not overpower the other recommendations disproportionately. This set is the "expert recommendation set", the set of URLs retrieved from inferring the learner's context and finding the set of URLs corresponding to that context.

A merging of both sets is used for GraphRank-based recommendations. This is meant to be akin to being given a set of Web pages, say from a search engine, and using GraphRank to order the results. For the purposes of this recommender system, the query is given in the form of browsing behavior and the set of Web pages we want ordered is the merging of our usage and expert recommendation URL sets. Each URL is then ranked according to each of the three ranks and a final score calculated using the USER Rank and a set of weights. The resulting ranked set is sorted in reverse order and concatenated to a length equal to the number of recommendations we want to give. This is the set of recommendations returned to the learner browsing our website.

6 Experiments and Results

First, we will describe the data and experimental setup. The usage logs and website graph are from Crimson's database, CLA Student Services' content management system. The College of Liberal Arts is the largest college at the University of Minnesota, serving over 14,500 students in nearly 70 majors. The "Main" CLASS website has over 400 Web pages. After cleaning of usage data cleaning, the data contained logs for over 250,000 visits.

Four sets of recommendation weights were used for each test case: one strictly ExpertRank, one strictly UsageRank, one strictly GraphRank and one mixing all three ranks evenly. The values of n_1, n_2, and n_3 were evaluated to be 0.0011, 0.1004, and 0.8985, respectively. Each test case also included 3 randomly-generated sets of recommendations for comparison, which were averaged to form a baseline measure of comparison. 6 different test cases of sample usage sequences, which were chosen to cover a wide range of possible situations, were generated for each of the 4 sets and were evaluated by a professional academic advisor who served as our domain expert.

The test case usage sequences are described in the tables that follow; the top-most URL representing the first page visited in the test session and the bottom-most URL representing the page the learner is currently at. For each set of recommendations, the expert was asked to determine how relevant, on a scale of 0 to 5, each link was given the learner's browsing behavior, defined by the usage sequence for each test case. The scale is as follows: 0 (Very Irrelevant), 1 (Moderately Irrelevant), 2 (Slightly Irrelevant), 3 (Slightly Relevant), 4 (Moderately Relevant), and 5 (Very Relevant).

6.1 Individual Test Cases and Descriptions

The first test case is meant to capture a common type of usage sequence whereby the learner ends up at a Web page with a list of all our major brochures. Given that there are almost 70 forms to choose from, it's important to give any guidance we can. The second URL ("Job Search Jump Start…") clues us in that, assuming the visitor is a student, they could be transferring in from another institution. That being said, Web pages with the word "job" in the title tend to get lots of hits from students in general.

Table 1. Test Case #1

URL	Title	
/index.html	advising web	
/advising/Job_Search_Jump....html	Job Search Jump Start…	
/mbrochures/index.html	major brochures	**Current URL**

Table 2. Test Case #2

URL	Title	
/index.html	advising web	
/degree_requirements/FAQs_About....html	FAQs About the…	
/majors/index.html	Majors	
/choosing_a_major/index.html	choosing a major	**Current URL**

The second test case is related to the first, in that there are Web pages related to major information, but this is less focused on a list of specific majors than it is about resources available to aid in choosing a major. Additionally, the sequence includes a visit to "FAQs About the Second Language Requirement", a commonly-visited URL that often influences the choice between a Bachelor of Arts or a Bachelor of Science (when the choice exists for a particular major).

Table 3. Test Case #3

URL	Title	
/index.html	advising web	
/advising/index.html	advising	
/registration/index.html	registration	
/canceling_and_adding/index.html	canceling and adding	**Current URL**

The third test case is a great example of a usage sequence where we wouldn't want a strictly usage-based recommendation system. If it is the case that the learner is looking for information on canceling courses (instead of adding them, which is less common), then usage-based recommendations risk providing links to more information about canceling courses instead of course load planning or time management strategies.

Table 4. Test Case #4

URL	Title	
/index.html	advising web	**Current URL**

This test case is the equivalent of a learner walking into an advising office and asking an advisor for advice regarding student services – an extremely general case. Here, usage-based recommendations have an advantage, because if the advisor were to reply to the learner, it would likely take the form of our most-asked questions. This case is also necessary in that recommendations must be given at the home page despite there being a lack of contextual information to utilize.

Table 5. Test Case #5

URL	Title	
/degree_requirements/FAQs_About....html	FAQs About the...	
/advising/Schedule_an_Advising....html	Schedule an Advising Appointment	
/degree_requirements/index.html	degree requirements	**Current URL**

Not all learners enter a website through the home page, so this test case (and the following one) is meant to simulate a link being followed to the "FAQs About the Second Language Requirement" Web page. Perhaps feeling overwhelmed by the large amount of text in the FAQ, they visit the Web page to find out how to schedule an advising appointment. Finally, they arrive at the gateway Web page for information about degree requirements.

Table 6. Test Case #6

URL	Title	
/transfer_student_guide/index.html	transfer student guide	
/choosing_a_major/index.html	choosing a major	
/steps/index.html	steps to a liberal arts...	**Current URL**

The final test case demonstrates the information gain possible from leveraging learner context from a usage sequence. The most likely case is that this learner is planning on transferring to the University of Minnesota, as evidenced not only by a visit to the Transfer Student Guide, but also the following visit to "Choosing a Major" (students intending to transfer must declare a major upon admission to the College of Liberal Arts). This gives the current page in the session – "Steps to a Liberal Arts Degree" – much more contextual information, which will be helpful to leverage when providing recommendations.

6.2 Results

For each set of results, the following metrics were calculated:

- **Average Relevance:** the average recommendation quality for a set of recommendations, on a scale of 0 to 5.

- **Average "First 5" Relevance:** the average recommendation quality for the first five recommendations, which are the ones most likely to be read and acted upon.
- **Standard Deviation**
- **# of Unique URLs Recommended:** of the 60 total recommendations made for each ranking method, this is the total number of unique URLs that were recommended.

In the descriptions below, "gateway" pages are Web pages that are typically link-heavy and refer to no particular piece of content. Most of these pages end in "index.html". At the other end of the spectrum are "content" pages, which are centered on a single document or concept and are typically text-heavy. Additionally, bolded and underlined entries indicate the highest/lowest value for a case (depending on the type of measure). Italicized and underlined indicate the second highest/lowest value for a case (again, this is context dependant).

Table 7.

Average Relevance	Test Case #						
Weight Settings	One	Two	Three	Four	Five	Six	Avg
UR: 1, ER: 0, PR: 0	**3.2**	**4.8**	3.1	**4.7**	2.6	*4.3*	*3.783*
UR: 0, ER: 1, PR: 0	*3*	3.8	3.2	*4.6*	2.7	4.2	3.583
UR: 0, ER: 0, PR: 1	2.8	*4.3*	**3.7**	*4.6*	**3.4**	**4.5**	**3.883**
UR: .33, ER: .33, PR: .33	2.6	*4.3*	3.3	**4.7**	*2.9*	*4.3*	3.683
RANDOM	1.466	2.766	*3.4*	2.9	2.1	2.6	2.539

From Table 7., GraphRank-ordered recommendations give the highest average relevance score, closely followed by UsageRank. Among the individual test cases, note the variance in scores from test case to test case, particularly from case #4 to case #5. Test case #4, while meant to be unfair to the recommendation system because of its lack of contextual information, has almost uniformly high relevance scores for all weight settings (aside from the random recommendations, of course). A closer examination of this test case and the ranking methods suggests an explanation. Essentially, the pool of candidate recommendations for both the usage and expert sets is comprised of a large number of gateway pages with higher than normal rule confidences (because the user is at the home page and hasn't traversed the Web graph any further yet). And since the user is at the home page, many of those gateway pages are considered relevant, because we don't know enough about them to say that a particular content-oriented (or "authority") page is relevant (with limited exceptions, such as the page for "scheduling an advising appointment").

Contrast this with test case #5, in which almost every weight setting (except for GraphRank) does worse than a relevance value of 3, somewhere between "Slightly Irrelevant" and "Slightly Relevant", which is not the kind of performance we'd like to have. In the case of UsageRank, most of the results were less relevant because the rules weren't very strong for that usage sequence to begin with and none of the top recommendations mentioned anything about major information. ExpertRank did slightly better, but could have improved had it not made recommendations about major information from the "Classroom Grading & Examination Procedures" website, which is geared towards faculty. GraphRank returned gateway pages, primarily (9 out of 10), playing it safe. Most of its recommendations were moderately relevant.

Table 8.

Average "First 5" Relevance	Test Case #						
Weight Settings	One	Two	Three	Four	Five	Six	**Avg**
UR: 1, ER: 0, PR: 0	*3.4*	**4.6**	*3.6*	*4.6*	2.4	4	*3.77*
UR: 0, ER: 1, PR: 0	**3.8**	*4.4*	3.2	*4.6*	*3*	**4.6**	**3.93**
UR: 0, ER: 0, PR: 1	1.6	3.8	**4.4**	4.2	**3.6**	*4.4*	3.67
UR: .33, ER: .33, PR: .33	2.6	*4.4*	3.4	**5**	*3*	4.2	*3.77*
RANDOM	1.266	2.73	*3.6*	2.87	1.93	2.13	2.42

Table 8 shows the relevance results when using only the first five recommendations. Here it can be seen that, ExpertRank is the overall leader in relevance, but it is very closely followed by UsageRank and the mixed weights setting. GraphRank would have been lower had it not done particularly well in test case #3, where it – again – recommended many of the gateway pages from the "how to guides" section rather than content pages, which the other ranking methods were more apt to do (4 out of 10 and 9 out of 10 for UsageRank and ExpertRank, respectively, were content page recommendations, in contrast to GraphRank which was 1 out of 10). In contrast, for test case #1, GraphRank's gateway page recommendation approach backfired as its first 4 recommendations were terrible given the user's context, leading to it's abysmal average of 1.6 for that case. The next 5 recommendations were much better.

Test case #1 was also interesting with respect to the other ranking methods as well. 6 of UsageRank's recommendations were for individual major brochures, which were all deemed "slightly relevant". The others were for major information gateway pages, 2 of them in the top 5, which helped boost its score. ExpertRank's first 5 recommendations contained 3 of the best links, helping its score considerably.

In general, ExpertRank is the most consistently-good ranking when it comes to the first 5 recommendations, and it never dips below a score of 3 for any of the test cases, which cannot be said for the other ranking methods. Another interesting note about ExpertRank is that it is the only ranking method that is at least as good as or better than its overall average relevance (see Table 7) for every test case. It is better than the overall average 4 out of 6 test cases, a good indication of its consistency in making the best recommendations in the first 5.

Table 9.

Standard Deviation	Test Case #						
Weight Settings	One	Two	Three	Four	Five	Six	**Avg**
UR: 1, ER: 0, PR: 0	**1.14**	**0.42**	1.97	**0.48**	**1.07**	0.95	**1.01**
UR: 0, ER: 1, PR: 0	1.89	1.03	**0.63**	*0.70*	1.95	**0.79**	1.16
UR: 0, ER: 0, PR: 1	2.10	*0.95*	*0.95*	*0.70*	*1.17*	0.85	*1.12*
UR: .33, ER: .33, PR: .33	2.17	*0.95*	1.42	**0.48**	1.29	*0.82*	1.19
RANDOM	*1.80*	1.77	1.75	1.50	1.71	1.65	1.70

From Table 9, the standard deviation for each of the test cases is given. As expected, the random recommendations all have large standard deviations. However, it can also be seen that test cases #1 and #5 have very high standard deviations for all ranking methods, not just for the random recommendations. Perhaps not surprisingly, these are the two worst-scoring test cases overall, having 0's and 1's dragging down the 4's and 5's for each ranking method. In general, we would want to see consistently high-scoring recommendations, but for problem cases like #1 and #5, a better first five is preferable as it is more likely the user will choose one of those links over the last five. Given that, ExpertRank for case #1 and GraphRank for case #5 would be preferable, despite UsageRank being higher for case #1 overall.

Table 10.

# of Unique URLs Recommended	
Weight Settings	**# Unique (out of 60 possible)**
UR: 1, ER: 0, PR: 0	_39_
UR: 0, ER: 1, PR: 0	**42**
UR: 0, ER: 0, PR: 1	17
UR: .33, ER: .33, PR: .33	29

Table 10 shows how many unique URLs were recommended for each ranking method overall. From the table, it is easy to see that ExpertRank recommends the highest number of unique URLs and GraphRank the lowest number. While not directly a measure of recommendation quality, recommendation diversity is certainly an indirect measure of the quality of the overall navigation experience, because at some point, recommendations to specific pages containing relevant content should be made. In the case of GraphRank, only 3 of its 17 recommended URLs are to content pages; the rest are gateway pages. After some time of receiving these recommendations, it is doubtful the user will find much utility in going back to the same gateway pages for information they don't necessarily know how to find in the first place. If an expert-driven recommendation system is to provide real navigational assistance, it should try to give the most relevant **specific** recommendations it can.

6.3 Summary

In general, all three ranking methods did well in terms of individual test case relevancy measures. GraphRank scored the highest on overall relevancy and ExpertRank led the "First 5" scores, while UsageRank trailed closely in both cases. The mixed weights also scored high. However, there are problems with just taking the highest-scoring measure and calling it a day. When considering the overall user experience, GraphRank is clearly recommending the same pages over and over again, leading to questions about its usefulness in such knowledge-dense Web environments. It is, after all, only using the GraphRank obtained from the Web graph to determine the order of recommendations; no contextual information is directly incorporated into such an ordering, despite using the same pool of URLs to choose from as ExpertRank. If the same gateway pages keep showing up in the pool, GraphRank will recommend them every time, no matter what the users' context is.

UsageRank, on the other hand, will always make recommendations reflecting the most popular 'next' URLs to users and, as such, is susceptible to the problems of usage-based recommendation systems outlined in section 1, namely the "cold start" and "bias" issues. If a bad recommendation appears in the list – and UsageRank has its fair share of 0's – then there is a risk that the system itself will propagate bad recommendations by making them appear to the user as though they were relevant to the current context. Additionally, though UsageRank scores well in terms of absolute relevance, it has a tendency to recommend some URLs that appear on the same page the user is already at. In some cases, such as when the user visits a text-heavy page, this can be desirable. If not, it risks obvious redundancy and, thus, wasted recommendation space. This could be filtered out, but it is uncertain that the remaining URLs will be sufficiently relevant given the decreasing confidence values as you move further down the list.

ExpertRank, on the other hand, tends to recommend more content pages than gateway pages, while still scoring very well overall, and particularly so in the first five recommendations. At its worst, it is an average ranking method, but at its best, it is the superior in providing variety while ensuring consistent relevancy. Given the stated goals of an expert-driven recommendation system, this ranking method is, unsurprisingly, the furthest ahead in terms of their fulfillment. It is also more resilient to the problems suffered by UsageRank and other purely usage-based recommendation approaches.

The mixed ranks method is a mixed bag. It scores well overall, but not spectacularly so or in a consistent fashion. However, this approach holds a great deal of promise if a way can be found to mitigate the ill-effects of the other ranking methods, while ensuring the best parts remain. This we leave to future work.

7 Conclusions

From these test cases, it should be clear that expert-driven rankings offer an advantage for recommender systems operating in knowledge-dense environments. ExpertRank, in particular, offers a "best of both worlds" solution in which the learner intent is used to help inform expert's response, much as it is in a real world interaction. As a recommendation ranking method, ExpertRank scores well on a consistent basis, offering excellent recommendation diversity while remaining relevant.

There are, of course, improvements to be made. Further work includes the development of a more fine-grained approach to content network ranking, further study and experimentation using the mixed ranks method, and aligning the recommendation system more closely with the learning model by examining the possible queries an expert may pose to the learner to understand the learner intent better.

Acknowledgements

We would like to thank Dr. Nathanial Paradise, Academic Advisor for the Society & Culture Student Community in the College of Liberal Arts, University of Minnesota, for providing us valuable feedback as our domain expert. We would also like to thank

Dr. Chris Kearns, Assistant Dean of Student Services for the College of Liberal Arts, University of Minnesota, for providing the epistemological framework from which our recommender system could be built. Additionally, we thank the reviewers of this paper for pointing us towards areas needing clarification and further elaboration. We finally thank the research group members of Data Analysis and Management Group, who have provided valuable feedback and suggestions. This work was supported by AHPCRC contract number DAAD19-01-2-0014. The content of the work does not necessarily reflect the position or policy of the government and no official endorsement should be inferred.

References

1. http://www.atg.com/en/products/engine/
2. http://digimine.com/our_service_as_rev.asp
3. http://www.triplehop.com/ie/product_demos/tripmatcher.html
4. G. Adomavicius, A. Tuzhilin, "Towards the Next Generation of Recommender Systems: A Survey of the State-of-the-Art and Possible Extensions." IEEE Transactions on Knowledge and Data Engineering, vol 17, June 2005.
5. R.Burke, "Hybrid recommender systems: Survey and experiments". In User Modeling and User-Adapted Interaction, 2002.
6. M. Balabanovic and Y. Shoham, "Fab: Content-Based, Collaborative Recommendation," Comm. ACM, vol. 40, no. 3, pp. 66-72, 1997.
7. Gray, M. Haahr, "Personalised, Collaborative Spam Filtering", Proceedings of First Conference on Email and Anti-Spam (CEAS) July 2004
8. W. Hill, L. Stead, M. Rosenstein, and G. Furnas, "Recommending and Evaluating Choices in a Virtual Community of Use," Proc. Conf. Human Factors in Computing Systems, 1995.
9. H. Ishikawa, M. Ohta, S. Yokoyama, J. Nakayama, K. Katayama: On the Effectiveness of Web Usage Mining for Page Recommendation and Restructuring. Web, Web-Services, and Database Systems 2002: 253-267.
10. J.A. Konstan, B.N. Miller, D. Maltz, J.L. Herlocker, L.R. Gordon, and J. Riedl, "GroupLens: Applying Collaborative Filtering to Usenet News," Comm. ACM, vol. 40, no. 3, pp. 77-87, 1997.
11. J. Li and O.R. Zaïane, "Combining Usage, Content, and Structure Data to Improve Web Site Recommendation," Proc. Fifth Int'l Conf. Electronic Commerce and Web Technologies (EC-Web '04), pp. 305-315, 2004.
12. Mobasher, "Web Usage Mining and Personalization", In Practical Handbook of Internet Computing Munindar P. Singh (ed.), CRC Press, 2005.
13. B.N. Miller, I. Albert, S.K. Lam, J.A. Konstan, and J. Riedl, "MovieLens Unplugged: Experiences with an Occasionally Connected Recommender System," Proc. Int'l Conf. Intelligent User Interfaces, 2003.
14. Mobasher, R. Cooley and J. Srivastava, "Automatic Personalization Based On Web Usage Mining", Communication of ACM Volume 43, Issue 8, August, 2000.
15. L. Page, S. Brin, R. Motwani and T. Winograd "The PageRank Citation Ranking: Bringing Order to the Web" Stanford Digital Library Technologies, January 1998.
16. S. Perugini, M. A. Goncalves and E.A. Fox, "A connection centric survey of recommender system research", Journal of Intelligent Information Systems, 2004.

17. P. Resnick, N. Iakovou, M. Sushak, P. Bergstrom, and J. Riedl, "GroupLens: An Open Architecture for Collaborative Filtering of Netnews," Proc. 1994 Computer Supported Cooperative Work Conf, 1994.
18. P. Resnick and H.R. Varian,, 'Recommender Systems'. Communications of the ACM, 40 (3), 56-58, 1997.
19. M. Spiliopoulou, "Web usage mining for Web site evaluation". Communications of the ACM, 43(8):127-134, 2000.
20. J.Srivastava, P. Desikan and V.Kumar. "Web Mining - Concepts, Applications and Research Directions", Book Chapter in Data Mining: Next Generation Challenges and Future Directions, MIT/AAAI 2004.
21. J.B. Schafer, J. Konstan and J. Riedl, 'Recommender Systems in E-Commerce'. In: EC '99: Proceedings of the First ACM Conference on Electronic Commerce, Denver, CO, pp. 158-166.
22. J.B. Schafer, J.A. Konstan, and J. Riedl, "E-Commerce Recommendation Applications," Data Mining and Knowledge Discovery, vol. 5, nos. 1/2, pp. 115-153, 2001.
23. L. Terveen and W. Hill, "Human-Computer Collaboration in Recommender Systems". In: J. Carroll (ed.): Human Computer Interaction in the New Millenium. New York: Addison-Wesley, 2001.
24. J. Li, OR Zaiane, "Using Distinctive Information Channels for a Mission-based Web Recommender System," Proc. of WebKDD, 2004
25. C. DeLong, P. Desikan and J. Srivastava, "USER (User Sensitive Expert Recommendation): What Non-Experts NEED to Know," Proc. of WebKDD, 2005
26. http://dev.mysql.com/doc/refman/4.1/en/fulltext-stopwords.html
27. Z. Huang, H. Chen, and D. Zeng, "Applying Associative Retrieval Techniques to Alleviate the Sparsity Problem in Collaborative Filtering", ACM Transactions on Information Systems, Vol. 22, No. 1, January 2004, Pages 116–142.
28. Z. Huang, W. Chung, and H. Chen, "A Graph Model for E-Commerce Recommender Systems", JASIST, 55(3):259–274, 2004

Analysis and Detection of Segment-Focused Attacks Against Collaborative Recommendation⋆

Bamshad Mobasher, Robin Burke, Chad Williams, and Runa Bhaumik

Center for Web Intelligence
School of Computer Science, Telecommunication and Information Systems
DePaul University, Chicago, Illinois
(mobasher, rburke, cwilli43, rbhaumik)@cs.depaul.edu

Abstract. Significant vulnerabilities have recently been identified in collaborative filtering recommender systems. These vulnerabilities mostly emanate from the open nature of such systems and their reliance on user-specified judgments for building profiles. Attackers can easily introduce biased data in an attempt to force the system to "adapt" in a manner advantageous to them. Our research in secure personalization is examining a range of attack models, from the simple to the complex, and a variety of recommendation techniques. In this chapter, we explore an attack model that focuses on a subset of users with similar tastes and show that such an attack can be highly successful against both user-based and item-based collaborative filtering. We also introduce a detection model that can significantly decrease the impact of this attack.

1 Introduction

Recent research has begun to examine the vulnerabilities and robustness of different recommendation techniques, such as collaborative filtering, in the face of what has been termed "shilling" attacks [1,2,3,4], but we call *profile injection attacks*, since promoting a particular product is only one way such attack might be used. In a profile injection attack, an attacker interacts with the recommender system to build within it a number of profiles associated with fictitious identities with the aim of biasing the system's output.

It is easy to see why collaborative filtering is vulnerable to profile injection attacks. A user-based collaborative filtering algorithm collects user profiles, which are assumed to represent the preferences of many different individuals and makes recommendations by finding peers with like profiles. If the profile database contains biased data (many profiles all of which rate a certain item highly, for example), these biased profiles may be considered peers for genuine users and result in biased recommendations. This is precisely the effect found in [3] and [4]. This vulnerability of collaborative filtering has been the focus of some recent

⋆ This research was supported in part by the National Science Foundation Cyber Trust program under Grant IIS-0430303.

O. Nasraoui et al. (Eds.): WebKDD 2005, LNAI 4198, pp. 96–118, 2006.

studies directed at better understanding the weakness of these recommendation algorithms. These explorations have shown that high-knowledge [2] attack models can be very effective at attacking user-based collaborative filtering, but the item-based collaborative filtering algorithm [5] appears to be more robust. These findings have been further supported by the lack of success of reduced knowledge attacks against the item-based algorithm.

Researchers who have examined this phenomenon have concentrated on broad attack models whose profiles contain ratings across the spectrum of available objects and have measured their results by looking at how all of the users of the system are affected in the aggregate. However, it is a basic truism of marketing that the best way to increase the impact of a promotional activity is to target one's effort to those already predisposed toward one's product. In other words, it is more likely that an attacker wishing to promote a particular product will be interested not in how often it is recommended to all users, but how often it is recommended to the particular market segment that is likely to already have a propensity to purchase it.

We explore a new style of attack model that shifts the focus from trying to impact the complete user set to instead targeting a segment of profiles with specific interests. We call such an attack a *Segment Focused attack* (or simply a *segment attack*). As we show, an attack based on this approach can not only be highly effective against the user-based algorithm, but can also have a significant impact on the item-based algorithm, which is generally considered more robust. Furthermore this attack model demonstrates both algorithms are vulnerable to attacks requiring only a limited amount of system knowledge. Our experiments compare the segment attacks with the standard attack models previously studied, and demonstrate the segment attack model's effectiveness against item-based collaborative filtering algorithm.

The paper concludes with an examination of how a system might insulate itself from such an attack through detection and response. Recently a few researchers have focused on detecting and preventing shilling attacks. Chirita et al. [6] proposed several metrics for analyzing rating patterns of malicious users and evaluate their potential for detecting such shilling attacks. Su et al. [7] developed a spreading similarity algorithm in order to detect groups of very similar shilling attackers which is applied to a simplified attack scenario. O'Mahony et al. [8] developed several techniques to defend against the attacks proposed in [3] [4]. We show empirically that previous detection algorithms that have been effective against more traditional attacks are not necessarily effective against the segment attack. In response, we introduce a new classification-based detection algorithm, called the *Segment Model Detection* which uses a set of detection attributes for classifying attack profiles. We show that the proposed detection model when combined with either collaborative technique can greatly increase the system's robustness in the face of a segment attack.

The paper is organized as follows. In Section 2 we provide a general formal framework for profile injection attacks against collaborative systems, and we present the details of our proposed segment attack model. Section 3 includes some background information and the specific details of the user-based and item-based recommendation algorithms used in our experiments. In Section 4 we describe our evaluation methodology, including two evaluation metrics use to determine the effectiveness of the segmented attack against each algorithm. We then present our experimental results, with a detailed analysis of the proposed segmented attack model, and show that it can be effective against both user-based and item-based algorithms. In Section 5 we provide a brief introduction to attack detection and response and work that has been done to address this need. Following this, we introduce a model based technique for detecting and responding to the segment attack. In Section 5.3 we present experimental results of our model-based approach compared with the Chirita algorithm.

2 Attack Models

We have considered attacks where the attacker's aim is to introduce a bias in the recommender system by injecting fake user ratings. We call such attacks *profile injection attacks*. Our goal is to identify different types of profile injection attacks, and to study their characteristics and their impact on common collaborative filtering recommendation algorithms. An attack against a collaborative filtering recommender system consists of a set of attack profiles, biased profile data associated with fictitious user identities, and a *target item*, the item that the attacker wishes the system to recommend more or less highly. In this paper, our focus is on "shilling" attacks in which the aim of the attacker is to promote the target item. Hence, we call such attacks, *push* attacks. An attack model is an approach to constructing the attack profile, based on knowledge about the recommender system, its rating database, its products, and/or its users. The general form of a push attack profile consists of an m-dimensional vector of ratings, were m is the total number of items in the system. The rating given to the pushed item, i_t, is r_t. Generally, in a push attack, $r_t = r_{max}$, i.e., the maximum rating on the rating scale. On the other hand, in a *nuke* attack, in which the goal is to reduce the likelihood of the target item being recommended, $r_t = r_{min}$, where r_{min} is the minimum allowable rating.

We begin by presenting a formal framework for characterizing attack models and attack profiles. We then turn our attention to several specific attack models that we have introduced or studied in this work and discuss their properties. In Section 4, we present our detailed experimental results corresponding to these attack models.

2.1 Framework for Characterizing Profile Injection Attacks

Let I be a set of items, U a set of users, R a set of rating values, r_{max} is the maximum rating in R, and r_{min} is the minimum rating in R, and $UP = \{up_1, up_2, \cdots, up_d\}$ a set of user profiles, where each $up_i = \{\langle i, r \rangle \mid i \in I, r \in R \cup \{\texttt{null}\}\}$, with $\texttt{null}$ representing a missing or undefined rating.

An *attack model* partitions the set of items, I, into 4 groups i_t, I_S, I_F, and $I_\emptyset$, such that i_t is the *target item*; I_S is a set of *selected items*; I_F is a set of randomly

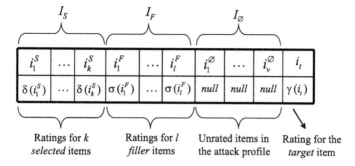

Fig. 1. The general form of an attack profile in a profile injection attack

selected *filler items*; and $I_\emptyset = I - (I_S \uplus I_F \uplus \{i_t\})$ is the set of *unrated items*. The set of parameters that define the partitioning and assignment of ratings for each partition are specific to the particular attack model. The functions δ and σ assign ratings to the elements I_S and I_F, respectively, while γ assigns a rating to the target item, i_t. These functions, and the manner in which I is partitioned, depend on the particular attack model, as described below.

The generic form of an attack profile, as described above, is depicted pictorially in Figure 1. Generally speaking, specific attack models vary based on the parameters or methods used to identify the *selected items*, the proportion of the remaining items that are used as *filler items*, and the way that specific ratings are assigned to each of these sets of items and to the target item. In most cases, the set of selected items, I_S, is either empty or represents a small group of items that have been selected because of their association with the target item (or a targeted segment of users). These items may be selected according to a number of factors that may include the distribution of rating values among items or users, the likelihood that a particular item is highly or frequently rated, or the expected characteristics associated with a particular segment of users. On the other hand, the set of filler items, I_F, represent a group of randomly selected items in the database which are assigned ratings within the attack profile.

We next focus our attention on a number of specific attack models and discuss some of their characteristics.

2.2   Basic Attack Models

Two attack models, introduced originally in Lam and Reidl [3] are the *random* and *average* attack models. Both of these attack models involve two groups of items, the target item i_t and a set of filler items I_F where all items in I_F are assigned ratings based on the same amount of system knowledge. In [3], these models assumed that the filler items consisted of all items in the databases (except the target items), potentially requiring substantial knowledge and effort on the part of the attacker. We introduce a more general form of these attacks that allows for varying degrees of knowledge about the items in the system. We have also introduced a more sophisticated attack model, *Bandwagon attack* [2],

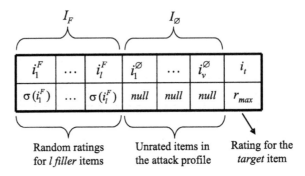

Fig. 2. An attack profile based on the random or the average attack model

that is designed to be more practical in terms of the knowledge or the effort involved by the attacker.

Both random and average attack profiles consist of ratings assigned to the filler items, as described above, and a pre-specified rating assigned to the target item. In the random attack the assigned ratings are based on the overall distribution of user ratings in the database, while in the average attack the rating for each filler item is computed based on its average rating for that item. Although we generally treat this attack model as a push attack, it can also be used as a nuke attack by changing the assigned rating for the target item from r_{max} to r_{min}. In both of these attack models, the set of selected items is empty. More formally, the average and random attack models have the following general characteristics:

- $I_S = \emptyset$;
- I_F is a set of randomly chosen filler items drawn from $I - \{i_t\}$, where the ratio of filler items $|I_F|/|I - \{i_t\}|$ is a pre-specified parameter.
- $\forall i \in I_F, \sigma(i) \sim \mathcal{N}(\mu, s)$, where $\sigma(i)$ is the rating given to item i. For average attack, $\mu = \mu_i$ and $s = s_i$, where μ_i and s_i are the mean and standard deviation of ratings or item i across all users, i.e., the rating value for each item $i \in I_F$ is drawn from a normal distribution around the mean rating for i. In the random attack $\mu = \mu_I$ and $s = s_I$, where μ_I and s_I are the mean and standard deviation of ratings for all items in I, i.e., the rating value for each item $i \in I_F$ is drawn from a normal distribution around the mean rating value across all items and users in the database;
- $\gamma(i_t) = r_{max}$, where r_{max} is the maximum rating value in R.

It should also be noted that the only difference between the average attack and the random attack is in the manner in which ratings are assigned to the filler items in the profile. Figure 2 depicts the general form for both the random and the average attacks.

The knowledge required to mount random attack is quite minimal, especially since the overall rating mean in many systems can be determined by an outsider empirically (or, indeed, may be available directly from the system). However, as Lam and Reidl [3] show, and our results confirm [2], the attack is not particularly effective.

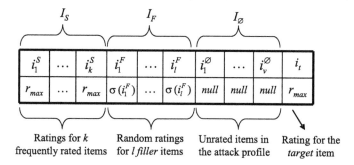

Fig. 3. A *Bandwagon* attack profile

Average attack which is more powerful uses the individual mean for each item rather than the global mean (except for the pushed item). In addition to the effort involved in producing the ratings, the average attack also has a considerable knowledge cost of order $|I_F|$ (the number of filler items in the attack profile). Our experiments, however, have shown that, in the case of user-based collaborative filtering algorithms, the average attack can be just as successful even when using a small filler item set, i.e., by assigning the average ratings to only a small subset of items in the database. Thus, the knowledge requirements for this attack can be substantially reduced [2]. This attack model, however, is not, in general, effective against an item-based collaborative algorithm, as we will show in Section 4.

The bandwagon attack [2] is based on the random attack, except that an additional group of items is selected to increase effectiveness with a minimal amount of additional knowledge. The goal of the bandwagon attack is to associate the attacked item with a small number of frequently rated items. This attack takes advantage of the Zipf's law distribution of popularity in consumer markets: a small number of items, best-seller books for example, will receive the lion's share of attention and also ratings. The attacker using this model will build attack profiles containing those items that have high visibility. Such profiles will have a good probability of being similar to a large number of users, since the high visibility items are those that many users have rated. This attack can be considered to have low knowledge cost since it does not require any system-specific data, because it is usually not difficult to independently determine what the "blockbuster" products are in any product space.

More formally, the *Bandwagon attack model* is an attack model, with the following characteristics:

- I_S is a set of selected items, such that for each $i \in I_S$, $|\{\langle i, r \rangle \in up_j \mid up_j \in UP, r \neq \mathtt{null}\}| \geq c$, where c is a pre-specified threshold constant (i.e., the total number of non-null ratings for all elements of I_S exceed a pre-specified constant).
- $\forall i \in I_S, \delta(i) = r_{max}$, where r_{max} is the maximum rating value in R.
- I_F is a set of randomly chosen filler items drawn from $I - \{i_t\}$, where the ratio of filler items is of size $|I_F|/|I - \{i_t\}|$ and is a pre-specified parameter;

- $\forall i \in I_F, \sigma(i) \sim \mathcal{N}(\mu_I, s_I)$, μ_I and s_I are the mean and standard deviation of ratings for all items in I, i.e., the rating value for each item $i \in I_F$ is drawn from a normal distribution around the mean rating value across the whole database;
- $\gamma(i_t) = r_{max}$.

Figure 3 depicts a typical attack profile for the bandwagon attack. Items i_1^S through i_k^S in I_S are selected because they have been rated by a large number of users in the database. These items are assigned the maximum rating value together with the target item, i_t. The ratings for the filler items i_1^F through i_l^F in I_F are determined randomly in a similar manner as in the random attack. The bandwagon attack therefore can be viewed as an extension of the random attack.

We showed in Burke et al. [2] that, despite the reduced knowledge, the bandwagon attack can still very successful against user based collaborative filtering. However, as we show below, none of these attacks are particularly effective against the item based algorithm.

2.3   The Segment Attack Model

Previous work [3] concluded that item-based algorithms were more robust than user-based ones and the average attack has been found to be most effective. From a cost-benefit point of view, however, such attacks are sub-optimal; they require a significant degree of system-specific knowledge to mount, and they push items to users who may not be likely purchasers. To address this, we introduce the *segment attack* model as a reduced-knowledge push attack specifically designed for the item-based algorithms [9].

It is a basic truism of marketing that the best way to increase the impact of a promotional activity is to target one's effort to those already predisposed towards one's product. In other words, it is likely that an attacker wishing to promote a particular product will be interested not in how often it is recommended to all users, but how often it is recommended to likely buyers. The segment attack model is designed to push an item to a targeted group of users with known or easily predicted preferences. For example, suppose that Eve, in our previous example, had written a fantasy book for children. She would no doubt prefer that her book be recommended to buyers who had expressed an interest in this genre, for example buyers of *Harry Potter* books, rather than buyers of books on Java programming or motorcycle repair. Eve would rightly expect that the "fantasy book buyer" segment of the market would be more likely to respond to a recommendation for her book than others. In addition, it would be to the benefit of the attacker to reduce the impact to unlikely buyers since a broad attack will be easier to detect.

We can frame this intuition as a question of utility. We assume that the attacker has a particular item i that she wants recommended more highly because she has a personal stake in the success of this product. The attacker receives some positive utility or profit p_i each time i is purchased. Let us denote the event that a recommendation of product i is made to a user u, by $R_{u,i}$ and the event that a user buys an item by $B_{u,i}$. The probability that a user will purchase i if it is recommended we can describe as a conditional probability: $P(B_{u,i}|R_{u,i})$. Over all users U that visit the system over some time period, the expected profit would be

$$P = \sum_{u \in U} p_i * P(R_{u,i}) * P(B_{u,i}|R_{u,i}) \tag{1}$$

The attacker of a recommender system hopes to increase her profit by increasing $P(R_{u,i})$, the probability that the system will recommend the item to a given user.

However, preferences for most consumer items are not uniformly distributed over the population of buyers. For many products, there will be users (like "Harry Potter" buyers) who would be susceptible to following a recommendation for a related item (another fantasy book for children) and others who would not. In other words, there will be some segment of users S that are distinguished from the rest of the user population $N = U - S$, by being likely recommendation followers:

$$\forall s \in S, \forall n \in N, P(B_{s,i}|R_{s,i}) \gg P(B_{n,i}|R_{n,i})) \tag{2}$$

Let us consider an extreme case of a niche market in which $P(B_{n,i}|R_{n,i})$ is zero. The only customers worth recommending to are those in the segment S. Everyone else will ignore the recommendation. It is in the attacker's interest to make sure that the attacker item is recommended to the segment users; it does not matter what happens to the rest of the population. The attacker will be only interested in manipulating the quantity $P(R_{s,i})$. In other words, the quantity that matters to an attacker may not be the overall impact of an attack, but rather its impact on a segment of the market distinguished as likely buyers. This may even be true if $P(B_{n,i}|R_{n,i}) > 0$ because these out-of-segment buyers contribute relatively little to the expected utility compared to the in-segment ones.

More formally, the *segment attack model* is an attack model, with the following characteristics:

- I_S is a set of selected items the attacker has chosen to define the segment, and all items in I_S are given the rating r_{max} (i.e., $\delta(i_j^S) = r_{max}$).
- I_F is a set of randomly chosen filler items drawn from $I - \{I_S \uplus i_t\}$, where the ratio of filler items $|I_F|/|I - \{i_t\}|$ is a pre-specified parameter, and all items in I_F are given the rating r_{min} (i.e., $\delta(i_j^F) = r_{min}$);
- $\gamma(i_t) = r_{max}$.

The target group of users (segment) in the segment attack model can then be defined as the set $U_S = \{UP_1^S...UP_t^S\}$ of user profiles in the database such that: $\forall UP_j^S \in U_S, \forall i \in I_S, Rating(UP_j^S, i) \geq r_c$, where $Rating(UP_j^S, i)$ is the rating associated with item i in the profile UP_j^S, and r_c is a pre-specified minimum rating threshold.

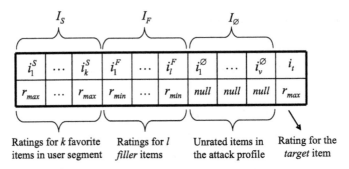

Fig. 4. A *Segment* attack profile

Figure 4 depicts a typical attack profile based on the segment attack model. The selected segment items, i_1^S through i_k^S in I_S represent the items that are (likely to be) favored by the targeted segment of users, like the Harry Potter books in the above example. These items are assigned the maximum rating value together with the target item. To provide the maximum impact on the item-based CF algorithm, the minimum rating was given to the filler items, thus maximizing the variations of item similarities used in the item-based algorithm.

The detailed experimental results for this attack model are presented in Section 4. The result show that this attack model is quite effective against both item-based and user-based collaborative filtering.

3   Recommendation Algorithms and Evaluation Metrics

We have focused on the most commonly-used algorithms for collaborative filtering, namely user-based and item-based. Previous work had suggested that item-based collaborative filtering might provide significant robustness compared to the user-based algorithm, but, as this paper shows, the item-based algorithm also is still vulnerable in the face of some of the attacks we introduced in the previous section. In the rest of this section we provide the details of the standard CF algorithms we have used in our experiments.

3.1   User-Based Collaborative Filtering

The standard collaborative filtering algorithm is based on user-to-user similarity [10]. This kNN algorithm operates by selecting the k most similar users to the target user, and formulates a prediction by combining the preferences of these users. kNN is widely used and reasonably accurate. The similarity between the target user, u, and a neighbor, v, can be calculated by the Pearson's correlation coefficient defined below:

$$sim_{u,v} = \frac{\sum_{i \in I} (r_{u,i} - \bar{r}_u) * (r_{v,i} - \bar{r}_v)}{\sqrt{\sum_{i \in I} (r_{u,i} - \bar{r}_u)^2} * \sqrt{\sum_{i \in I} (r_{v,i} - \bar{r}_v)^2}} \tag{3}$$

where I is the set of all items that can be rated, $r_{u,i}$ and $r_{v,i}$ are the ratings of some item i for the target user u and a neighbor v, respectively, and $\bar{r}_u$ and $\bar{r}_v$ are the average of the ratings of u and v over I, respectively.

Once similarities are calculated, the most similar users are selected. In our implementation, we have used a value of 20 for the neighborhood size k. We also filter out all neighbors with a similarity of less than 0.1 to prevent predictions being based on very distant or negative correlations. Once the most similar users are identified, we use the following formula to compute the prediction for an item i for target user u.

$$p_{u,i} = \bar{r}_a + \frac{\sum\limits_{v \in V} sim_{u,v} * (r_{v,i} - \bar{r}_v)}{\sum\limits_{v \in V} |sim_{u,v}|} \tag{4}$$

where V is the set of k similar users and $r_{v,i}$ is the rating of those users who have rated item i, $\bar{r}_v$ is the average rating for the target user over all rated items, and $sim_{u,v}$ is the mean-adjusted Pearson correlation described above. The formula in essence computes the degree of preference of all the neighbors weighted by their similarity and then adds this to the target user's average rating: the idea being that different users may have different "baselines" around which their ratings are distributed. Note also that if the denominator of the above equation is zero, our algorithm replaces the prediction by average rating of that user u.

3.2 Item-Based Collaborative Filtering

Item-based collaborative filtering works by comparing items based on their pattern of ratings across users. Again, a nearest-neighbor approach can be used. The kNN algorithm attempts to find k similar items that are have a similar pattern of ratings across different users.

For our purpose we have adopted the adjusted cosine similarity measure introduced by Sarwar et al. [5]. The adjusted cosine similarity formula is given by:

$$sim_{i,j} = \frac{\sum\limits_{u \in U} (r_{u,i} - \bar{r}_u) * (r_{u,j} - \bar{r}_u)}{\sqrt{\sum\limits_{u \in U} (r_{u,i} - \bar{r}_u)^2} * \sqrt{\sum\limits_{u \in U} (r_{u,j} - \bar{r}_u)^2}} \tag{5}$$

where $r_{u,i}$ represents the rating of user u on item i, and $\bar{r}_u$ is the average of the user u's ratings as before. After computing the similarity between items we select a set of k most similar items to the target item and generate a predicted value by using the following formula:

$$p_{u,i} = \frac{\sum\limits_{j \in J} r_{u,j} * sim_{i,j}}{\sum\limits_{j \in J} sim_{i,j}} \tag{6}$$

where J is the set of k similar items, $r_{u,j}$ is the prediction for the user on item j, and $sim_{i,j}$ is the similarity between items i and j as defined above. We consider a neighborhood of size 20 and ignore items with negative similarity. 'The idea here is to use the user's own ratings for the similar items to extrapolate the prediction for the target item. As in the case of user-based algorithm, if the denominator of the above equation is zero, our algorithm replaces the prediction by average rating of that user u.

3.3   Evaluation Metrics

There has been considerable research in the area of recommender systems evaluation [11]. Some of these concepts can also be applied to the evaluation of the security of recommender systems, but in evaluating security, we are interested not in raw performance, but rather in the change in performance induced by an attack. In O'Mahony et al. [4] two evaluation measures were introduced: *robustness* and *stability*. Robustness measures the performance of the system before and after an attack to determine how the attack affects the system as a whole. Stability looks at the shift in system's ratings for the attacked item induced by the attack profiles.

Our goal is to measure the effectiveness of an attack - the "win" for the attacker. The desired outcome for the attacker in a "push" attack is of course that the pushed item be more likely to be recommended after the attack than before. In the experiments reported below, we follow the lead of O'Mahony et al. [4] in measuring stability via prediction shift. However, we also measure hit ratio, the average likelihood that a top N recommender will recommend the pushed item [5]. This allows us to measure the effectiveness of the attack on the pushed item compared to all other items.

Average prediction shift is defined as follows. Let U and I be the sets of target users and items, respectively. For each user-item pair (u, i) the prediction shift denoted by $\Delta_{u,i}$, can be measured as $\Delta_{u,i} = p'_{u,i} - p_{u,i}$, where p' represents the prediction after the attack and p before. A positive value means that the attack has succeeded in making the pushed item more positively rated. The average prediction shift for an item i over all users can be computed as:

$$\Delta_i = \sum_{u \in U} \Delta_{u,i} / |U|. \tag{7}$$

Similarly the average prediction shift for all items tested can be computed as:

$$\bar{\Delta} = \sum_{i \in I} \Delta_i / |I|. \tag{8}$$

Note that a strong prediction shift is not a guarantee that an item will be recommended - it is possible that other items' scores are affected by an attack as well or that the item scores so low to begin with that even a significant shift does not promote it to "recommended" status. Thus, in order to measure the effectiveness of the attack on the pushed item compared to other items, we introduce the hit ratio metric. Let R_u be the set of top N recommendations for user u. For each push attack on item i, the value of a recommendation hit for user u denoted by H_{ui}, can be evaluated as 1 if $i \in R_u$; otherwise H_{ui} is evaluated to 0. We define hit ratio as the number of hits across all users in the test set divided by the number of users in the test set. The hit ratio for a pushed item i over all users in a set can then be computed as:

$$HitRatio_i = \sum_{u \in U} H_{ui}/|U|. \tag{9}$$

Likewise average hit ratio can then calculated as the sum of the hit ratio for each item i following an attack on i across all items divided by the number of items:

$$\overline{HitRatio} = \sum_{i \in I} HitRatio_i/|I|. \tag{10}$$

4   Experimental Results

In our experiments we have used the publicly-available Movie-Lens 100K dataset[1]. This dataset consists of 100,000 ratings on 1682 movies by 943 users. All ratings are integer values between one and five where one is the lowest (disliked) and five is the highest (most liked). Our data includes all the users who have rated at least 20 movies.

In all experiments, we used a neighborhood size of 20 in the k-nearest-neighbor algorithms for user-based and item-based systems. To perform our attack experiments, we must average over a number of different attack items, so we selected 50 movies from a wide range of ratings. We also generally selected a sample of 50 users as our test data, again mirroring the overall distribution of users in terms of number of movies seen and ratings provided. The results reported below represent averages over the combinations of test users and test movies. We use the metrics of prediction shift and hit ratio, as described earlier, to measure the relative performance of various attack models. Generally, the values of these metrics are plotted against the size of the attack reported as a percentage of the total number of profiles in the system.

For all the attacks, we generated a number of attack profiles and inserted them into the system database and then generated predictions. We measure "size of attack" as a percentage of the pre-attack user count. There are approximately 1000 users in the database, so an attack size of 1% corresponds to 10 attack profiles added to the system.

In the results below, we present the vulnerabilities of both user-based and item-based collaborative filtering against push attacks.

4.1   Attacks Against User-Based Collaborative Filtering

Figure 5 shows the results of a comparative experiment examining three algorithms at different attack sizes. The algorithms include the average attack

---

[1] http://www.cs.umn.edu/research/GroupLens/data/

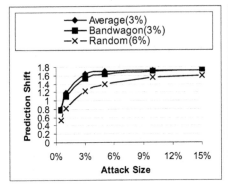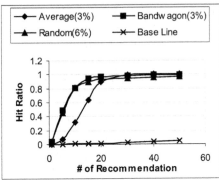

Fig. 5. Comparison of attacks against user-based algorithm, prediction shift (left) and hit ratio(right). The baseline in the right panel indicates the hit ratio results without any attack.

(3% filler sizes), the bandwagon attack (using 1 frequently rated item and 3% filler size), and the random attack (6% filler size). We see that even without system-specific data an attack like the bandwagon attack can be successful at higher attack sizes. The best performance is achieved with profiles with relatively small filler sizes. The average attack is obviously quite powerful - recall that the rating scale in this domain is 1-5 with an average of 3.6, so a rating shift of 1.5 is enough to lift an average-rated movie to the top of the scale. On the other hand, the bandwagon attack is able to come very close to the average attack in performance, even with minimal knowledge requirements. All that is necessary for an attacker is to identify a few items that are likely to be rated by many users.

4.2   Attacks Against Item-Based Collaborative Filtering

Our earlier investigation [1], as well as the study reported in Lam and Reidl [3], suggest that while the average and random attacks can be successful against user-based collaborative systems, they generally fall short of having a significant impact in the stability of item-based algorithms. For example, Figure 6 shows that item-based CF approach is more robust than the standard user-based algorithms in terms of the overall prediction shift on target items. Note the difference in the y-axis scales. Similar results are seen with the hit ratio metric.

Should we conclude then that an item-based algorithm is a successful defense against profile injection attacks, or are there specific attack models that can have a practical impact on such systems? Our experiments with the segment attack (see Figure 4) suggest that the answer to the later question is yes.

Recall that in the segment attack a set of items are selected for co-rating with the target item based on how they define a segment of users. Furthermore, the selection of the segment is done implicitly (without direct knowledge about the individual users within the segment) by the virtue of selecting highly rated movies with similar characteristics. The bandwagon attack uses general

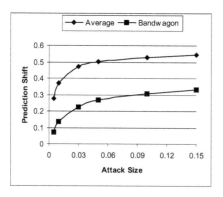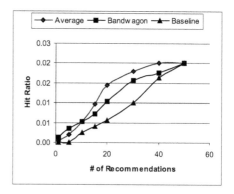

Fig. 6. Prediction Shift(left) and HitRatio(right) results for Average and Bandwagon Attack against Item-Based Collaborative Filtering. The Baseline in the right panel indicates the hit ratio results without any attack.

knowledge about the popularity of items. The segmented attack is based on a different type of knowledge. It uses domain knowledge about the similarity of items in order to target users that prefer items of a particular type. If we evaluate the segmented attack based on its average impact on all users, there is nothing remarkable. The attack has an effect but does not approach the numbers reached by the average attack. However, we must recall our market segment assumption: namely, that recommendations made to in-segment users are much more useful to the attacker than recommendations to other users. Our focus must therefore be with the "in-segment" users, those users who have rated the segment movies highly and presumably are desirable customers for pushed items that are similar: an attacker using the Harrison Ford segment might be interested in pushing a new movie featuring the star in an action role.

To build our segmented attack profiles, we identified the segment of users as all users who had given above average scores (4 or 5) to any three of the five most popular horror movies, namely, *Alien, Psycho, The Shining, Jaws,* and *The Birds.*[2] For this set of five movies, we then selected all combinations of three movies that had at least 50 users support, and chose 50 of those users randomly as our target segment and averaged the results.

The power of the segmented attack is emphasized in Figure 8 in which the impact of the attack is compared within the targeted user segment and within the set of all users. Left panel in the figure shows the comparison in terms of prediction shift and varying attack sizes, while the right panel depicts the hit ratio at 1% attack. While the segmented attack does show some impact against the system as a whole, it truly succeeds in its mission: to push the attacked movie precisely to those users defined by the segment. Indeed, in the case of in-segment users, the hit ratio is much higher than average attack.The chart also depicts the

---

[2] The list was generated from on-line sources of the popular horror films: http://www.imdb.com/chart/horror and http://www.filmsite.org/afi100thrillers1. html

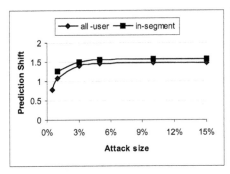 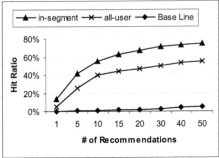

Fig. 7. Prediction shift and hit ratio results for the Horror Movie Segment in user-based algorithm

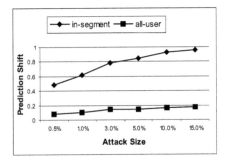 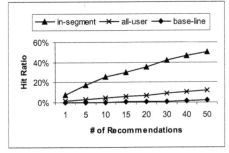

Fig. 8. Prediction shift and hit ratio results for the Horror Movie Segment in item-based algorithm

effect of hit ratio before any attack. Clearly the segmented attack has a bigger impact than any other attack we have previously examined against the item-based algorithm. Our prediction shift results show that the segmented attack is more effective against in-segment users than even the more knowledge-intensive average attack for the item-based collaborative algorithm. These results were also confirmed with a different segment based on a selection of Harrison Ford's movies (*Star Wars, Return of the Jedi, Indiana Jones and the Last Crusade,* and *Raiders of the Lost Ark*), which for the sake of brevity we do not include. Figure 7 also shows that segmented attack is also successful against user-based algorithm.

5   Attack Profile Classification

In this section, we present our approach to attack detection and response based on profile classification: we analyze the characteristics of profiles and label each profile either as an authentic or an attack profile. We introduce two attributes that we have determined to be particularly effective at detecting segment attack, and show that a classifier based on these attributes can be extremely effective at detecting attack profiles that use the segment attack template. Prior work in detecting attacks in collaborative filtering systems have mainly focused on ad hoc algorithms for identifying basic attack models such as the random attack [6]. In contrast, we propose an alternate technique based on more traditional supervised learning. We show that a C4.5 classifier, using the proposed classification attributes, and built on a training set created through injecting system data with segment attack profiles, can be applied to unseen segment attack data with impressive results.

For this approach, a user's profile is examined and based on characteristics of the profile, the entry is given a classification or Probability of Attack (PA) for the profile. Once each profile has been classified, this factor can be used to discount likely attack profiles to minimize their impact on other users. In Chirita et al. [6], a simple calculation was used to to discard likely attack profiles in user-based collaborative filtering by discounting the similarity with the PA through the following computation:

$$sim'_{u,v} = sim_{u,v} * (1 - PA_v) \qquad (11)$$

where $sim_{u,v}$ is the Pearson correlation for profile u and neighbor profile v as calculated in equation (3), and PA_v is the PA for profile v. We apply a similar process to discount the attack profiles. For item-based algorithm, however, the discounting is slightly more complicated since similarity is being tabulated over items rather than users. As a result, we must incorporate the PA into the adjusted cosine similarity from equation (5) to discount the weight applied to each specific user profile in calculating the similarity between the items. The resulting item similarity is computed as follows:

$$sim'_{i,j} = \frac{\sum_{u \in U} (r_{u,i} - \bar{r}_u) * (r_{u,j} - \bar{r}_u) * (1 - PA_u)}{\sqrt{\sum_{u \in U} (r_{u,i} - \bar{r}_u)^2 * (1 - PA_u)} * \sqrt{\sum_{u \in U} (r_{u,j} - \bar{r}_u)^2 * (1 - PA_u)}} \qquad (12)$$

where $r_{u,i}$ represents the rating of user u on item i, $\bar{r}_u$ is the average of the user u's ratings, and PA_u is the PA score for profile u as before.

5.1   Generic Attributes for Detection

The hypothesis behind using generic attributes is based on the expectation that the overall signature of attack profiles differs from authentic profiles. This difference comes from two sources: the rating given the target item, and the distribution of ratings among the filler items. As many researchers in the area have theorized [3,6,4,9], it is unlikely if not unrealistic for an attacker to have complete knowledge of the ratings in a real system. As a result generated profiles often deviate from rating patterns seen for authentic users. This variance may be manifested in many ways, including an abnormal deviation from the system average rating, or an unusual number of ratings in a profile. As a result, an attribute that captures these anomolies is likely to be informative in identifying reduced knowledge attack profiles (i.e., attack profiles with few filler items).

Prior work in attack profile classification has focused on detecting the general anomolies in attack profiles. Chirita et al. [6] introduced such a detection and response scheme. Their scheme focused heavily on an attribute they introduced for detecting the high rating deviations often associated with attack profiles. They referred to this attributes as *Rating Deviation from Mean Agreement* (RDMA), computed in the following way:

$$RDMA_u = \frac{\sum_{i=0}^{N_u} \frac{|r_{u,i} - Avg_i|}{NR_i}}{N_u} \tag{13}$$

where N_u is the number of ratings in user u's profile, $r_{u,i}$ is the rating given item i in user u's profile, and NR_i is the number of overall ratings given to item i. In addition, their work hypothesised that attack profiles were likely to have a higher similarity with their top 25 closest neighbors than real users using Pearson correlation [12]. Their detection algorithm leveraged this by basing the mean agreement (Avg_i and NR_i) used in the RDMA on the subgroup of profiles whose average similarity over their top 25 neighbors was less than half of the maximum average top 25 similarity in the system. This value is then used to calculate the PA for profile u, by applying the following activation function:

$$PA_u = \begin{cases} 0, \text{if} RDMA_u < RDMA_{Avg} \\ \frac{1}{e^\alpha - 1}(e^{\alpha \frac{RDMA_u - RDMA_{Avg}}{1 - RDMA_{Avg}}} - 1), \text{otherwise} \end{cases} \tag{14}$$

These probabilities are then used to discount the weights of suspected attack profiles as described above. Their work showed this technique to be successful in detecting basic attacks with large filler sizes. As we will show, however, this algorithm has difficulty detecting the segment attack, and generally, low knowledge attacks attacks that have small filler sizes.

Instead, we propose using a variation of the RDMA measure which we call *Weighted Degree of Agreement* (WDA) that uses only the numerator of the RDMA equation. This captures the sum of the differences of the profile's ratings from the item's average rating divided by the item's rating frequency. The overall average $\overline{WDA}$ is then subtracted from the profile's value, WDA_u, as a normalizing factor.

5.2   Model-Specific Attributes for Detection

One weakness of generic attributes is that for smaller profile sizes, they have more difficulty in distinguishing an attack profile from an eccentric, but authentic, profile. To address the detection coverage gap at smaller filler sizes, we present an alternative approach for detection based on attack model similarity. In our appeoach, we detect attack profiles by comparing profile similarity to known attack models as done in traditional pattern classification. For this approach, known models could be used to build a training set where standard data mining techniques could then be applied to build a classifier. With a pattern matching approach, the closer an attacker mimics a known attack model, the greater the chance of detection. As a result, to avoid detection an attacker would theoretically have to deviate from the most effective models. By eliminating the benefit of the most effective profiles, the cost of an attack would increase since a larger attack would be required for a similar effect.

As shown in Section 2 attacks can be characterized based on the characterisitcs of their partitions I_{target} (the target item), I_S (selected items), and I_F (filler items). Model-specific attributes are those that aim to recognize the distinctive signature of a particular attack model. These attributes are based on partitioning each ratings profile in such a way as to maximize the profile's similarity to a known attack model. Statistical features of the ratings that make up the partition can then be used as detection attributes. One useful property of partition-based features is that their derivation can be sensitive to additional information (such as time-series or critical mass data) that suggests likely attack targets.

Our detection model discovers partitions of each profile that maximizes its similarity to the attack model. To model this partitioning, each profile is split into two sets. The set P_{target} contains all items in the profile with the profile's maximum rating; the set P_{filler} consists of all other ratings in the profile. Thus the intention is for P_{target} to approximate $I_{target} \cup I_S$ and P_{filler} to approximate I_F. We will not attempt to differentiate I_{target} from I_S. We can then use statistical features of the partitions as detection attributes. For the segment attack model, the partitioning feature that maximizes the attack's effectiveness is the difference in ratings of items in the $I_{target} \cup I_S$ compared to the items in I_F. Thus we introduce the *Filler Mean Target Difference* (FMTD) attribute. The attribute is calculated as follows:

$$FMTD_u = \left| \left(\frac{\sum\limits_{i \in P_{target}} r_{u,i}}{|P_{target}|} \right) - \left(\frac{\sum\limits_{k \in P_{filler}} r_{u,k}}{|P_{filler}|} \right) \right| \tag{15}$$

where $r_{u,i}$ is the rating given by user u to item i. The overall average $\overline{FMTD}$ is then subtracted from $FMTD_u$ as a normalizing factor.

5.3   Detection Experimental Results

For our detection experiments, we used the same Movie-Lens 100K dataset[3] used in Section 4. To minimize over-training, the dataset was split into two equal-sized partitions. The first partition was made into a training set, while the second was used for testing and was unseen during training. The training data was created by inserting a variety of segment attacks at various filler sizes that ranged from 3% to 100%. Once again to minimize over-training, all training data was created using the Harrison Ford segment while testing was executed on the 6 combinations of Horror segment movies. Specifically the training data

---

[3] http://www.cs.umn.edu/research/GroupLens/data/

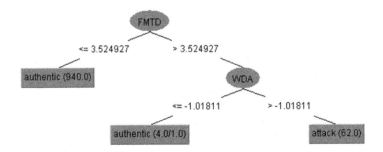

Fig. 9. C4.5 Decision tree using the proposed FMTD and WDA attributes

Table 1. Comparison of confusion matrices for the Chirita et al. and the Segment Model algorithms, using 1% Horror segment attack averaged across filler sizes

Segment Model Detection			Chirita et al. Detection		
Authentic	Attack		Authentic	Attack	
942.3	0.7	Authentic	794.1	148.9	Authentic
0.0	9.0	Attack	2.7	6.3	Attack

was created by inserting a 1% segment attack against the Harrison Ford segment at a particular filler size, and generating the detection attributes for the authentic and attack profiles. This process was repeated 6 more times with 1% segment attacks against the same segment at a different filler size, and generating the detection attributes. For all these subsequent attacks, the detection attributes of only the attack profiles were then added to the original detection attribute dataset. This approach combined with the average attribute normalizing factor described above, allowed a larger attack training set to be created while minimizing over training for larger attack sizes that would affect the WDA distribution.

Based on the training data described above, C4.5 was used to build a binary profile classifier with $PA_u = 0$ if classified as *authentic* and $PA_u = 1$ if classified as *attack*. The resulting tree was used for all subsequent detection runs labeled *Segment Model Detection* and is depicted in Figure 9. The Chirita et al. algorithm was also implemented for comparison purposes (with $\alpha = 10$), and run on the test set described above and labeled *Chirita et al. Detection* [6]. To measure the effectiveness of the classification algorithms we used attack *precision* and *recall*. Attack precision is the ratio of true positives to all (true and false) positives, while attack recall is defined as the ratio of true positives to the sum of true positives and false negative. All segment attack results reflect the average over the 6 combinations of Horror segment movies described in Section 4. All prediction shift numbers for both user-based and item-based recommendation algorithms use the same parameters as in Section 4.

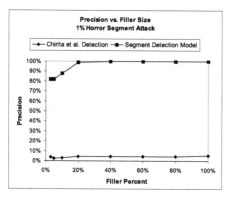
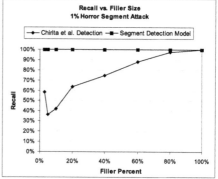

Fig. 10. Detection performance vs. filler size for 1% Horror segment attack

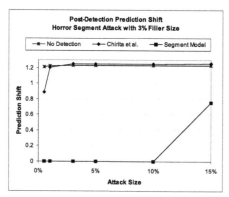
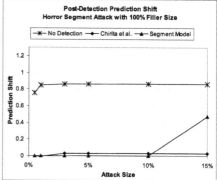

Fig. 11. User-based in-segment prediction shift for Horror segment attack at 100% filler size

In our results, we present the detection capabilities of the proposed attributes for increasing the robustness of both user-based and item-based collaborative filtering against segment push attacks. Table 1 depicts the average confusion matrix for each detection algorithm averaged over filler sizes of 3%, 5%, 10%, 20%, 40%, 60%, 80%, and 100% for a segment attack of size 1% (i.e., containing attack profiles numbering to 1% of the original profile database).

As the confusion matrices show, both algorithms perform fairly well on average over the range of filler sizes although our Attack Similarity Model's classification resulted in fewer false positives. A more in depth look at the performance of the Chirita et al. algorithm reveals the biggest gap in attack profile recall is at lower filler sizes while it performs very well at higher filler sizes. For the Attack Similarity Model, the precision improved from 81% at 3% filler size to 100% for filler sizes 40% or greater with the recall remaining at 100% throughout the range. The precision and recall results comparing these algorithms are depicted in Figure 10.

These detection algorithms were then used with user-based and item-based collaborative filtering as described in Section 5. As Figure 11 shows, although the Chirita et al. detection performs very well at higher filler sizes it has difficulty at lower filler sizes for even small attack sizes. The results also show the effect of training in the Segment Similarity Detection Model solely on small attack sizes. It should be noted that when the training data included higher attack sizes the overall classification performance at high attack sizes greatly improved, but at the cost of lower recall at small attack sizes. Based on these results, the low attack size biased training set was kept as the smaller attack sizes are likely to be more realistic. For item-based both detection methods significantly increased robustness resulting in insignificant prediction shift regardless of filler size up to an attack size of 15%.

To summarize, the Chirita et al. algorithm performs well in detecting basic attack models (such as the random attack) involving profiles with large filler sizes. However, it falls short when faced with more sophisticated attack profiles such as those based on the segment attack. Our classification-based approach using the proposed model-specific classification attribute is far more successful in detecting such attack profiles.

6   Conclusions

The open and interactive nature of collaborative filtering is both a source of strength and vulnerability for recommender systems. As our research and that of others has shown, biased profile data can easily sway the recommendations of a collaborative system towards inaccurate results that serve the attacker's ends. We have been able to model and empirically demonstrate successful attacks against the most common collaborative algorithms. We also have shown that although segment attack is effective against both user-based and item-based collaborative filtering, attack profile detection can be an effective way of increasing robustness for this type of attack.

This paper has shown several key findings in the area of attacks against recommender systems. We have shown that it is possible to mount successful attacks against such systems without a substantial knowledge of the system or users. The examination of segment attack, a very effective reduced knowledge attack, also demonstrated the vulnerability of the more robust item-based algorithm. In addition we proposed a profile classification and discounting algorithm which we call *Attack Similarity Model*, that can effectively identify attack profiles and provide a significant increase in robustness of collaborative filtering. Detection enhanced recommender systems, which combine collaborative recommendation with profile detection and discounting, seem likely to provide significant defensive advantages for recommender systems.

In our future work, we plan to deepen and extend our study of profile injection attacks. We will further develop ideas on detection and response and to evaluate their effectiveness against simulated and (given the availability of appropriate data) real-world attacks. In particular, we will develop detection algorithms that can automatically identify injected attack profiles based on many of the attack models described in this work. This will likely include additional generic and model-specific detection attributes to identify more general attack models. We are also exploring combining model-based attributes with time-series analysis to further improve robustness.

Our evaluation methodology relies on attack profiles that are generated in a fairly straightforward way from our attack models. We know that these attacks are effective, so they represent vulnerabilities that should be addressed. We plan to investigate what happens when an attack deviates from the attack model. Is the decrease in attack efficiency ameliorated by a decreased chance of detection from our model-based classifier? If we can ensure that the efficiency of attacks falls off faster than our ability to detect, then the model-based approach will represent an effective all-around defense.

References

1. Burke, R., Mobasher, B., Zabicki, R., Bhaumik, R.: Identifying attack models for secure recommendation. In: Beyond Personalization: A Workshop on the Next Generation of Recommender Systems, San Diego, California (2005)
2. Burke, R., Mobasher, B., Bhaumik, R.: Limited knowledge shilling attacks in collaborative filtering systems. In: Proceedings of the 3rd IJCAI Workshop in Intelligent Techniques for Personalization, Edinburgh, Scotland (2005)
3. Lam, S., Reidl, J.: Shilling recommender systems for fun and profit. In: Proceedings of the 13th International WWW Conference, New York (2004)
4. O'Mahony, M., Hurley, N., Kushmerick, N., Silvestre, G.: Collaborative recommendation: A robustness analysis. ACM Transactions on Internet Technology **4**(4) (2004) 344–377
5. Sarwar, B., Karypis, G., Konstan, J., Riedl, J.: Item-based collaborative filtering recommendation algorithms. In: Proceedings of the 10th International World Wide Web Conference, Hong Kong (2001)
6. Chirita, P.A., Nejdl, W., Zamfir, C.: Preventing shilling attacks in online recommender systems. In: WIDM '05: Proceedings of the 7th annual ACM international workshop on Web information and data management, New York, NY, USA, ACM Press (2005) 67–74
7. Su, X.F., Zeng, H.J., Chen, Z.: Finding group shilling in recommendation system. In: Proceedings of the 14th international World Wide Web Conference (WWW05). (2005)
8. OMahony, M., Hurley, N., Silvestre, G.: Utility-based neighbourhood formation for efficient and robust collaborative filtering. In: Proceedings of the 5th ACM Conference on Electronic Commerce (EC04). (2004) 260–261
9. Mobasher, B., Burke, R., Bhaumik, R., Williams, C.: Effective attack models for shilling item-based collaborative filtering systems. In: Proceedings of the 2005 WebKDD Workshop, held in conjuction with ACM SIGKDD 2005, Chicago, Illinois (2005)

10. Herlocker, J., Konstan, J., Borchers, A., Riedl, J.: An algorithmic framework for performing collaborative filtering. In: Proceedings of the 22nd ACM Conference on Research and Development in Information Retrieval (SIGIR'99), Berkeley, CA (1999)

11. J.Herlocker, Konstan, J., Tervin, L.G., Riedl, J.: Evaluating collaborative filtering recommender systems. ACM Transactions on Information Systems **22**(1) (2004) 5–53

12. Resnick, P., Iacovou, N., Suchak, M., Bergstrom, P., Riedl, J.: Grouplens: an open architecture for collaborative filtering of netnews. In: CSCW '94: Proceedings of the 1994 ACM conference on Computer supported cooperative work, ACM Press (1994) 175–186

Adaptive Web Usage Profiling*

Bhushan Shankar Suryavanshi, Nematollaah Shiri, and Sudhir P. Mudur

Dept. of Computer Science and Software Engineering
Concordia University
Montreal, Quebec, Canada
{bs_surya, shiri, mudur}@cse.concordia.ca

Abstract. Web usage models and profiles capture significant interests and trends from past accesses. They are used to improve user experience, say through recommendation of pages, pre-fetching of pages, etc. While browsing behavior changes dynamically over time, many web usage modeling techniques are static due to prohibitive model compilation times and also lack of fast incremental update mechanism. However, profiles have to be maintained so that they dynamically adapt to new interests and trends, since otherwise their use can lead to poor, irrelevant, and mis-targeted recommendations in personalization systems. We present a new profile maintenance scheme, which extends the Relational Fuzzy Subtractive Clustering (RFSC) technique and enables efficient incremental update of usage profiles. An impact factor is defined whose value can be used to decide the need for recompilation. The results from extensive experiments on a large real dataset of web logs show that the proposed maintenance technique, with considerably reduced computational costs, is almost as good as complete remodeling.

1 Introduction

The world wide web has become an integral part of our lives being used by millions of people nowadays for a variety of e-commerce applications. The reasons for this popularity include 24×7 availability, seamless communication over any distance, fast and cheap information access. However, further sustained growth in e-commerce mandates significant improvements in the ease and the speed with which a layman can do a business transaction on the web. Understanding behaviors, characteristics, and preferences of users is essential for satisfactory user experience. This can help companies retain current customers, attract new customers, improve cross marketing and sales, judge the effectiveness of promotional campaigns, track leaving customers, and find an effective logical structure of their web space [1].

Profiles refer to information about the preferences of individuals. For a web site, user profiling is the process of building preference information specific to each visitor of the site. Profiles could be built explicitly or implicitly [11]. In explicit profiling, a profile is built through active involvement of the user, typically through fill-in forms and questionnaires. Each profile may contain generic information such as date of birth and area code, along with some dynamic information, which is likely to change over

---

* This work is an extended version of our earlier work presented at WebKDD 2005 [29].

O. Nasraoui et al. (Eds.): WebKDD 2005, LNAI 4198, pp. 119–138, 2006.
© Springer-Verlag Berlin Heidelberg 2006

time such as favorite television programs or football teams. Explicit profiling requires users to get involved directly and put in most of the effort, and hence depends much on the motivation of users. On the other hand, in implicit profiling users are not directly involved. The navigation behavior and preferences of the user are learnt typically through analysis of the user interaction logs recorded by the web server. The web logs have lots of information which can be used to identify the user's interests in the site. Web usage mining techniques [16, 17] discover usage profiles from server logs. We emphasize on 'usage' profiles rather than 'user' profiles because users cannot be identified from anonymous web server logs. This is due to proxy servers and local network gateways, use of a single computer by multiple users, and dynamic IPs [8]. The usage of the website on the other hand can be traced through the server logs, which are basically user access history datasets. Moreover, it is these anonymous users that every company wishes to attract and get involved with its website when they first visit the site. A personalized experience may lead the users to register and further use/reuse the site and its services.

The collection of usage profiles reflects the semantics of the historic user access dataset at particular point of time. An important application is in web personalization which provides content and services at the website tailored to the needs of individual users. Users are recommended objects which may include pages, products, advertisements, etc., depending on the type and taste of the user. Another important application is the use by content creators or web designers to identify which material is used more often, how long a material is viewed by which types of users, and in what order they are accessed. Profiles have also been used for path prediction, prefetching of pages, improving the structure of websites, and in a nutshell improving the user's experience.

An important characteristic to note is the dynamic nature of the usage of websites. A popular website is visited frequently by a large number of users with various needs. The browsing behavior of users of such sites is not fixed or static. A user might browse the same page for different purposes. Each time the same user accesses the site, he/she may have different browsing goals. Moreover, user behavior and interest can change with time. If these profiles or models are fixed and do not adapt to new interests and usage, it may lead to degradation of the system performance over time. Irrelevant and mis-targeted recommendations annoy the users, leading to poor and ineffective personalization systems. Most existing techniques for modeling web usage are static or inefficient, mainly due to the fact that the time complexity to compile the data into a model is in general prohibitive and adding one new data point may sometime require a full recompilation of the model [24]. If personalized recommendations have to succeed, it is vital to develop maintenance techniques, which can adapt to changes in the usage model in non-stationary web environments. This forms the main focus of this chapter.

Clustering techniques have been used extensively to extract usage profiles that capture different interests and trends among users accessing the site. We present a new maintenance scheme, based on a new algorithm, called *Incremental Relational Fuzzy Subtractive Clustering (Incremental* RFSC), that can track evolution of the clustering model. We study the similarity of the clustering model obtained using the Incremental RFSC algorithm and compare it with the model obtained from a complete reclustering (using RFSC) to show the validity of our proposed maintenance scheme. It should be noted that Incremental RFSC does not completely replace reclustering but enables adaptability which can reduce the number of times reclustering has to be performed. Any maintenance technique based on incremental update of the profile requires a measure to indicate, to the web analyst, when reclustering is required. For this purpose we introduce a quantitative measure, called *impact factor*. Reclustering is recommended when the impact factor exceeds a predefined threshold. We have conducted extensive experiments, which show effectiveness of the proposed technique for adaptive usage profiling to provide personalized recommendations.

2   Related Work

In the context of discovering usage profiles, we can distinguish two cases: clustering of user transactions or access sessions and clustering of page views. A session is typically the set of pages that a user accessed from the moment s/he entered the site till the moment s/he leaves it.

Mobasher et al. [17] proposed a technique for capturing aggregate usage profiles based on association rules discovery and usage based clustering. This technique directly computes overlapping clusters of URL references based on their co-occurrence patterns across user transactions. A hypergraph is constructed whose hyperedges are frequent itemsets that are found by the *a priori* algorithm. The weight of a hyperedge in this hypergraph is calculated by averaging all the confidences of association rules found in these frequent itemsets. Clusters are obtained by applying the hypergraph partitioning algorithm to this hypergraph. Yan et al. [34] used K–means clustering algorithm to cluster user sessions. Xie et al. [33] exploit belief functions for finding similarity between sessions and then cluster them using a greedy algorithm. Shahabi and Banaei-Kashani [26] propose dynamic clustering to adapt to changes in user's behaviors in real time. Hierarchical clustering methods have also been applied to web logs. For instance, Fu et al. [11] suggest a technique, called generalization-based clustering, which uses page URLs to construct a hierarchy, which is then used to categorize the pages. The sessions are generalized according to the page hierarchy and clustered using BIRCH algorithm [36].

All the above are "hard" partitioning techniques, while web log data is inherently soft and fuzzy in nature. A user's browsing behavior on the web is highly uncertain [33]. It is therefore inappropriate to capture such overlapping interests of the users in crisp partitions. To deal with this fuzziness and uncertainty, Nasraoui et al. [20] proposed to extract profiles using an unsupervised relational clustering algorithm based on the competitive agglomeration algorithm. They [21] further extend this approach with fuzzy clustering algorithms such as Relational Fuzzy C-Maximal Density Estimator (RFC-MDE) and Fuzzy C Medoids algorithm (FCMdd). The basis of these techniques is the Fuzzy C-means (FCM) [3] method of clustering which allows an object to belong to two or more clusters at the same time.

All the aforementioned fuzzy C-means based algorithms need to convert non-Euclidean relations into Euclidean using the β-spread transformation. This transformation consists of adding a positive number β to all off-diagonal elements of the relational matrix R, and involves expensive eigenvalue computations [9]. Moreover, the spread could be so large that the structure in the original relational matrix R might not be mirrored by the β-spread transformed matrix [9]. Another point that should be mentioned here is that the success of most of the Fuzzy C-Means based techniques depends on a number of input parameters such as number of clusters C, fuzzifier factor m, and an initial partition U(0). While some methods do not require number of clusters to be user specified, [21, 22], it is not always possible to have a priori knowledge of all the above parameters for large datasets such as web logs. Due to such user control parameters, these clustering techniques may not manifest the true structure or groups in the data. Relational Fuzzy Subtractive Clustering (RFSC) [27] is an alternative fuzzy clustering technique proposed by us. It is a highly scalable algorithm for extracting usage profiles. The input parameters needed by RFSC are programmatically set using a heuristic which has worked well in all our experiments. Two of the parameters, namely accept ratio and reject ratio (explained in more detail in section 4) are specifically used as part of the termination condition for the algorithm, however it is important to note that this termination condition does not negatively affect the discovery of significant structure in the dataset. RFSC finds clusters in decreasing order of significance. Therefore, changing the terminating conditions will only lead to not finding the less significant areas; but the high significant areas which form the real structure in data will always be found. Overall, RFSC is relatively immune to noise, works well on large datasets and also reduces the concern over the prohibitively long time taken for compiling the model. We also proposed a cluster validity index for RFSC. For completeness, the RFSC algorithm is briefly described in Section 4.

3   An Overview of Cluster Maintenance

A clustering algorithm should have the following desirable properties [31, 5]:

(1) *Stability* -- produce a clustering which is unlikely to be altered drastically when new objects are added.
(2) *Robustness* -- small errors in the description of the objects may only lead to small changes in the clustering.
(3) *Order insensitivity* -- composition of clusters is independent of the order in which objects are processed.
(4) *Maintainability* -- handle growth efficiently, i.e., maintenance of clusters should be practical and efficient.

Most existing clustering algorithms are not well-suited for maintaining clusters in a dynamic environment, and often the problem of updating clusters is solved only by complete reclustering [31, 6, 5, 30]. Also most clustering algorithms suffer from limitations such as requiring the specification of the number of clusters, sensitivity to initialization of clusters and to noise [19].

One of the early works proposed in dynamic cluster maintenance in information retrieval is [5], which is based on the notion of cover coefficient. An incremental document clustering algorithm is proposed in [6], which attempts to maintain small diameter clusters as new points are inserted in the dataset. They also studied the dual clustering problem, where the clusters are of fixed diameter, and the goal is to minimize the number of clusters. Ester et al. [10] proposed an extension of GDBSCAN algorithm for large updates in a data warehouse environment. Tasoulis et al. [30] introduced an extension of the k-windows algorithm that can discover clustering rules from a dataset in a dynamic environment. Their experiments showed that their extension could effectively and efficiently identify the changes in the pattern structure. In web usage mining, Shahabi et al. [26] studied dynamic clustering as an approach to make the cluster model adaptive to short-term changes in users' behaviors. They argue that web usage mining systems should compromise between scalability and accuracy to be applicable to web sites with numerous visitors,. They also show that even with lower accuracy, dynamic clustering helps achieve adaptability. Nasraoui et al. [19] were among the first to propose a framework of mining evolving user profiles through a new scalable clustering methodology, inspired from the natural immune system, which is capable of continuously learning and adapting to new incoming patterns. The Web server plays the role of the human body, and the incoming requests play the role of foreign antigens, bacteria, or viruses that need to be removed by the proposed immune-based clustering technique. Baraglia and Silvestri [2] propose a recommender system, called SUGGEST 3.0 that dynamically generates links to pages that have not yet been visited by a user and might be of his potential interest. Differently from other recommender systems, their system does not make use of any off-line component, and is able to manage web sites made up of pages dynamically generated. For this purpose, SUGGEST 3.0 incrementally builds and maintains historical information using an incremental graph partitioning algorithm, requiring no off-line component.

Our work in this paper differs from earlier maintenance schemes in several ways, most notably the following:

- Many of the aforementioned maintenance schemes are for crisp clustering. Our maintenance scheme is for RFSC, which is a fuzzy clustering algorithm. There has been little work reported is this area.
- We strongly believe that computation of similarity between the clustering obtained after application of any maintenance algorithm and complete reclustering is necessary to validate a maintenance scheme. Unlike in many of the above, we show the validity of incremental RFSC by computing similarity.
- To the web analyst, it is often unknown as to when a complete remodeling is required. It is also useful to know when the user access patterns have drastically changed. This would help the analyst to set historic time windows when remodeling operation is applied. For this we provide a quantitative definition of an "impact factor." Thresholding of this factor can indicate as to when complete remodeling becomes necessary.

The main motivation for developing an incremental RFSC comes from the advantages which RFSC offers for web usage profiling over previously used clustering algorithms. For instance, RFSC works very well with large datasets which is an absolute requirement for modeling real world data. Further, RFSC can handle noise which is inherent in web usage data and is independent of user specified input parameters that often causes bias in modeling. Incremental RFSC with impact factor neatly extends RFSC to a full fledged maintenance scheme.

4   Relational Fuzzy Subtractive Clustering (RFSC)

We briefly describe the RFSC algorithm in this section. Interested readers are referred to [27] for a detailed description along with experimental results showing its effectiveness in web usage profiling. RFSC is based on the subtractive clustering algorithm proposed by Chiu, 1994 [7], a technique widely used in fuzzy systems modeling. Subtractive clustering is in turn based on mountain method proposed by Yager and Filev, 1992 [35] for estimating the number and initial location of cluster centers. A relational extension of mountain method has been proposed in [23].

Numerical relational data describes the set of objects to be clustered, less directly by giving a measurement of the dissimilarity (or similarity) between each pair of objects [13]. The RFSC algorithm starts by considering each object x_i as a potential cluster center. The potential P_i of each object x_i is calculated as follows:

$$P_i = \sum_{j=1}^{N_U} e^{-\alpha R_{ij}^2} \text{ , where } \alpha = 4/\gamma^2$$

in which R_{ij} is the dissimilarity between objects x_i and x_j, N_U is the total number of objects to be clustered, and γ is essentially the neighborhood calculated from the relational matrix R. It also holds that $R_{ij} \geq 0$, $R_{ij} = R_{ji}$, and $R_{ii} = 0$. In [27] we proposed a heuristic method for estimating a value for γ as follows. We define neighborhood-dissimilarity value (γ_i) of each object x_i from every other object as the median of dissimilarity values of x_i to all other objects. The neighborhood-dissimilarity value (γ) for the entire dataset is defined as the median of all γ_i's, for i in $[1..N_U]$. Based on our experiments, this heuristic seems to work fine for web usage datasets.

An object with the highest potential (P_1^*) is selected as the first cluster center. Next, the potential of each object is reduced proportional to the degree of similarity with this previous cluster center. Thus there is larger subtraction in potential of objects that are closer to this cluster center compared to those which are farther away. After this subtractive step, an object (x_t) with the next highest potential (P_t) is selected as the next candidate cluster center. Now to determine whether this can be accepted as an actual cluster center or not, we make use of two threshold values $\overline{\in}$ (accept ratio) and $\underline{\in}$ (reject ratio), where we have that $0 < \overline{\in}, \underline{\in} < 1$, and $\underline{\in} < \overline{\in}$. If $P_t > \overline{\in} P_1^*$, then x_t is selected as the next cluster center, and this is followed by the subtractive step described above. If $P_t < \underline{\in} P_1^*$, then x_t is rejected, and the clustering algorithm terminates. If the potential P_t lies between $\overline{\in} P_1^*$ and $\underline{\in} P_1^*$, then we say that potential has fallen in the gray region, in which case we check whether x_t provides a good trade-off between having a sufficient potential and being sufficiently far from existing cluster centers. If this holds, then x_t is selected as the next cluster center. This process of subtraction and selection continues until $P_t < \underline{\in} P_1^*$, which is the termination condition. After finding C cluster centers, we can find the membership degree of different x_j to each cluster c_i using the formula:

$$u_{ij} = e^{-\alpha R_{c_i j}^2} \text{ , } i = [1..C] \& j = [1..N_U],$$

in which $R_{c_i j}$ is the dissimilarity of the ith cluster center x_{c_i} with the jth session x_j. When $x_j = x_{c_i}$, we have $R_{c_i j} = 0$ and that the membership $u_{ij} = 1$. We have relaxed the constraint imposed by fuzzy C-means based algorithms, namely that $\sum_{i=1}^{C} u_{ij} = 1$. This effectively makes RFSC less sensitive to noise, as shown by our experiments in [27].

4.1 A Cluster Validity Index for RFSC

Any clustering algorithm is incomplete without a validity index that gives a measure of the "goodness" of the clustering. Good clustering of data results in low intra-cluster distance and large inter-cluster distance. In [27], we introduced a goodness index for the RFSC algorithm based on the Xie-Beni index [32]. The Xie- Beni index is basically the ratio of compactness to separation of the clusters, but requires the aforementioned constraint imposed by fuzzy C-means algorithms, which is a condition not mandatory in RFSC. We define *compactness* as follows in which c_i is the ith cluster center:

$$Compactness = \sum_{i=1}^{C} \left(\frac{\sum_{j=1}^{N_U} u_{ij}^2 * R_{c_i j}^2}{\sum_{j=1}^{N} u_{ij}} \right) \Bigg/ C.$$

Separation is defined as the $\min_{i \neq k} R_{c_i c_k}^2$, for i=1 to C and k=1 to C, where c_i and c_k are the ith and kth cluster centers respectively, and $R_{c_i c_k}$ is the dissimilarity between these cluster centers. Using compactness and separation values, our validity index for the RFSC clustering technique is defined as the ratio of compactness to separation.

We obtain a best clustering by searching and selecting those values of $\overline{\in}$ and $\underline{\in}$ which result in a minimum value for this index.

5 Maintenance Scheme for RFSC

Though the clusters obtained from usage data manifest the interests and trends among the users accessing the site at the time the clustering operation was applied, the interests and needs of users change dynamically over time. New logs are continuously created as users access the website. We thus require a cluster maintenance scheme by which these changing trends and patterns can be captured without having to frequently carry out this relatively expensive operation of reclustering of large volume of old and new data together.

Cluster maintenance is not a complete alternative to reclustering. By its very definition, cluster maintenance tries to incorporate newly arrived data into the existing model, while maintaining the profiles created earlier from the original set of data. This at best can result in a close approximation to clustering of the complete data, including both old and new. Clearly, reclustering will always give more accurate results and is required to be done periodically. Cluster maintenance however enables us to continuously adapt to the dynamic and changing environment in a much less expensive manner in terms of computation times and resources, and which also allows subsequent maintenance even after reclustering. Thus a "balanced" combination of full data clustering and cluster maintenance is ideally suited for dynamic environments. In this section, we introduce an extension of the RFSC algorithm, to which we refer as the *incremental RFSC* algorithm, used as the main component for our usage profile maintenance scheme. We will also introduce a measure that helps decide the stage at which a complete reclustering is required.

Suppose we have a dataset of N_U objects and have C clusters. Also let $u(C \times N_U)$ be the membership matrix, which contains the membership values of every object to each of the C clusters. To begin with, these C clusters and the matrix u are obtained using the RFSC algorithm. Subsequently, these are updated using incremental RFSC until reclustering of the complete dataset is required. This sequence of incremental RFSC and reclustering constitutes the maintenance scheme we propose in this work.

Let $W = \{Z_1, Z_2, ..., Z_C\}$ be the set of C prototypes representing the C clusters. We also store the corresponding potentials using which these C prototypes were chosen as the cluster centers, $P = \{P_1, P_2, ..., P_C\}$. These potentials have a natural ordering (i.e., descending) as RFSC finds the cluster with the highest potential first, followed by the next highest potential, and so on.

Let x_{new} be a new object (session) added to the dataset. Depending on x_{new}, we have three possible situations:

Case i) x_{new} has a high membership value with respect to one of the existing C clusters, and hence its potential is such that it becomes a core member of that cluster. Or x_{new} has a very low potential in which case it is probably a noise.

Case ii) The potential of x_{new} is such that it is not a core member of any of the C clusters, and its potential is lower than all the potentials of these clusters, but is high enough to become a new cluster center.

Case iii) The potential of x_{new} is such that it is better than the potential of an existing cluster center.

The process of determining the case that is applicable to the new object x_{new} and the actions taken are described in the following steps.

1. First, the stored potentials of all previous cluster prototypes P_i are raised by the degree to which this x_{new} is close to these previously known cluster prototypes. Hence the potential of the cluster prototype will increase more if x_{new} is closer to it (as x_{new} makes that cluster more dense) compared to when x_{new} is farther away. The maximum increase in potential is 1, i.e., when x_{new} coincides with an existing cluster center. Let P'_i be these updated potentials.

2. We check if the potential of x_{new} is better than the first cluster center, that is whether $P_{new} > P'_1$. If true, then case (iii) holds and the actions taken are described later below. If not, we then proceed with the subtractive step, i.e., potential of x_{new} will be reduced depending on its similarity with the first cluster center. After this subtractive step, if P_{new} becomes negative, it means that x_{new} is a core element or very close to the first cluster center, and hence case (i) holds. No further comparison or subtraction is required.

3. If the potential does not become negative, then we continue to compare the updated potential of x_{new} with the potential of next cluster prototype. Again if the potential of x_{new} is less than this cluster center, we perform the subtractive step as described above. If the potential of x_{new} is greater than the current cluster center, i.e., x_{new} has potential better than the potential of an existing cluster center, then case (iii) holds and we continue with step 4a below; otherwise we proceed with the subtractive step. Also it might so happen that after comparison with the potentials of all existing C cluster prototypes and going through the corresponding subtractive steps, x_{new} has a potential good enough to become a new cluster center, which indicates case (ii) holds and we continue with step 4b.

4a If case (iii) holds, we calculate the impact factor for not making x_{new} as one of the existing cluster centers. Computation of impact factor is discussed below. If the impact factor exceeds a threshold value, specified by a web administrator, then a complete reclustering has to be performed.

4b If case (ii) holds, x_{new} becomes a new cluster center and the model now has C+1 prototypes. Additionally, the membership of all the existing objects is also calculated with respect to this new cluster and stored in matrix u which will now have one more row to store the membership values for the newly generated cluster.

5. Irrespective of the case at hand, we calculate the membership of x_{new} with all the existing clusters.

5.1 Impact Factor

This parameter, denoted I, is a measure of the degree to which the cluster model is affected by not making the new incoming object as one of the existing cluster centers, when its potential is such that using the regular RFSC (for clustering of the complete dataset) it would have been a cluster center. Impact factor is calculated only when we have case (iii). We next explain the notion of impact factor with the help of an example and then provide a formal definition. Fig. 1(a) shows a clustering of N_U objects obtained using RFSC. As can be seen, there are three clusters with their centers marked. Now suppose a new object x_{new} arrives and has to be included in the existing

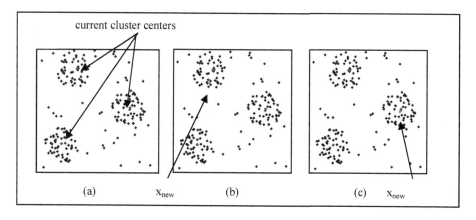

Fig. 1. Examples for impact factor calculation

clustering. If we have case (iii), then it means the potential of x_{new} is better than one of the existing cluster centers. Two situations can arise. Fig. 1(b) illustrates the first situation wherein x_{new} lies very close to an existing cluster center. Making x_{new} the cluster center of this cluster will not change much the clustering we have because there already exists a cluster center very close to x_{new} and the membership of x_{new} will be very close to 1. Hence the impact of not making this a cluster center is very low. The other situation is shown in Fig. 1(c), wherein we see that x_{new} is sufficiently far from any of the existing cluster centers. This would mean that the impact of not making this object as a cluster center will be much greater.

We shall now give a quantitative measure for impact factor. The impact factor I is initialized to 0 the first time the incremental RFSC algorithm is applied and also every subsequent time that RFSC is used to perform reclustering of the entire dataset. When a new object x_{new} is to be included in an existing cluster, if case (iii) holds, we find the minimum of the dissimilarity of x_{new} to existing cluster centers and increase the impact factor. Hence when there is a cluster center near x_{new}, the impact is less, whereas the impact is more if the cluster centers are far away. When the impact factor reaches a pre-defined threshold, reclustering of the entire dataset is required.

We next present our maintenance algorithm with the impact factor considered.

Incremental RFSC Algorithm

1. Calculate the potential P_{new} of the new object x_{new} to be inserted
2. Raise the potentials of all existing cluster prototypes;
$D_{i, new}$ = dissimilarity between x_{new} and i^{th} cluster center

$$P_i = P_i + e^{-\alpha D^2_{i,new}};$$

3. d_{min} = min. of the dissimilarity values between x_{new} and all the previously found cluster centers.
for i=1 to C **do**   **if** $(P_{new} > P_i)$ **then**

if $(P_{new} > \in P_1)$ **then** $I += d_{min}$ //case (iii)

else if $(P_{new} \geq \in P_1)$ **then**

if $(d_{min}/\gamma) + (P_{new}/P_1^{)} \geq 1$, **then** $I += d_{min}$ //case (iii)

end if
else

$$P_{new} = P_{new} - P_i \, e^{-\alpha D^2_{i,new}};$$

if $(P_{new} < 0)$, **then** goto step 5;   //case (i) -- no further comparisons required
end if

end for
4.   **if** $((P_{new} > 0)$ and (case (iii) is not true))   //check if x_{new} can become a new cluster center

if $(P_{new} \geq \in P_1)$, **then**

if $(d_{min}/\gamma) + (P_{new}/P_1^{)} \geq 1$, **then**   //case (ii) is true, x_{new} is the new cluster center
C = C+1; //increment cluster count
$P_C = P_{new}$;
Calculate the membership of N_U old objects
with respect to this new cluster;
end if

end if
end if
5.   Increment N_U by 1 as a new object is added; Calculate membership of x_{new} with C clusters.
End algorithm;

6 Experiments and Results

In this section, we first present the evaluation metrics used by us to measure the similarity between clustering obtained by applying the Incremental RFSC maintenance algorithm and the one obtained by complete reclustering using RFSC. This is followed by an analysis of our experimental results and the values obtained for these metrics.

6.1 Evaluation Metrics

For similarity metrics, we have used the Rand, Corrected Rand, and Jaccard coefficients. Details of these metrics can be found in Jain and Dubes, 1988 [15] and in [29]. Basically, Rand and Jaccard values are in the range [0, 1]. The maximum value of 1 may not be achievable when the two clusterings have different number of clusters. Hubert et al. [14] suggested use of "rand index corrected for chance", called as "corrected" Rand (CR) coefficient. Correcting a statistic for chance means normalization such that its value is 0 when the partitions are selected by chance, and is 1 when a perfect match is achieved.

6.2 Data Preparation

For our experiments, we used the access logs from the web server of the Computer Science department at Concordia University from December 31, 2004 to March 5, 2005. This is a different and a much larger dataset than the one we used in [29]. The access log records from a web server are at a very fine granularity. Cleaning [8, 16] is required to remove log entries for image files and other such components within a web page. Log records for accesses by web crawlers and failed requests are also removed from the dataset. A session (as defined in section 2) is typically a collection of URLs of pages visited by a user from the moment she/he enters a web site to the moment the same user leaves the site. Each distinct URL in the site is assigned a unique number j ranging from 1 to M, the total number of URLs. The collection of the user accesses in the kth session is represented as a binary vector of size M, in which the jth entry is 1 if the user accessed the jth URL during this session, and is 0 otherwise. Sessions were identified from the log records by considering the elapsed time between two consecutive accesses from the same IP address. We considered 45 minutes as the maximum elapsed time. The root "/" was filtered out from all the sessions as it appeared in more than 80% of the sessions. We also removed short sessions of length 1 or 2, as they do not carry much information related to users' access patterns. After this pre-processing of the data, we obtained 64,529 user sessions with 10,424 distinct URLs. The average length of the sessions determined was 6.997 pages and sparsity level was 0.999329, defined as 1- (nonzero entries / total entries). Also, in all our experiments we use the similarity measure proposed in [20, 21] for construction of relational matrix R.

6.3 Similarity Analysis

We now evaluate our maintenance algorithm by comparing the clusterings obtained with those obtained by complete reclustering. Let N_{old} denote the number of sessions in the initial set of sessions clustered by RFSC, and N_{new} denote the number of new sessions which are to be added to the cluster model of the N_{old} sessions. Sessions are strictly ordered by time, i.e., in the order in which they were formed when users accessed the website. We created 9 experimental case studies by choosing different values for N_{old} as 30000 (46.49%), 34000 (52.68%), 38000 (58.88%), 42000 (65.08%), 46000 (71.28%), 50000 (77.48%), 54000 (83.68%), 58000 (89.88%) and 62000 (96.08%). For each case, the number of increment is N_{new} = 64529 - N_{old}. These (N_{old}, N_{new}) pairs can also be seen in Table 1.

For each of the above 9 cases, we applied RFSC to cluster the sessions in N_{old} and used the validity index mentioned above to achieve the best clustering for these N_{old} sessions. We then applied our maintenance algorithm in each case to include the new N_{new} sessions into the existing clustering. For validation and comparison purposes, we also performed reclustering of the entire dataset, i.e., N_{old} + N_{new} = 64529 sessions, using validity index to achieve the best clustering for the entire dataset. We obtained C=46 clusters. Since Rand, CR, and Jaccard coefficients are defined for crisp clustering, we defuzzified the clusters obtained by applying the maintenance and reclustering techniques. Each session is assigned to a cluster to which its degree of membership is the highest (nearest prototype). Also noise sessions, which have low membership with all the prototypes are put into one extra cluster, called *noise* cluster. That is, if a clustering yields C clusters, we add the $(C+1)^{th}$ cluster as the noise cluster during the defuzzication step. After defuzzification, we measure the similarity of clustering obtained from the incremental RFSC and reclustering operations. Fig. 2 shows the results of these experiments for measuring similarities.

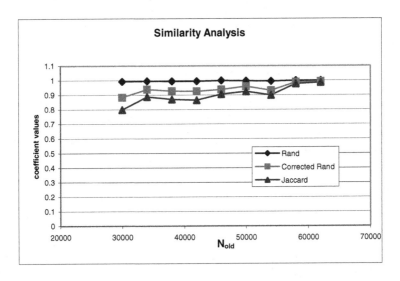

Fig. 2. Comparing the results of incremental RFSC and reclustering

Particularly interesting is the Corrected Rand (CR) coefficient since it has the maximum value of 1 when the clustering structures (partitions) compared are identical. It has the value 0 when they are generated by chance (i.e., CR is corrected for chance). The CR values obtained are 0.883, 0.938, 0.928, 0.925, 0.937, 0.959, 0.931,

0.988 and 0.992, respectively, for the 9 cases studied in these experiments. These are very high values of CR (high similarity) noting that the first case had $N_{old} = 30000$, which is even less than 50% of the entire dataset under consideration. We see that increase in N_{old} or decrease in the number of newly added sessions N_{new} leads to higher similarity of the clusterings generated. These results indicate that the similarity between the clustering obtained from incremental RFSC and complete reclustering did not, in a statistical sense, happen by chance. High values of CR for very small increments (0.992 for case 9 with $N_{old}= 62000$) indicate that RFSC is stable when the dataset grows with addition of new objects. This is a desirable clustering property as discussed in Section 3.

Table 1 shows the computation time for adding these N_{new} sessions. Although, having a high similarity with the cluster model obtained by complete reclustering is a necessary condition for any maintenance algorithm, this should not come at a prohibitive cost. We observed that on an average, Incremental RFSC takes around 4 seconds to add 100 new sessions. While the time taken for clustering of the entire dataset of 64529 sessions is around one and a half hour, adaptation of this cluster model to accommodate 100 new sessions can be accomplished in just a few seconds. In the absence of such a maintenance algorithm, a complete reclustering would have been required, clearly showing the importance of our maintenance algorithm.

Table 1. Timings for incremental RFSC

N_{old}	N_{new}	time (sec)
30000	34529	3219
34000	30529	2965
38000	26529	2675
42000	22529	2358
46000	18529	1999
50000	14529	1625
54000	10529	1210
58000	6529	776
62000	2529	301

6.4 Detection of New Interest Areas

While the above experiments clearly show that Incremental RFSC maintains existing clusters with varying number of new sessions (N_{new}) being added, it does not demonstrate whether new interest areas will also be detected, if the newly added data has that characteristic. Indeed, Incremental RFSC is very capable of detecting new interest areas. For demonstrating this, we consider the following experimental case. Clustering of the entire dataset of 64,529 sessions yields C=46 clusters as discussed above. RFSC detects clusters according to its order of significance in the dataset i.e., the most prominent cluster (interest area) is found first, followed by the next prominent cluster, and so on. We defuzzified these clusters and created 7 pairs of (N_{old}, N_{new}) partitions of the entire dataset by hiding clusters 1, 3, 5, 10, 26, 32, and 44, one at a time. These clusters were chosen at random. Hence in this process we hide the most prominent as well as lower potential clusters found by RFSC in the entire dataset. For each such partition, we apply RFSC to N_{old} sessions to get C_{old} clusters. The cardinalities of these (N_{old}, N_{new}) partitions and the values of C_{old} are shown in Table 2, in which the first column indicates the hidden cluster /profile.

Table 2. New interest areas detected with incremental RFSC

Hidden Cluster	N_{old}	N_{new}	C_{old}	No. of new clusters	Impact factor I	Corrected Rand (CR)
1	60964	3565	47	1	1845.2	0.881
3	61799	2730	45	1	1261.7	0.949
5	62697	1832	47	0	221.7	0.885
10	62184	2345	45	1	1316.0	0.988
26	63745	784	45	1	95.7	0.998
32	64032	497	45	1	72.8	0.997
44	64033	496	45	1	68.8	0.996

Next, we use Incremental RFSC to add the hidden N_{new} sessions to the cluster model, respectively. Table 2 shows the impact factor I. Considering that N_{new} is relatively a small addition compared to N_{old}, we note that the values for impact factor is quite high especially for the more prominent clusters that were hidden like 1,3 and 10. This is because the new cluster formed is quite prominent (significant new trend or interest among users) with respect to the existing cluster model and if I keeps increasing at the same rate, then a complete reclustering of the entire dataset may be required. Noteworthy is the fact that in each of the above cases, we could recover the cluster that was hidden. Also, high CR values indicate a close similarity between the model obtained from the maintenance algorithm and the original clustering of 64529 sessions in each case. One such example is shown below. The left column in Table 3 shows the original profile 3 which was hidden in the second case above, and the right

Table 3. Example of profile hidden and profile recovered with incremental RFSC

Original profile (profile 3)	Profile detected with incremental RFSC
/~comp471/main.htm - 0.941	/~comp471/main.htm - 0.865
/~comp471/ - 0.932	/~comp471/ - 0.860
/~comp471/General/ASSIGNS.htm - 0.343	/~comp471/General/ASSIGNS.htm - 0.324
/~comp471/General/NOTES.htm - 0.313	/~comp471/General/NOTES.htm - 0.294
/~comp471/General/LAB.htm - 0.245	/~comp471/General/LAB.htm - 0.243
/~comp471/outline/outline.htm - 0.145	/~ha_l/comp471.html - 0.206
/programs/ugrad/cs/comp471.shtml - 0.131	/~ha_l/ - 0.180
/~ha_l/comp471.html - 0.130	/~comp471/outline/outline.htm - 0.131
/~comp471/General/PROJECT.htm - 0.125	/programs/ugrad/cs/comp471.shtml - 0.119
/~comp471/slides/ - 0.124	/~comp471/slides/ - 0.116

shows its detection with incremental RFSC. The top 10 URLs are shown with their popularity scores in the profile. This profile is related to course comp471 offered in Winter 2005. We also see that one of the highly accessed pages by students taking this course is of the tutor of this course.

We also observed an apparent discrepancy in the near faithful recovery of clusters when we hide cluster 5. When we add cluster 5, no new cluster is formed. We tried to understand why this had happened. Profile 5 is related to a student who took both comp239 (Mathematics for Computer Science II) and comp352 (Data Structures and Algorithms). This profile is shown in Table 4 (a). Now, in the clustering obtained by applying RFSC to N_{old} = 62,697 sessions, we saw that profile 13 is related to the instructor and students of comp352, while profile 21 is related to the instructor (shown as Prof1) and students of comp 239. Hence, the sessions that were hidden got split into these two clusters and no new cluster was formed. This is also suggested by the low impact factor value, i.e., the impact of not making this a new cluster is very low. Profiles 13 and 21 after the addition of N_{new} =1832 sessions is shown in Table 4 (b) and (c), respectively, in which we only show the top 5 most popular pages.

Table 4. Explaining apparent discrepancy for hidden profile 5

Profile 5 (hidden)
/current_students.shtml - 0.616 /~comp239/ - 0.559 /~comp239/2005W/ - 0.552 /~comp352/ - 0.459 /~comp352/2005w/ - 0.449

(a)

Profile 13 (after maintenance)	Profile 21(after maintenance)
/~comp352/2005w/ - 0.775 /~comp352/ - 0.645 /~cc/COMP352/index.html - 0.410 /~cc/COMP352/announcements.html - 0.279 /current_students.shtml - 0.256	/~Prof1/ - 0.738 /~comp239/2005W/ - 0.706 /~Prof1/239/ - 0.556 /~comp239/ - 0.303 /programs/ugrad/cs/comp239.shtml - 0.115

(b)   (c)

Another interesting experiment is when we hide the first cluster. Procedurally, RFSC finds subsequent clusters according to their potential with respect to the first prominent cluster. In this case, however, we are hiding the first cluster itself and then clustering the remaining sessions to obtain C_{old}=47 clusters. With addition of N_{new} with 3565 sessions, using our incremental RFSC, we recover the cluster even though we see a high impact factor. Again, this is because of the fact that had the entire dataset been clustered, this interest area would have been the most prominent one.

We have also verified this property visually, by running experiments using several synthetically generated datasets consisting of points in two-dimensional Euclidean space. One such dataset has been shown in the WebKDD workshop paper [29]. Please refer to the same for details.

6.5 Adaptive Usage Profiling for Web Personalization

An important application of usage profiling is in web personalization. Collaborative filtering (CF) is the most widely used technique in building recommender systems [25]. The goal of CF is to predict the preferences of a current user, called the *active user*, based on the preferences of a group of "like-minded" users. The key idea in CF is that the active user will prefer those items that like-minded individuals prefer or even those items that dissimilar individuals do not prefer. CF techniques are either memory-based or model-based [4]. While the former is more accurate, its scalability compared to model-based is poor. To overcome these problems, we proposed a technique [28], which is a hybrid of memory-based and model-based CF approaches and includes the complementary advantages of both. It is important to note that the term hybrid has been used in different senses in recommender systems earlier. Our sense of hybrid is to combine both memory-based and model-based approaches to provide more accurate predictions at reasonable cost. We showed that while memory-based CF has slightly higher accuracy, efficiency of fuzzy hybrid CF is much better (30 to 40 times) than memory-based CF. Interested readers are referred to [28] for a detailed description of our hybrid technique and the experimental results.

The main goal of adapting the model to the dynamic changes in the web environment is to increase the relevance and accuracy of recommendations to the user. We now discuss the results of the experiments performed to determine the recommendation quality when using the maintenance algorithm. Incremental RFSC fits in well with our fuzzy hybrid CF technique and hence we compare recommendation quality for the following three techniques: (i) Fuzzy hybrid CF using incremental RFSC; (ii) Fuzzy hybrid CF using Reclustering; and (iii) Memory-based CF.

For this study, we divided the entire dataset of sessions into two: the training set with 42,000 sessions (65.08%), and the test set with the remaining (22,529 sessions). Again the sessions are ordered according to their creation time and the division was also made considering this order. We applied the RFSC algorithm and the cluster validity index. In all, 47 clusters were found, i.e., C=47. For experimentation, Breese et al. 1998 [4] proposed two protocols. In the first, called All-but-1 protocol, one of the pages is randomly selected and withheld from each session in the test set. The CF algorithm is then used to predict this page. In the second protocol, called *Given t*, some *t* number of pages are selected from each session in the test set and then CF algorithm is used to predict the rest of the pages. In our experiments, we used a protocol similar to these, described as follows. We randomly selected approximately 80% of the pages in each session in the test set as seen, and tried to predict the other 20% of pages, which were hidden, using the above algorithms. For each of the above, we checked to see if the hidden pages are present in the top-N pages recommended by the respective algorithms. For fuzzy hybrid CF with incremental RFSC, after every 4000 new sessions that were seen from the test set, these sessions were added to the model using incremental RFSC. Similar to fuzzy hybrid CF with reclustering, complete reclustering was performed in steps of 4000 sessions, i.e., at 46000, 50000, 54000, 58000, and 62000.

Fig. 3 shows the comparison of recommendation effectiveness, using recall, precision, and F1, which are widely used for measuring effectiveness [4, 25]. For these experiments, we kept the parameter k-nearest neighbor, k=100; fuzzy K-nearest prototype, K=5; and varied the parameter TOPN from 5 to 30.

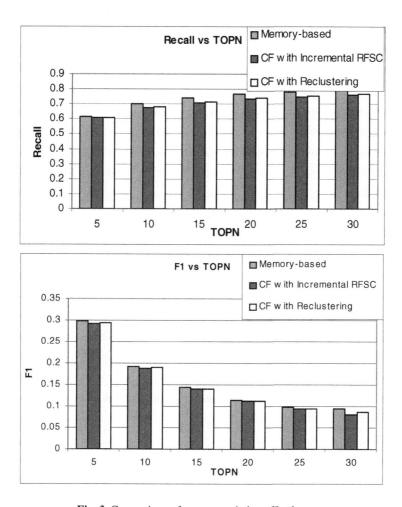

Fig. 3. Comparison of recommendation effectiveness

We observed that recommendation quality obtained using incremental RFSC and complete reclustering is almost the same. Also as TOPN increases, even though we note an increase in recall, we see that precision decreases and the overall combined effect (captured by F1 measure) decreases as well. On the other hand, fuzzy hybrid CF is much more efficient and its effectiveness approaches that of memory-based CF.

7   Conclusions and Future Work

The browsing behavior of users on the web is not fixed or static but rather users' interests change dynamically with time. If models or profiles learned from usage data do not adapt to the new interest and usage, this may lead to degradation of the system over time. As this has to be done online, correctness, robustness, and efficiency of adaptation are crucial for the success of personalization. In this paper, we proposed a profile maintenance scheme based on a new algorithm, Incremental RFSC, for adaptive usage profiling. Our maintenance scheme consists of the following components:

1. RFSC algorithm for initial clustering and reclustering;
2. Incremental RFSC algorithm for adapting the profile model efficiently to newly arriving web usage data; and
3. An impact factor whose value can be used to decide on when reclustering is recommended.

We have implemented this maintenance scheme. Using a large web usage data of 64,529 user sessions with 10,424 distinct URLs, we have conducted extensive experiments to evaluate its performance. For demonstrating correctness, we compute similarity of the results from Incremental RFSC clustering with the results from complete reclustering using RFSC. Our experiments show that the similarity is very high. Incremental RFSC is also very robust. We experimented with different batch sizes for adding new sessions ranging from 2,529 to 34,529 sessions. Even for truly large number of new additions, the cluster model using Incremental RFSC was very similar to the reclustered model. Most important of all, our experiments also show that Incremental RFSC does not fail to discover new Interest areas (clusters) when they ought to be found in the newly added data. We computed Impact factors in each case. The values obtained for Impact factor match very well to our intuition about the newly added data. When a significantly new interest area develops and continues to evolve over time with addition of new usage data, we observe a high impact factor indicating reclustering of the entire dataset would achieve a better model. Lastly, our experiments also clearly indicate that the quality of recommendation obtained using this algorithm is almost as good as complete reclustering of the entire dataset. Incremental RFSC is very fast, taking only a few seconds for adapting the usage profile model with 100 new user sessions. This is what makes it a powerful technique for online web usage profiling. We are not aware of any other maintenance scheme that works with fuzzy clustering and provides this quality of performance. As future work, we plan to experimentally investigate thresholds for impact factors in different dynamic situations. Also we would like to apply this incremental clustering algorithm in different domains such as document clustering.

Acknowledgements

This work was supported in part by Natural Sciences and Engineering Research Council (NSERC) of Canada, and by ENCS Faculty, Concordia University. We also thank anonymous reviewers for their useful comments.

References

1. Abraham, A.: Business Intelligence from Web Usage Mining. J. of Information and Knowledge Management (JIKM), World Scientific Publishing, 2(4), pp. 375-390, 2003.
2. Baraglia, R., Silvestri, F.: An Online Recommender System for Large Web Sites. In Proc. IEEE/WIC/ACM Int'l Conference on Web Intelligence, Beijing, China, September, 2004.

3. Bezdek, J.C.: Pattern Recognition with Fuzzy Objective Function Algorithms. Plenum, New York, 1981.

4. Breese, J., Heckerman, D., Kadie, C.: Empirical Analysis of Predictive Algorithms for Collaborative Filtering. In Proc. of UAI-98, pp. 43-52, 1998.

5. Can, F., Ozkarahan, E.A.: A Dynamic Cluster Maintenance System for Information Retrieval. In Proc. 10th Annual International ACM-SIGIR Conference, pp. 123-131, 1987.

6. Charikar, M., Chekuri, C., Feder, T., Motwani, R.: Incremental clustering and dynamic information retrieval. In SIAM Journal on Computing 33 (6), pp. 1417-1440, 2004.

7. Chiu, S.L.: Fuzzy model identification based on cluster estimation. J. of Intelligent and Fuzzy Systems, 2(3), 1994.

8. Cooley, R., Mobasher, B. and Srivastava, J.: Data Preparation for Mining World Wide Web Browsing Patterns. J. of Knowledge and Information Systems, 1, pp. 1-27, 1999.

9. Corsini, P., Lazzerini, B., Marcelloni, F.: A New Fuzzy Relational Clustering Algorithm Based on Fuzzy C-means Algorithm. Soft Computing, Springer-Verlag, 2004.

10. Ester, M., Kriegel, H., Sander, J., Wimmer, M., Xu, X.: Incremental Clustering for Mining in a Data Warehousing Environment. In Proc. of VLDB 1998, Morgan Kaufmann Publishers Inc., pp. 323-333, 1998.

11. Fu, Y., Sandhu, K., Shih, Asho, M.: Generalization-Based Approach to Clustering of Web Usage Sessions. In Proc. WebKDD 1999, pp. 21-38, 1999.

12. Huang, J.Z., Ng, M.K., Wai-Ki Ching, Joe Ng, David Wai-Lok, C.: A Cube Model and Cluster Analysis for Web Access Sessions. In Proc. WebKDD 2001, pp. 48-67, 2001

13. Hathaway, R.J., Bezdek, J.C., Davenport, J.W.: On relational data version of c-means algorithm. Pattern Recognition Letters, 17, pp. 607-612, 1996.

14. Hubert, L. & Arabie, P.: Comparing partitions. J. of Classification, 2, pp. 193-198, 1985.

15. Jain, A. K., Dubes, R. C.: Algorithms for Clustering Data. Prentice-Hall, Englewood Cliffs, NJ, 1988.

16. Mobasher, B.: Web Usage Mining and Personalization. Practical Handbook of Internet Computing, Munindar P. Singh (ed.), CRC Press, 2004.

17. Mobasher, B., Cooley, R., Srivastava, J.: Automatic personalization based on web usage mining. Comm. ACM, 43, 8 (August), pp. 142–151, 2000.

18. Nasraoui, O.: World Wide Web Personalization. Encyclopedia of Data Mining and Data Warehousing, J. Wang, (ed.), Idea Group, 2005.

19. Nasraoui O., Cardona C., Rojas C., and Gonzalez F.: Mining Evolving User Profiles in Noisy Web Clickstream Data with a Scalable Immune System Clustering Algorithm. In Proc. WebKDD, Washington DC, August, 2003.

20. Nasraoui O., Krishnapuram R., Joshi A., Kamdar T.: Automatic Web User Profiling and Personalization using Robust Fuzzy Relational Clustering. In E-Commerce and Intelligent Methods, Springer-Verlag, 2002.

21. Nasraoui O., Frigui H., Krishnapuram R., Joshi A.: Extracting Web User Profiles Using Relational Competitive Fuzzy Clustering. International Journal on Artificial Intelligence Tools, Vol. 9, No. 4, pp. 509-526, 2000.

22. Nasraoui O. and Krishnapuram R.: One Step Evolutionary Mining of Context Sensitive Associations and Web Navigation Patterns. In Proc. SIAM conference on Data Mining, Arlington, VA, pp. 531-547, April 2002.

23. Pal, K., Pal, N., Keller, J. M., Bezdek, J.: Relational mountain (density) clustering method and web log analysis. Int'l J. of Intelligent Systems 20(3), pp. 375-392, 2005.

24. Pennock, D. M., Horvitz, E., Lawrence, S., Giles, C. L.: Collaborative filtering by personality diagnosis: A hybrid memory- and model-based approach. In Proc. of UAI-2000, pp. 473-480, Stanford, CA, 2000.

25. Sarwar, B. M., Karypis, G., Konstan, J. A., Riedl, J.: Analysis of recommender algorithms for e-commerce. In Proc. 2nd ACM E-commerce Conference, Minnesota, USA, 2000.
26. Shahabi, C., Banaei-Kashani, F.: A Framework for Efficient and Anonymous Web Usage Mining Based on Client-Side Tracking. In Proc. WebKDD 2001, Springer-Verlag, New York, 2002.
27. Suryavanshi, B.S., Shiri, N., Mudur, S.P.: An Efficient Technique for Mining Usage Profiles using Relational Fuzzy Subtractive Clustering. In Proc. of IEEE Int'l Workshop on Challenges in Web Information Retrieval and Integration (WIRI' 05), Tokyo, Japan, April 8-9, 2005.
28. Suryavanshi, B.S., Shiri, N., Mudur, S.P.: A Fuzzy Hybrid Collaborative Filtering Technique for Web Personalization. In Proc. of 3rd Workshop on Intelligent Techniques for Web Personalization (ITWP'05), Edinburgh, Scotland, August, 2005.
29. Suryavanshi, B.S., Shiri, N., Mudur, S.P.: Incremental Relational Fuzzy Subtractive Clustering for Dynamic Web Usage Profiling. In Proc. WebKDD Workshop, Chicago, August, 2005.
30. Tasoulis, D., Vrahatis, M.: Unsupervised Clustering on Dynamic Databases. Pattern Recognition Letters (to appear), 2005.
31. Van Rijsbergen, C. J.: Information Retrieval. 2nd ed. Butterworths, London, 1979.
32. Xie, X. L., Beni, G.: A validity measure for fuzzy clustering. IEEE Trans. on PAMI, 13(8), pp. 841-847, 1991.
33. Xie, Y. and Phoha, V.V.: Web User Clustering from Access Log Using Belief Function, In Proc. 1st International Conference on Knowledge Capture (K-CAP 2001), pp. 202–208. ACM Press, 2001.
34. Yan, T. W., Jacobsen, M., Garcia-Molina, H., Dayal, U.: From User Access Patterns to Dynamic Hypertext Linking. Proc. 5th International World Wide Web Conf., 1996.
35. Yager R.R., Filev D.P.: Approximate clustering via the mountain method. IEEE Transaction on System Man Cybern, 24(8), pp. 1279–1284, 1994.
36. Zhang, T., Ramakrishnan, R., Livny, M.: BIRCH: an efficient data clustering method for very large databases. In Proc. 1996 ACM SIGMOD Int. Conf. Management of Data, pp. 103–114, Montreal, Canada, June 1996.

On Clustering Techniques for Change Diagnosis in Data Streams

Charu C. Aggarwal and Philip S. Yu

IBM T. J. Watson Research Center
19 Skyline Drive, Hawthorne, NY 10532
{charu, psyu}@us.ibm.com

Abstract. In recent years, data streams have become ubiquitous in a variety of applications because of advances in hardware technology. Since data streams may be generated by applications which are time-changing in nature, it is often desirable to explore the underlying changing trends in the data. In this paper, we will explore and survey some of our recent methods for change detection. In particular, we will study methods for change detection which use clustering in order to provide a concise understanding of the underlying trends. We discuss our recent techniques which use micro-clustering in order to diagnose the changes in the underlying data. We also discuss the extension of this method to text and categorical data sets as well community detection in graph data streams.

1   Introduction

The results of many data stream mining applications such as clustering and classification [3,6,23] are affected by the changes in the underlying data. In many applications, change detection is a critical task in order to understand the nature of the underlying data. In many applications, it is desirable to have a concise description of the changes in the underlying data [1,2,9,14,15,23]. This can then be leveraged in order to make changes in the underlying task. A natural choice for creating concise descriptions of the change is the method of clustering. In this paper, we will examine a number of our recent techniques for change diagnosis of streams which utilize clustering as an approach. In particular, we will examine the method of micro-clustering, which can be used to examine changes in quantitative, categorical, or text data. We will also examine the technique of community detection in graph data streams.

The fast nature of data streams results in several constraints in their applicability to data mining tasks. For example, it means that they cannot be re-examined in the course of their computation. Therefore, all algorithms need to be executed in only one pass of the data. Clustering is a natural choice for summarizing the evolution of most kinds of data streams [3,23], since it provides a conduit for summarization of the data. These summaries can be used for a variety of tasks which depend upon the change diagnosis. We note that a different method for change diagnosis is discussed in [1], which provides visual summaries of the changing trends in the data. This can be very helpful for a

O. Nasraoui et al. (Eds.): WebKDD 2005, LNAI 4198, pp. 139–157, 2006.

variety of data mining tasks. In other applications in which the change needs to be reported in the context of a particular kind of segmentation, it is also helpful to use clustering for summarization methods. This paper will concentrate on such techniques.

One important fact about change detection applications is that most users apply these techniques only in the context of user-specific horizons. For example, a business analyst may wish to determine the changes in the data over a period of days, months, or years. This creates a natural challenge since a data stream does not allow the natural flexibility of re-examining the previous portions of the data. In this context, the use of clustering in conjunction with a pyramidal time frame can be very useful. The concept of the pyramid time frame has been discussed in [3], and turns out to be very useful for a number of applications.

The methods discussed in this paper are applicable to a wide variety of data types such as text, categorical data, and quantitative data. We will discuss the algorithms and methods in detail for each case. We will also discuss the extension of the method to graph data streams and the use of the technique for community detection and evolution.

This paper is organized as follows. In the next section, we will discuss the overall stream summarization framework, and its use for quantitative change detection. We will also provide a specific example of an intrusion detection application. In section 3, we will discuss how the technique can be used for text and categorical data. In section 4, we will discuss the use of the method for community detection and evolution. Section 5 discusses the conclusions and summary.

2   Micro-clustering and Quantitative Change Detection

The method of micro-clustering uses an extension of the cluster feature method discusses in [26]. Since data streams have a temporal component, we also need to keep track of the time stamps of arriving data points. In addition, we need to store the data periodically in a systematic way in order to access it later for the purposes of change diagnosis. Therefore, the data needs to be saved periodically on disk. A key issue is the choice of time periods over which the data should be saved. n this section, we will discuss both issue.

In order to store the current *state* of the clusters, we use a summary statistical representation which are referred to as *microclusters* [3]. The summary information in the microclusters is used by an offline component which is dependent upon a wide variety of user inputs such as the time horizon or the granularity of clustering. In order to define the micro-clusters, we will introduce a few concepts. It is assumed that the data stream consists of a set of multi-dimensional records $\overline{X}_1 \ldots \overline{X}_k \ldots$ arriving at time stamps $T_1 \ldots T_k \ldots$. Each $\overline{X}_i$ is a multi-dimensional record containing d dimensions which are denoted by $\overline{X}_i = (x_i^1 \ldots x_i^d)$.

We will first begin by defining the concept of microclusters and pyramidal time frame more precisely.

Definition 1. *A microcluster for a set of d-dimensional points $X_{i_1} \ldots X_{i_n}$ with time stamps $T_{i_1} \ldots T_{i_n}$ is the $(2 \cdot d + 3)$ tuple $(\overline{CF2^x}, \overline{CF1^x}, CF2^t, CF1^t, n)$,* *wherein* $\overline{CF2^x}$ *and* $\overline{CF1^x}$ *each correspond to a vector of d entries. The definition of each of these entries is as follows:*

- *For each dimension, the sum of the squares of the data values is maintained in* $\overline{CF2^x}$. *Thus,* $\overline{CF2^x}$ *contains d values. The p-th entry of* $\overline{CF2^x}$ *is equal to* $\sum_{j=1}^{n}(x_{i_j}^p)^2$.
- *For each dimension, the sum of the data values is maintained in* $\overline{CF1^x}$. *Thus,* $\overline{CF1^x}$ *contains d values. The p-th entry of* $\overline{CF1^x}$ *is equal to* $\sum_{j=1}^{n} x_{i_j}^p$.
- *The sum of the squares of the time stamps* $T_{i_1} \ldots T_{i_n}$ *is maintained in* $CF2^t$.
- *The sum of the time stamps* $T_{i_1} \ldots T_{i_n}$ *is maintained in* $CF1^t$.
- *The number of data points is maintained in n.*

We note that the above definition of microcluster maintains similar summary information as the cluster feature vector of [26], except for the additional information about time stamps. We will refer to this temporal extension of the cluster feature vector for a set of points $\mathcal{C}$ by $\overline{CFT}(\mathcal{C})$. We note that the micro-clusters have a number of properties such as the *additivity property*, and the *linear update* property which makes them particularly suited to data streams:

- The additivity property ensures that it is possible to compute the microcluster statistics over a specific time horizon in order to determine the nature of the changes in the data.
- The linear update property is a direct consequence of the additivity property. Since each additional point can be incorporated into the cluster statistics by using additive operations pver the different dimensions, it ensures that the time required to maintain micro-cluster statistics increases linearly with the number of data points and dimensionality. This is an important property, since it ensures that the micro-cluster statistics are efficiently updateable.

Since recent data is more relevant than historical data, it is desirable to use a layered approach to saving the data at specific snapshots. For this purpose, we divide the snapshots into different *orders*, which follow the below rules:

- Snapshots of order i are stored at time intervals which are divisible by α^i.
- The last $\alpha + 1$ snapshots of order i are always stored.

We make the following observations about this pattern of storage:

- For a data stream, the maximum order of any snapshot stored at T time units since the beginning of the stream mining process is $\log_\alpha(T)$.
- For a data stream the maximum number of snapshots maintained at T time units since the beginning of the stream mining process is $(\alpha + 1) \cdot \log_\alpha(T)$.
- For any user specified time window of h, at least one stored snapshot can be found within $2 \cdot h$ units of the current time.

While the first two facts are easy to confirm, the last needs to be validated explicitly. A proof of the last point is provided in [3]. We also note that the bound $(\alpha + 1) \cdot \log_\alpha(T)$ is an upper bound, since there is some overlapping between snapshots of different orders. In practice, only one copy of the snapshots need be maintained when there is overlap between snapshots of different orders.

The maintenance of snapshots is a fairly straightforward task. We only need to maintain the micro-cluster statistics dynamically, and update the cluster centers when necessary. In each iteration, we determine the closest micro-cluster center and assign the incoming data point to it. The cluster statistics are updated using this incoming data point. Because of the additivity property, this is a straight-forward operation. The detailed clustering maintenance algorithm is discussed in [3]. Once the cluster statistics have been updated, we can periodically store them using the pyramidal time frame. The stored snapshots can then be used in order to determine the summary of the data evolution.

In the work of [1] and [12], the problem of change detection has been stud-ied from the point of view of understanding how the data characteristics have changed over time. However, these papers do not deal with the problem of study-ing the changes in clusters over time. In the context of the clustering problem, such evolution analysis also has significant importance. For example, an analyst may wish to know how the clusters have changed over the last quarter, the last year, the last decade and so on. For this purpose, the user needs to input a few parameters to the algorithm:

- The two clock times t_1 and t_2 over which the clusters need to be compared. It is assumed that $t_2 > t_1$. In many practical scenarios, t_2 is the current clock time.
- The time horizon h over which the clusters are computed. This means that the clusters created by the data arriving between $(t_2 - h, t_2)$ are compared to those created by the data arriving between $(t_1 - h, t_1)$.

Another important issue is that of deciding how to present the changes in the clusters to a user, so as to make the results appealing from an intuitive point of view. We present the changes occurring in the clusters in terms of the following broad objectives:

- Are there new clusters in the data at time t_2 which were not present at time t_1?
- Have some of the original clusters been lost because of changes in the be-havior of the stream?
- Have some of the original clusters at time t_1 shifted in position and nature because of changes in the data?
- Find the nature of the changes in the clusters at time t_1 till the time t_2.
- Find all the transient clusters from t_1 to time t_2. The transient clusters are defined as those which were born after time t_1, but expired before time t_2.

We note that the micro-cluster maintenance algorithm maintains the idlists which are useful for tracking cluster information. The first step is to compute $\mathcal{N}(t_1, h)$ and $\mathcal{N}(t_2, h)$ as discussed in the previous section. Therefore, we divide the micro-clusters in $\mathcal{N}(t_1, h) \cup \mathcal{N}(t_2, h)$ into three categories:

- Micro-clusters in $\mathcal{N}(t_2, h)$ for which none of the ids on the corresponding *idlist* are present in $\mathcal{N}(t_1, h)$. These are new micro-clusters which were cre-ated at some time in the interval (t_1, t_2). We will denote this set of micro-clusters by $\mathcal{M}^{added}(t_1, t_2)$.

- Micro-clusters in $\mathcal{N}(t_1, h)$ for which none of the corresponding ids are present in $\mathcal{N}(t_2, h)$. Thus, these micro-clusters were deleted in the interval (t_1, t_2). We will denote this set of micro-clusters by $\mathcal{M}^{deleted}(t_1, t_2)$.
- Micro-clusters in $\mathcal{N}(t_2, h)$ for which some or all of the ids on the corresponding *idlist* are present in the idlists corresponding to the micro-clusters in $\mathcal{N}(t_1, h)$. Such micro-clusters were at least partially created before time t_1, but have been modified since then. We will denote this set of micro-clusters by $\mathcal{M}^{retained}(t_1, t_2)$.

The macro-cluster creation algorithm is then separately applied to each of this set of micro-clusters to create a new set of higher level clusters. The macro-clusters created from $\mathcal{M}^{added}(t_1, t_2)$ and $\mathcal{M}^{deleted}(t_1, t_2)$ have clear significance in terms of clusters added to or removed from the data stream. The micro-clusters in $\mathcal{M}^{retained}(t_1, t_2)$ correspond to those portions of the stream which have not changed very significantly in this period. When a very large fraction of the data belongs to $\mathcal{M}^{retained}(t_1, t_2)$, this is a sign that the stream is quite stable over that time period. In many cases, the clusters in $\mathcal{M}^{retained}$ could change significantly over time. In such cases, we can utilize the statistics of the underlying data in order to calculate the shift in the corresponding centroid. This shift can be determined by computing the centroid of $\mathcal{M}^{retained}(t_1, t_2)$, and comparing it to $\mathcal{S}(t_1)$.

The process of finding transient clusters is slightly more complicated. In this case, we find the micro-clusters at each snapshot between t_1 and t_2. Let us denote this set by $\mathcal{U}(t_1, t_2)$. This is the *universal* set of micro-clusters between t_1 and t_2. We also find the micro-clusters which are present at either t_1 or t_2. This set is essentially equivalent to $\mathcal{N}(t_1, t_1) \cup \mathcal{N}(t_2, t_2)$. Any micro-cluster which is present in $\mathcal{U}(t_1, t_2)$, but which is not present in $\mathcal{N}(t_1, t_1) \cup \mathcal{N}(t_2, t_2)$. In other words, we report the set $\mathcal{U}(t_1, t_2) - \mathcal{N}(t_1, t_1) - \mathcal{N}(t_2, t_2)$ as the final result.

We also tested the micro-clustering method for evolution analysis on the network intrusion data set in [3]. This data set was obtained from the UCI machine learning repository [27]. First, by comparing the data distribution for $t_1 = 29, t_2 = 30, h = 1$ CluStream found 3 micro-clusters (8 points) in $\mathcal{M}^{added}(t_1, t_2)$, 1 micro-cluster (1 point) in $\mathcal{M}^{deleted}(t_1, t_2)$, and 22 micro-clusters (192 points) in $\mathcal{M}^{retained}(t_1, t_2)$. This shows that only 0.5% of all the connections in $(28, 29)$ disappeared and only 4% were added in $(29, 30)$. By checking the original data set, we find that all points in $\mathcal{M}^{added}(t_1, t_2)$ and $\mathcal{M}^{deleted}(t_1, t_2)$ are normal connections, but are outliers because of some particular feature such as the number of bytes of data transmitted. The fact that almost all the points in this case belong to $\mathcal{M}^{retained}(t_1, t_2)$ indicates that the data distributions in these two windows are very similar. This happens because there are no attacks in this time period.

More interestingly, the data points falling into $\mathcal{M}^{added}(t_1, t_2)$ or $\mathcal{M}^{deleted}(t_1, t_2)$ are those which have evolved significantly. These usually correspond to newly arrived or faded attacks respectively. Here are two examples: (1) During the period $(34, 35)$, all data points correspond to normal connections, whereas during $(39, 40)$ all data points belong to smurf attacks. By applying our change analysis procedure for $t_1 = 35, t_2 = 40, h = 1$, it shows that 99% of the smurf connections (i.e., 198 connections) fall into two $\mathcal{M}^{added}(t_1, t_2)$ micro-clusters, and 99% of the normal connections fall into 21 $M^{deleted}(t_1, t_2)$ micro-clusters. This means these normal connections are non-existent during $(39, 40)$; (2) By applying the change analysis procedure for $t_1 = 640, t_2 = 1280, h = 16$, we found that all the data points during $(1264, 1280)$ belong to one $\mathcal{M}^{added}(t_1, t_2)$ micro-cluster, and all the data points in $(624, 640)$ belong to one $\mathcal{M}^{deleted}(t_1, t_2)$ micro-cluster. By checking the original labeled data set, we found that all the connections during $(1264, 1280)$ are smurf attacks and all the connections during $(624, 640)$ are neptune attacks. In general, the micro-clustering method may be used to perform concise summarization and evolution analysis of data streams. This methodology can also be extended to categorical data. We discuss this method in the next section.

3   Change Detection for Text and Categorical Data

The problem of change detection for text data has been studied in [22], whereas some techniques for summarization of categorical data have been proposed in [16]. In this paper, we will use summarization as a tool for comprehensive change detection of text and categorical data. As in the case of quantitative data, we need to maintain a statistical representation of the summary structure of the data. We will refer to such groups as *cluster droplets*. This is analogous to the summary cluster feature statistics or micro-cluster statistics stored in [3,26]. We will discuss and define the cluster droplet differently for the case of text and categorical data streams respectively. For generality, we assume that a weight is associated with each data point. In some applications, this may be desirable, when different data points have different levels of importance, as in th ecase of a temporal fade function. First, we will define the cluster droplet for the categorical data domain:

Definition 2. *A cluster droplet $\mathcal{D}(t, \mathcal{C})$ for a set of categorical data points $\mathcal{C}$ at time t is referred to as a tuple $(\overline{DF2}, \overline{DF1}, n, w(t), l)$, in which each tuple component is defined as follows:*

- *The vector $\overline{DF2}$ contains $\sum_{i \in \{1...d\}, j \in \{1,...d\}, i \neq j} v_i \cdot v_j$ entries. For each pair of dimensions, we maintain $v_i \cdot v_j$ values. We note that v_i is number of possible categorical values of dimension i and v_j is the number of possible values of dimension j. Thus, for each of the $v_i \cdot v_j$ categorical value pairs i and j, we maintain the (weighted) counts of the number of points for each value pair which are included in cluster $\mathcal{C}$. In other words, for every possible pair of categorical values of dimensions i and j, we maintain the weighted number of points in the cluster in which these values co-occur.*
- *The vector $\overline{DF1}$ contains $\sum_{i=1}^{d} v_i$ entries. For each i, we maintain a weighted count of each of the v_i possible values of categorical attribute i occurring in the cluster.*
- *The entry n contains the number of data points in the cluster.*
- *The entry $w(t)$ contains the sum of the weights of the data points at time t. We note that the value $w(t)$ is a function of the time t and decays with time unless new data points are added to the droplet $\mathcal{D}(t)$.*

- *The entry l contains the time stamp of the last time that a data point was added to the cluster.*

We note that the above definition of a droplet assumes a data set in which each categorical attribute assumes a small number of possible values. (Thus, the value of v_i for each dimension i is relatively small.) However, in many cases, the data might actually be somewhat sparse. In such cases, the values of v_i could be relatively large. In those instances, we use a sparse representation. Specifically, for each pair of dimensions i and j, we maintain a list of the categorical value pairs which have *non-zero* counts. In a second list, we store the actual counts of these pairs. In many cases, this results in considerable savings of storage space. For example, consider the dimension pairs i and j, which contain v_i and v_j possible categorical values. Also, let us consider the case when $b_i \le v_i$ and $b_j \le v_j$ of them have non-zero presence in the droplet. Thus, at most $b_i \cdot b_j$ categorical attribute pairs will co-occur in the points in the cluster. We maintain a list of these (at most) $b_{ij} < b_i \cdot b_j$ value pairs along with the corresponding counts. This requires a storage of $3 \cdot b_{ij}$ values. (Two entries are required for the identities of the value pairs and one is required for the count.) We note that if the number of distinct non-zero values b_i and b_j are substantially lower than the number of possible non-zero values v_i and v_j respectively, then it may be more economical to store $3 \cdot b_{ij}$ values instead of $v_i \cdot v_j$ entries. These correspond to the list of categorical values which have non-zero presence together with the corresponding weighted counts. Similarly, for the case of $\overline{DF1}$, we only need to maintain $2 \cdot b_i$ entries for each dimension i.

Next, we consider the case of the text data set which is an example of a *sparse numeric* data set. This is because most documents contain only a small fraction of the vocabulary with non-zero frequency. The only difference with the categorical data domain is the way in which the underlying cluster droplets are maintained.

Definition 3. *A cluster droplet $\mathcal{D}(t, \mathcal{C})$ for a set of text data points $\mathcal{C}$ at time t is defined to as a tuple $(\overline{DF2}, \overline{DF1}, n, w(t), l)$. Each tuple component is defined as follows:*

- *The vector $\overline{DF2}$ contains $3 \cdot wb \cdot (wb - 1)/2$ entries. Here wb is the number of distinct words in the cluster $\mathcal{C}$. For each pair of dimensions, we maintain a list of the pairs of word ids with non-zero counts. We also maintained the sum of the weighted counts for such word pairs.*
- *The vector $\overline{DF1}$ contains $2 \cdot wb$ entries. We maintain the identities of the words with non-zero counts. In addition, we maintain the sum of the weighted counts for each word occurring in the cluster.*
- *The entry n contains the number of data points in the cluster.*
- *The entry $w(t)$ contains the sum of the weights of the data points at time t. We note that the value $w(t)$ is a function of the time t and decays with time unless new data points are added to the droplet $\mathcal{D}(t)$.*
- *The entry l contains the time stamp of the last time that a data point was added to the cluster.*

The concept of cluster droplet has some interesting properties that will be useful during the maintenance process. These properties relate to the additivity and decay behavior of the cluster droplet. As in the case of quantitative micro-clustering, it is possible to perform the cluster droplet maintenance using an incremental update algorithm. The methodology is examining the evolving clusters can also be extended to this case. Details are discussed in [5] with an example of its application to text and market basket data sets.

4   Online Community Evolution in Data Streams

In this section, we discuss the problem of detecting patterns of interaction among a set of entities in a stream environment. Examples of such entities could be a set of businesses which interact with one another, sets of co-authors in a dynamic bibliography data base, or it could be the hyperlinks from web pages. In each of these cases, the interaction among different entities can rapidly evolve over time. A convenient way to model the entity interaction relationships is to view them as graphs in which the nodes correspond to entities and the edges correspond to the interactions among the nodes. The weights on these edges represent the level of the interaction between the different participants. For example, in the case when the nodes represent interacting entities in a business environment, the weights on the edges among these entities could represent the volume of business transactions. A *community of interaction* is defined to be a set of entities with a high degree of interaction among the participants.

The problem of finding communities in dynamic and evolving graphs been discussed in [10,11,17,19,20,21,24,25]. Since most of the current techniques are designed for applications such as the web, they usually assume a *gradually evolving* model for the interaction. Such techniques are not very useful for a fast stream environment in which the entities and their underlying relationships may quickly evolve over time. In addition, it is important to provide a user the *exploratory capability* to query for communities over different time horizons. Since individual points in the data streams cannot be processed more than once, we propose a framework which separates out the *offline exploratory* algorithms from the online stream processing part. The online stream processing framework creates summaries of the data which can then be further processed for exploratory querying. Therefore, as in the case of micro-clustering, we focus on the use of an Online Analytical Processing (OLAP) approach for providing offline exploratory capabilities to users in performing *change detection* across communities of interest over different time horizons.

Some examples of exploratory queries in which a user may be interested are as follows:

(1) Find the communities with substantial increase in interaction level in the interval $(t - h, t)$. We refer to such communities as *expanding communities*.
(2) Find the communities with substantial decrease in interaction level in the interval $(t - h, t)$ We refer to such communities as *contracting communities*.

(3) Find the communities with the most stable interaction level in the interval $(t - h, t)$.

We note that the process of finding an emerging or contracting community needs to be carefully designed in order to normalize for the behavior of the community evolution over different time horizons. For example, consider a data stream in which two entities n_1 and n_2 share a high level of interaction in the period $(t - h, t)$. This alone does not mean that the interaction level between n_1 and n_2 is stable especially if these entities had a even higher level of interaction in the previous period $(t - 2 \cdot h, t - h)$. Thus, a careful model needs to be constructed which tracks the behavior of the interaction graph over different time horizons in order to understand the nature of the change. In he next subsection we will discuss the process of online summarization of data streams, and leveraging this process for the purpose of data stream mining.

4.1   Online Summarization of Graphical Data Streams

In this subsection, we will discuss the overall interaction model among the different entities. We will also discuss the process of online summarization of the data stream. This interaction model is stored as a graph $G = (N, A)$, in which N denotes the set of nodes, and A denotes the set of edges. Each node $i \in N$ corresponds to an entity. The edge set A consists of edges (i, j), such that i and j are nodes drawn from N. Each edge (i, j) represents an interaction between the entities i and j. Each edge (i, j) also has a weight $w_{ij}(t)$ associated with it. This weight corresponds to the number of interactions between the entities i and j. For example, when the interaction model represents a bibliography database, the nodes could represent the authors and the weights on the edges could represent the number of publications on which the corresponding authors occur together as co-authors. As new publications are added to the database the corresponding weights on the individual edges are modified. It is also possible for new nodes to be added to the data as new authors are added to the original mix. In this particular example, the weight on each edge increases by one, each time a new co-authorship relation is added to the database. However, in many applications such as those involving business interaction, this weight added in each iteration can be arbitrary, and in some cases even negative.

In order to model the corresponding stream for this interaction model, we assume that a current graph $G(t) = (N(t), A(t))$ exists which represents the history of interactions at time t. At time $(t + 1)$ new additions may occur to the graph $G(t)$. Subsequently, each new arrival to the stream contains two elements:

- An edge (i, j) corresponding to the two entities between whom the interaction has taken place.
- An *incremental* weight $\delta w_{ij}(t)$ illustrating the additional interaction which has taken place between entities i and j at time t.

We refer to the above pair of elements as representative of an *interaction event*. We note that the nodes i, j, or the edge (i, j) may not be present in $N(t)$ and

$A(t)$ respectively. In such a case, the node set $N(t)$ and edge set $A(t)$ need to be modified to construct $N(t+1)$ and $A(t+1)$ respectively. In the event that a given edge does not exist to begin with, the original weight of (i,j) in $G(t)$ is assumed to be zero. Also, in such a case, the value of the edge set $A(t+1)$ is augmented as follows:

$$A(t+1) = A(t) \cup \{(i,j)\} \tag{1}$$

In the event that either the nodes i or j are not present in $N(t)$, the corresponding node set needs to be augmented with the new node(s). Furthermore, the weight of the edge (i,j) needs to be modified. If the edge (i,j) is new, then the weight of edge (i,j) in $G(t+1)$ is set to δw_{ij}. Otherwise, we add the incremental weight δw_{ij} to the current weight of edge (i,j) in $G(t)$. Therefore, we ave:

$$w_{ij}(t+1) = w_{ij}(t) + \delta w_{ij}(t) \tag{2}$$

We assume that the set of interaction events received at time t are denoted by $\mathcal{E}(t)$. In each iteration, the stream maintenance algorithm adds the interaction events in $\mathcal{E}(t)$ to $G(t)$ in order to create $G(t+1)$. We refer to the process of adding the events in $\mathcal{E}(t)$ to $G(t)$ by the $\oplus$ operation. Therefore, we have:

$$G(t+1) = G(t) \oplus \mathcal{E}(t) \tag{3}$$

At each given moment in time, we maintain the current graph of interactions $G(t)$ in main memory. In addition, we periodically store the graph of interactions on disk. We note that the amount of disk storage available may often be limited. Therefore, it is desirable to store the graph of interactions in an efficient way during the course of the stream arrival. We will refer to each storage of the graph of interactions at a particular moment as a *frame*. Let us assume that the storage limitation for the number of frames is denoted by S. In this case, one possibility is to store the last S frames at uniform intervals of t'. The value of S is determined by the storage space available. However, this is not a very effective solution, since it means that a history of larger than $S \cdot t'$ cannot be recalled.

One solution to this problem is to recognize that frames which are more stale need not be stored at the same frequency as more recent frames. Let t_c be the current time, and t_{min} be the minimum granularity at which 0th tier snapshots are stored. We divide the set of S frames into $\theta = \log_2(t_c/t_{min})$ tiers. The ith tier contains snapshots which are separated by a distance of $t_{min} \cdot 2^{i-1}$. For each tier, we store the last S/θ frames. This ensures that the total storage requirement continues to be S. Whenever it is desirable to access the state of the interaction graph for the time t, we simply have to find the frame which is temporally closest to t. The graph from this temporally closest frame is utilized in order to approximate the interaction graph at time t. The tiered nature of the storage process ensures that it is possible to approximate recent frames to the same degree of (percentage) accuracy than less recent frames. While this means that the (absolute) approximation of stale frames is greater, this is quite satisfactory fir a number of real scenarios. We make the following observations:

Lemma 1. *Let h be a user-specified time window, and t_c be the current time. Then a snapshot exists at time t_s, such that $h/(1+\theta/S) \le t_c - t_s \le (1+\theta/S) \cdot h$.*

Proof. This is an extension of the result in [6]. The proof is similar.

In order to understand the effectiveness of this simple methodology, let us consider a simple example in which we store (a modest number of) $S = 100,000$ frames for a stream over 10 years, in which the minimum granularity of storage t_{min} is 1 second. We have intentionally chosen an extreme example (in terms of the time period of the stream) together with a modest storage capability in order to show the effectiveness of the approximation. In this case, the number of tiers is given by $\theta = \log_2(10 * 365 * 24 * 3600) \approx= 29$. By substituting in Lemma 1, we see that it is possible to find a snapshot which is between 99.97% and 100.03% of the user specified value.

In order to improve the efficiency of edge storage further, we need to recognize the fact that large portions of the graph continue to be identical over time. Therefore, it is inefficient for the stream generation process to store the entire graph on disk in each iteration. Rather, we store only incremental portions of the graph on the disk. Specifically, let us consider the storage of the graph $G(t)$ for the ith tier at time t. Let the last time at which an $(i + 1)$th tier snapshot was stored be denoted by t'. (If no snapshot of tier $(i+1)$ exists, then the value of t' is 0. We assume that $G(0)$ is the null graph.) Then, we store the graph $F(t) = G(t) - G(t')$ at time t. We note that the graph $F(t)$ contains far fewer edges than the original graph $G(t)$. Therefore, it is more efficient to store $F(t)$ rather than $G(t)$. Another observation is that a snapshot for the ith tier can be reconstructed by summing the snapshots for all tiers larger than i.

Lemma 2. *We assume that the highest tier is defined by m. Let t_i be the time at which the snapshot for tier i is stored. Let t_{i+1}, t_{i+2} ... t_m be the last time stamps of tiers $(i + 1) \ldots m$ (before t_i) at which the snapshots are stored. Then the current graph $G(t_i)$ at the time stamp t_i is defined as follows:*

$$G(t_i) = \sum_{j=i}^{m} F(t_j) \tag{4}$$

Proof. This result can be proved easily by induction. We note that the definition of $F(\cdot)$ implies that:

$$G(t_i) - G(t_{i+1}) = F(t_i)$$
$$G(t_{i+1}) - G(t_{i+2}) = F(t_{i+1})$$

$$\ldots$$

$$G(t_{m-1}) - G(t_m) = F(t_{m-1})$$
$$G(t_m) - 0 = F(t_m)$$

By summing the above equations, we obtain the desired result.

The above result implies that the graph at a snapshot for a particular tier can be reconstructed by summing it with the snapshots at higher tiers. Since there are at most $\theta = \log_2(S/t_{min})$ tiers, it implies that the graph at a given time can be reconstructed quite efficiently in a practical setting.

4.2   Offline Construction and Processing of Differential Graphs

In this subsection, we will discuss the offline process of generating differential graphs and their application to the evolution detection process. The differential graph is generated over a specific time horizon (t_1, t_2) over which the user would like to test the behavior of the data stream. The differential graph is defined over the interval (t_1, t_2) and is defined as a fraction of the interactions over that interval by which the level of interaction has changed during the interval (t_1, t_2). In order to generate the differential graph, we first construct the *normalized graph* at the times t_1 and t_2. The normalized graph $G(t) = (N(t), A(t))$ at time t is denoted by $\overline{G(t)}$, and contains exactly the same node and edge set, but with different weights. Let $W(t) = \sum_{(i,j) \in A} w_{ij}(t)$ be the sum of the weights over all edges in the graph $G(t)$. Then, the normalized weight $\overline{w_{ij}(t)}$ is defined as $w_{ij}(t)/W(t)$. We note that the normalized graph basically comprises the fraction of interactions over each edge.

Let t_1' be the last snapshot stored just before time t_1 and t_2' be the snapshot stored just before time t_2. The first step is to construct the graphs $G(t_1')$ and $G(t_2')$ at time periods t_1' and t_2' by adding the snapshots at the corresponding tiers as defined by Lemma 2. Then we construct the normalized graph from the graphs at times t_1' and t_2'. The differential graph is constructed from the normalized graph by subtracting out the corresponding edge weights in the original normalized graphs. Therefore, the differential graph $\Delta G(t_1', t_2')$ basically contains the same nodes and edges as $\overline{G(t_2')}$, except that the differential weight $\Delta w_{ij}(t_1', t_2')$ on the edge (i, j) is defined as follows:

$$\Delta w_{ij}(t_1', t_2') = \overline{w_{ij}(t_2')} - \overline{w_{ij}(t_1')} \tag{5}$$

In the event that an edge (i, j) does not exist in the graph $\overline{G(t_1')}$, the value of $w_{ij}(t_1')$ is assumed to be zero. We note that because of the normalization process, the differential weights on many of the edges may be negative. These correspond to edges over which the interaction has reduced significantly during the evolution process. For instance, in our example corresponding to a publication database, when the number of jointly authored publications reduces over time, the corresponding weights in the differential graph are also negative.

Once the differential graph has been constructed, we would like to find clusters of nodes which show a high level of evolution. It is a tricky issue to determine the subgraphs which have a high level of evolution. A natural solution would be find the clustered subgraphs with high weight edges. However, in a given subgraph, some of the edges may have high positive weight while others may have high negative weight. Therefore, such subgraphs correspond to the entity relationships with high evolution, but they do not necessarily correspond to entity relationships with the greatest increase or decrease in interaction level. In order to find the community of interaction with the greatest increase in interaction level, we need to find subgraphs such that most interactions within that subgraph have either a high positive or high negative weight. This is a much more difficult problem than the pure vanilla problem of finding clusters within the subgraph $\Delta G(t_1', t_2')$.

4.3   Finding Evolving Communities

In this section, we will define the algorithm for finding evolution clusters in the interaction graph based on the user defined horizon. The process of finding the most effective clusters is greatly complicated by the fact that some of the edges correspond to an increase in the evolution level, whereas other edges correspond to a decrease in the evolution level. The edges corresponding to an increase in interaction level are referred to as the positive edges, whereas those corresponding to a reduction in the interaction level are referred to as the negative edges.

We design an algorithm which can effectively find subgraphs of positive or negative edges by using a partitioning approach which tracks the positive and negative subgraphs in a dynamic way. In this approach, we use a set of seed nodes $\{n_1 \ldots n_k\}$ in order to create the clusters. Associated with each seed n_i is a partition of the data which is denoted by N_i. We also have a bias vector B which contains $|N|$ entries of $+1$, 0, or -1. The bias vector is an indicator of the nature of the edges in the corresponding cluster. The algorithm utilizes an iterative approach in which the clusters are constructed around these seed nodes. The overall algorithm is illustrated in Figure 1. As illustrated in Figure 1, we first pick the k seeds randomly. Next, we enter an iterative loop in which we refine the initial seeds by performing the following steps:

- We assign each nodes to one of the seeds. The process of assignment of an entity node to a given seed node is quite tricky because of the fact that we would like a given subgraph to represent either increasing or decreasing communities. Therefore, we need to choose effective algorithms which can compute the distances for each community in a different way. We will discuss this process in detail slightly later. We note that the process of assignment is sensitive to the nature of the *bias* in the node. The bias in the node could

Algorithm *FindEvolvingCommunities*(Graph: (N, A),
   EdgeWeights: $\Delta w_{ij}(t_1, t_2)$, NumberOfClusters: k);
begin
   Randomly sample nodes $n_1 \ldots n_k$ as seeds;
   Let B be the bias vector of length $|N|$;
   Set each position in B to 0;
   while not(*termination_criterion*) **do**
     begin
     $(N_1 \ldots N_k) = AssignNodes(\ N, B, \{n_1 \ldots n_k\})$;
     $B = FindBias(N_1 \ldots N_k)$;
     $(N_1' \ldots N_k') = RemoveNodes(N_1 \ldots N_k)$;
     { Assume that the removed nodes are null partitions }
     $(n_1 \ldots n_k) = RecenterNodes(N_1 \ldots N_k)$;
     end
end

Fig. 1. Finding Evolving Communities

represent the fact that the cluster seeded by that node is likely to become one of the following: (1) An Expanding Community (2) A Contracting Community (3) Neutral Bias (Initial State). Therefore, we associate a *bias bit* with each seed node. This bias bit takes on the values of $+1$, or -1, depending upon whether the node has the tendency to belong to an expanding or contracting community. In the event that the bias is neutral, the value of that bit is set to 0. We note that an expanding community corresponds to positive edges, whereas a contracting community corresponds to negative edges. The process of assignment results in k node sets which are denoted by $N_1 \ldots N_k$. In the assignment process,we compute the distance of each seed node to the different entities. Each entity is assigned to its closest seed node. The algorithm for assignment of entities to seed nodes is denoted by *AssignNodes* in Figure 1.

- Once the assignment step has been performed, we re-assess the bias of that seed node. This is denoted by *FindBias* in Figure 1. The overall approach in finding the bias is to determine whether the interactions in the community attached to that seed node represent expansion or contraction. We will discuss the details of this algorithm slightly later. The bias bit vector B is returned by this procedure.

- Some of the seed nodes may not represent a coherent community of interaction. These seed nodes may be removed by the community detection algorithm. This process is achieved by the algorithm *RemoveNodes*. The new set of nodes is denoted by $N_1' \ldots N_k'$. We note that each N_i' is either N_i or null depending upon whether or not that node was removed by the algorithm.

- The final step is to re-center the seeds within their particular subgraph. The re-centering process essentially reassigns the seed node in a given subgraph N_i' to a more central point in it. In the event that N_i' is a null partition, the recentering process simply picks a random node in the graph as the corresponding seed. Once the recentering process is performed, we can perform the next iteration of the algorithm. The recentering procedure is denoted by *RecenterNodes* in Figure 1. The new set of seeds $n_1 \ldots n_k$ are returned by this algorithm.

4.4   Subroutines for Determination of the Communities

In the afore-mentioned discussion, we described the overall procedure for finding the communities of interaction. In this section, we will discuss the details of the subroutines which are required for determination of these communities. We will first discuss the procedure *AssignNodes* of Figure 1. The process of assigning the nodes to each of the centroids requires the use of the bias information stored in the bias nodes. Note that if a seed node has positive bias, then it needs to be ensured that the other nodes which are assigned to this seed node are related to it by positive interactions. The opposite is true if the bias on the seed node is negative. Finally, in the case of nodes with neutral bias, we simply need to find a path with high absolute interaction level. In this case, the positivity or negativity of the sign matters less than the corresponding absolute value. In order to achieve this goal, we define a *bias sensitive* distance function $f(n_1, n_2, b)$ between two nodes n_1 and n_2 for the bias bit b. For a given path P in the graph $\Delta G(t_1, t_2)$, we define the average interaction level $w(P)$ as the sum of the interaction levels on P divided by the number of edges on P. Therefore, we have:

$$w(P) = \sum_{(i,j) \in P} \Delta w_{ij}(t_1, t_2)/|P| \qquad (6)$$

We note that a path with high average *positive* weight corresponds to a set of edges with increasing level of interaction. This can also be considered an expanding community. The opposite is true of a path with high average *negative* weight, which corresponds to a contracting community. Therefore, the value of $w(P)$ is equal to the weight of the path divided by the number of edges on that path. We also define the average *absolute* average interaction level $w^+(P)$ as follows:

$$w^+(P) = \sum_{(i,j) \in P} |\Delta w_{ij}(t_1, t_2)|/|P| \qquad (7)$$

Note that the absolute interaction level does not have any bias towards a positive or negative level of interaction. Once we have set up the definitions of the path weights, we can also define the value of the interaction function $f(n_1, n_2, b)$. This interaction function is defined over all possible pairs of nodes (n_1, n_2).

$f(n_1, n_2, b) =$ Most positive value of $w(P)$ $\forall$ paths
$\qquad\qquad\quad P$ between n_1 and n_2 $\qquad$ if $b = 1$
$\qquad\qquad$ Modulus of most negative value of $w(P)$
$\qquad\qquad\quad \forall P$ between n_1 and n_2 $\qquad$ if $b = -1$
$\qquad\qquad$ Largest value of $w^+(P)$ $\forall$ paths
$\qquad\qquad\quad P$ between n_1 and n_2 $\qquad$ if $b = 0$

We note that the above interaction function is defined on the basis of the sum of the interaction values over a given path. In some cases, this interaction function can provide skewed results when the path lengths are long. This could result in less effective partitioning of the communities. A different interaction function is defined as the minimum interaction on the path between two entities. However, the bias of the corresponding centroid on that path is used in order to define the interaction function. This minimum interaction $w(P)$ is defined as follows:

$w(P) = \min_{(i,j) \in P} \max\{\Delta w_{ij}(t_1, t_2), 0\}$
$\qquad\qquad$ if $b = 1$
$\qquad\quad \max_{(i,j) \in P} \min\{\Delta w_{ij}(t_1, t_2), 0\}$
$\qquad\qquad$ if $b = -1$
$\qquad\quad \min_{(i,j) \in P} |\Delta w_{ij}(t_1, t_2)|$
$\qquad\qquad$ if $b = 0$

We note that the above mentioned function simply finds the minimum (absolute) weight edge of the corresponding sign (depending on the bias) between the two nodes. The corresponding interaction function $f(n_1, n_2, b)$ is defined in the same way as earlier. Henceforth, we will refer to the two above-defined functions as the average-interaction function and minimum interaction function respectively. In the latter case, the interaction distance corresponds to the interaction on the weakest link between the two nodes. As our experimental results will show, we found the minimum function to be slightly more robust than the average interaction function.

During the assignment phase, we calculate the value of the function $f(n_i, n, b)$ from each node n_i to the seed node n using the bias bit b. Each node n_i is assigned to the seed node n with the largest *absolute* value of the above-mentioned function. This process ensures that nodes are assigned to seeds according to their corresponding bias. The process of computation of the interaction function will be discussed in some detail slightly later.

Next, we determine the bias of each seed node in the procedure *FindBias*. In order to do so, we calculate the bias-index of the community defined by that seed node. The bias index of the community N_i is denoted by $\mathcal{I}(N_i)$, and is defined as the edge-weight fraction of the expanding portion of N_i. In order to do, so we divide the positive edge weights in the community by the total absolute edge weight in the same community. Therefore, we have:

$$\mathcal{I}(N_i) = \frac{\sum_{(p,q) \in N_i} \max\{0, \Delta w_{pq}(t_1, t_2)\}}{\sum_{(p,q) \in N_i} |\Delta w_{pq}(t_1, t_2)|} \tag{8}$$

We note that the bias index is 1 when all the edges in the community corresponding to increasing interaction, and is 0 when all the edges correspond to reducing interaction. Therefore, we define a threshold $t \in (0, 0.5)$. If the value of $\mathcal{I}(N_i)$ is less than t then the bias bit is set to -1. Similarly, if the value of $\mathcal{I}(N_i)$ is larger than $1 - t$, the bias bit is set to 1. Otherwise, the bias bit is set to zero.

Once the bias bits for the nodes have been set, we remove those seeds which have very few nodes associated with them. Such nodes usually do not correspond to a coherent community of interaction. This procedure is referred to as *RemoveNodes*. Thus, each set of nodes N_i is replaced by either itself or a null set of nodes. In order to implement this step, we use a minimum threshold on the number of nodes in a given partition. This threshold is denoted by mn_t. All partitions with less than mn_t entities are removed from consideration, and replaced by the null set.

The last step is to recenter the nodes within their corresponding partition. This denoted by the procedure *RecenterNodes* in Figure 1. The process of re-centering the nodes requires us to use a process in which the central points of subgraphs are determined. In order to recenter the nodes, we determine the node which minimizes the maximum distance of any node in the cluster. This is achieved by computing the distance of all points in the cluster starting at each node, and finding the minimax distance over these different values. The process of recentering helps to adjust the centers of the nodes in each iteration such that the process of partitioning the community sets becomes more effective over time.

4.5   Approximating Interaction Distances Among Nodes

The only remaining issue is to discuss the methodology for determining the interaction distances among nodes. We would like our algorithm to be general enough to find the maximum interaction distance for general functions. It is important to understand that the problem of finding the maximum interaction distance between two nodes is NP-hard.

Observation 4.1. *The problem of determining the maximum interaction distance between two nodes is NP-hard for arbitrary interaction functions.*

This observation is easily verified by observing that the problem of finding the longest path in a graph is NP-hard [7]. Since the particular case of picking the interaction function as the edge weight is NP-hard, the general problem is NP-hard as well.

However, it is possible to approximate the interaction distance of a maximum length using dynamic programming. Let wn_{ij}^t be the maximum interaction distance between two nodes using at most t nodes on that path. Let P_{ik}^t be the maximum length path between i and k using t edges. Let $PS_{ikj}^\oplus$ denote the path obtained by concatenating P_{ik}^t with the edge (k, j). Then, we define wn_{ij}^t recursively as follows:

$$wn_{ij}^0 = 0;$$
$$wn_{ij}^{t+1} = \max_k\{wn_{ij}^t, w(PS_{ikj}^\oplus)\}$$

We note that this dynamic programming algorithm does not always lead to an optimal solution in the presence of cycles in the graph [7]. However, for small values of t, it approximates the optimal solution well. This is because cycles are less likely to be present in paths of smaller length. It is also important to understand that if two entities are joined only by paths containing a large number of edges, then such pairs of entities should not be regarded as belonging to the same community. Therefore, we imposed a threshold *maxthresh* on the maximum length of the (shortest interaction distance) path between two nodes for them to belong to the same community. For a pair of nodes in which the corresponding path length was exceeded, the value of the interaction distance is set to 0. In [4], we have tested the method extensively over a number of real and synthetic data sets. These results show that the technique is scalable and provides insights about significantly evolving communities in the data stream.

5   Conclusions and Summary

In this paper, we examined the application of clustering for change diagnosis and detection in data streams. We showed how clustering can be used in order to determine summaries of the underlying change in the data. The overall framework is motivated by the micro-clustering technique [3], which provides a summary of the data for future change diagnosis. This summary can be used for text and categorical data, as well as community evolution in data streams. Such information has considerable value in a number of applications which require a clear understanding of the underlying data.

References

1. Aggarwal C. C.: A Framework for Diagnosing Changes in Evolving Data Streams, ACM SIGMOD Conference, (2003) 575–586.
2. Aggarwal C. C.: An Intuitive Framework for Understanding Changes in Evolving Data Streams, ICDE Conference, (2002).
3. Aggarwal C. C., Han J., Wang J., Yu P.: A Framework for Clustering Evolving Data Streams, VLDB Conference, (2003) 81–92.
4. Aggarwal C. C., Yu P. S.: Online Analysis of Community Evolution in Data Streams. *ACM SIAM Data Mining Conference*, (2006).
5. Aggarwal C. C., Yu P. S.: A Framework for Clustering Massive Text and Categorical Data Streams. *ACM SIAM Data Mining Conference*, (2006).
6. Aggarwal C, Han J., Wang J., Yu P.: On-Demand Classification of Data Streams. *ACM KDD Conference*, (2004).
7. Ahuja R., Magnanti T., and Orlin J.: *Network Flows: Theory, Algorithms and Applications*, Prentice Hall, Englewood Cliffs, New Jersey, (1992).
8. Babcock B., Babu S., Datar M., Motwani R., Widom J.: Models and Issues in Data Stream Systems, *ACM PODS Conference*, (2002) 1–16.
9. Chawathe S., and Garcia-Molina H.: Meaningful Change Detection in Structured Data. *ACM SIGMOD Conference Proceedings* (1997).
10. Cortes C., Pregibon D., and Volinsky C.: Communities of Interest, *Proceedings of Intelligent Data Analysis*, (2001).
11. Cortes C., Pregibon D., and Volinsky C.: Computational Methods for Dynamic Graphs, *Journal of Computational and Graphical Statistics*, 12, (2003), pp. 950-970.
12. Dasu T., Krishnan S., Venkatasubramaniam S., Yi K.: An Information-Theoretic Approach to Detecting Changes in Multi-dimensional data Streams. *Duke University Technical Report CS-2005-06* (2005).
13. Domingos P., and Hulten G.: Mining High-Speed Data Streams, *ACM SIGKDD Conference*, (2000).
14. Ganti V., Gehrke J., Ramakrishnan R.: A Framework for Measuring Changes in Data Characteristics. *ACM PODS Conference* (1999) pp. 126-137.
15. Ganti V., Gehrke J., Ramakrishnan R.: Mining and Monitoring Evolving Data. *IEEE ICDE Conference* (2000) pp. 439–448.
16. Ganti V., Gehrke J., Ramakrishnan R.: CACTUS- Clustering Categorical Data Using Summaries. *ACM KDD Conference* (1999) pp. 73–83.
17. Gibson D., Kleinberg J., and Raghavan P.: Inferring Web Communities from Link Topology, *Proceedings of the 9th ACM Conference on Hypertext and Hypermedia*, (1998).
18. Hulten G., Spencer L., and Domingos P.: Mining Time Changing Data Streams, *ACM KDD Conference*, (2001).
19. Imafuji N., and Kitsuregawa M.: Finding a Web Community by Maximum Flow Algorithm with HITS Score Based Capacity, *DASFAA*, (2003), pp. 101–106.

20. Kempe D., Kleinberg J., and Tardos E.: Maximizing the Spread of Influence Through a Social Network, *ACM KDD Conference*, (2003).
21. Kumar R., Novak J., Raghavan P., and Tomkins A.: On the Bursty Evolution of Blogspace, *Proceedings of the WWW Conference*, (2003).
22. Mei Q., Zhai C.: Discovering evolutionary theme patterns from text: an exploration of temporal text mining. *ACM KDD Conference*, (2005) pp. 198-207.
23. Nasraoui O., Cardona C., Rojas C., Gonzlez F.: TECNO-STREAMS: Tracking Evolving Clusters in Noisy Data Streams with a Scalable Immune System Learning Model, *ICDM Conference*, (2003) pp. 235-242.
24. Rajagopalan S., Kumar R., Raghavan P., and Tomkins A.: Trawling the Web for emerging cyber-communities, *Proceedings of the 8th WWW conference*, (1999).
25. Toyoda M., and Kitsuregawa M.: Extracting evolution of web communities from a series of web archives, *Hypertext*, (2003) pp. 28–37.
26. Zhang T., Ramakrishnan R., Livny M.: BIRCH: An Efficient Data Clustering Method for Very Large Databases. *ACM SIGMOD Conference*, (1996), pp. 103–114.
27. http://www.ics.uci.edu/~mlearn.

Personalized Search Results with User Interest Hierarchies Learnt from Bookmarks

Hyoung-rae Kim[1] and Philip K. Chan[2]

[1] Web Intelligence Laboratory
Hongje-dong, 158 bungi, Prugio 101dong 104ho
Gangneung-shi, Gangwon-do 210-948, South Korea
goddoes8@gmail.com
[2] Department of Computer Sciences
Florida Institute of Technology
Melbourne, FL. 32901, USA
pkc@cs.fit.edu

Abstract. Personalized web search incorporates an individual user's interests when deciding relevant results to return. While, most web search engines are usually designed to serve all users, without considering the interests of individual users. We propose a method to (re)rank the results from a search engine using a learned user profile, called a user interest hierarchy (UIH), from web pages that are of interest to the user. The user's interest in web pages will be determined implicitly, without directly asking the user. Experimental results indicate that our personalized ranking methods, when used with a popular search engine, can yield more potentially interesting web pages for individual users.

1 Introduction

Web personalization is the process of adapting a web site to the needs of specific users. Web personalization is used mainly in four categories: predicting web navigation, assisting personalization information, personalizing content, and personalizing search results. Predicting web navigation anticipates future requests or provides guidance to client. If a web browser or web server can correctly anticipate the next page that will be visited, the latency of the next request will be greatly reduced [11,20,325,2,13,38,39]. Assisting personalization information helps a user organize his or her own information and increases the usability of the Web [24,26]. Personalizing content focuses on personalizing individual pages, site-sessions (e.g., adding shortcut), or entire browsing sessions [1]. Personalized web search results provide customized results depending on each user's interests [19,18,25,2,17,29,4]. In this work, we focus on personalizing web search by ordering search engine results based on the interests of each individual user, which can greatly aid the search through massive amounts of data on the Internet.

There are two main techniques for performing web personalization: collaborative filtering [2,5] and user profiles [28,33]. Collaborative filtering uses information from many different users to make recommendations. Collaborative filtering assumes that people have common interests, and would suggest web pages that are the most popular. Disadvantages of this method are that it cannot predict whether a user will like a

O. Nasraoui et al. (Eds.): WebKDD 2005, LNAI 4198, pp. 158–176, 2006.
© Springer-Verlag Berlin Heidelberg 2006

new page, and it requires a large amount of data from many users to determine what pages are the most popular. Obtaining data on the web pages visited by many different users is often difficult (or illegal) to collect in many application domains. In contrast, user profiles require the web page history of only a single user. There are two techniques for building a user profile: explicit and implicit. The explicit approach takes time and effort for a user to specify his or her own interests, and the user's interests could change significantly over time. Alternatively, an implicit approach can identify a user's interests by inference, and can automatically adapt to changing or short-term interests. However, the implicit approach is not as accurate as the explicit approach.

In this paper, we propose a method to personalize web search by ranking the pages returned from a search engine. Pages are ranked based on their "score," where higher scores are considered to be more interesting to the user after comparing the text of the page to the user's profile that is learnt implicitly. For example, if a user searches for "aviation" and is interested in "job," then links related to "job" will be scored higher; but if a user is interested in "universities," then pages related to "universities" will be scored higher. We wish to devise a scoring function that is able to reorder the results from Google [14], based on a user's implicitly learned interests, such that web pages that the user is most interested in appear at the top of the page. A User Interest Hierarchy (UIH) is built from a set of interesting web pages using a divisive hierarchical clustering algorithm (DHC). A UIH organizes a user's interests from general to specific. The UIH can be used to build a scoring function for personalizing web search engines or e-commerce sites [6]. The web pages in a user's bookmarks are used as the set of interesting web pages for this work [24,26] in order to identify user interests.

While using a search engine, people find what they want. Often times they also find web pages they want to visit next time again. We define interesting web pages and potentially interesting web pages. The definition of *interest* is whether a user found what they want; the definition of *potential interest* is whether a web page will be interesting to a user in the future.

Our contributions are:

- We introduce personalized ranking methods – Weighted Scoring function (WS) and Uniform Scoring function (US) – that utilize an implicitly learned user profile (UIH);
- We identify four characteristics for terms that match the user profile and provide a probabilistic measure for each characteristic;
- Our experimental results indicate that WS method can achieve higher precision than Google for Top 1, 5, 10 and 20 potentially interesting web pages to the user that are relevant to the user search query;
- When incorporating the (*public*) ranking from the search engine, we found that equal weights for the public and personalized ranking can result in higher precision.

The rest of this paper is organized as follows: Section 2 presents related work regarding personalized search results and the use of bookmarks; Section 3 explains divisive hierarchical clustering algorithm that builds UIH; Section 4 details our approach to reorder search results; Section 5 provides a detailed description of our user-interest scoring methods; Section 6 discusses our evaluation; Section 7 analyzes our results; and Section 8 summarizes our work.

2   Related Work

Page et al. [29] first proposed personalized web search by modifying the global PageRank algorithm with the input of bookmarks or homepages of a user. their work mainly focuses on global "importance" by taking advantage of the link structure of the web. Haveliwala [17] determined that PageRank could be computed for very large subgraphs of the web on machines with limited main memory. Brin et al. [4] suggested the idea of biasing the PageRank computation for the purpose of personalization, but it was never fully explored. Bharat and Mihaila [2] suggested an approach called *Hilltop*, that generates a query-specific authority score by detecting and indexing pages that appear to be good experts for certain keywords, based on their links. Hilltop is designed to improve results for *popular* queries; however, query terms for which experts were not found will not be handled by the Hilltop algorithm. Haveliwala [18] used personalized PageRank scores to enable "topic sensitive" web search. They concluded that the use of personalized PageRank scores can improve web search, but the number of hub vectors (e.g., number of interesting web pages used in a bookmark) used was limited to 16 due to the computational requirements. Jeh and Widom [19] scaled the number of hub pages beyond 16 for finer-grained personalization. Our method does not use the structure of hyperlinks.

Liu et al. [25] also tried mapping user queries to sets of categories. This set of categories served as a context to disambiguate the words in the user's query, which is similar to Vivisimo [36]. They studied how to supply, for each user, a small set of categories as a context for each query submitted by the user, based on his or her search history. Our approach does not personalize the set of categories, but personalizes results returned from a search engine.

Another approach to web personalization is to predict forward references based on partial knowledge about the history of the session. Zukerman et al. [40] and Cadez et al. [5] use a Markov model to learn and represent significant dependencies among page references. Shahabi and Banaei-Kashani [32] proposed a web-usage-mining framework using navigation pattern information. They introduced a feature-matrices (FM) model to discover and interpret users' access patterns. This approach is different from ours since we use the contents of web pages, and not navigation patterns.

Teevan et al. [34] also use implicit interest from the user to re-rank search results. The presence of various files (e.g., Word documents, web pages) on the user's computer indicates the user is interested in those files. The user profile is essentially files of various types on the computer. However, we try to build a user profile by generalizing from web pages that have been bookmarked. Also, our user profile attempts to represent general to specific topics, each of which consists of related words.

PowerBookmarks [24] is a web information organization, sharing, and management tool, that monitors and utilizes users' access patterns to provide useful personalized services. PowerBookmarks provides automated URL bookmarking, document refreshing, bookmark expiration, and subscription services for new or updated documents. BookmarkOrganizer [26] is an automated system that maintains a hierarchical organization of a user's bookmarks using the classical HAC algorithm [37], but by applying "slicing" technique (slice the tree at regular intervals and collapse into one single level all levels between two slices). Both BookmarkOrganizer and PowerBookmarks reduce the effort required to maintain the bookmark, but they are insensitive to the context browsed by users and do not have reordering functions.

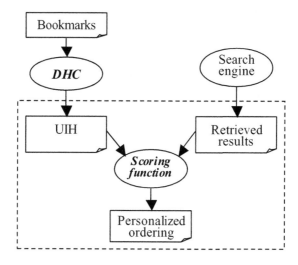

Fig. 1. Personalizing search results

3   Personalized Results

Personalization of web search involves adjusting search results for each user based on his or her unique interests. Our approach orders the pages returned by a search engine depending on a user's interests. Instead of creating our own web search engine, we retrieved results from Google [14]. Since the purpose of this paper is to achieve a personalized ordering of search engine results, we can score a page based on the user profile and the results returned by a search engine as shown in the dashed box in Fig. 1. This paper mainly focuses on the scoring function.

Table 1. Spample data set

Web page	Content
1	ai machine learning ann perceptron
2	ai machine learning ann perceptron
3	ai machine learning decision tree id3 c4.5
4	ai machine learning decision tree id3 c4.5
5	ai machine learning decision tree hypothesis space
6	ai machine learning decision tree hypothesis space
7	ai searching algorithm bfs
8	ai searching algorithm dfs
9	ai searching algorithm constraint reasoning forward checking
10	ai searching algorithm constraint reasoning forward checking

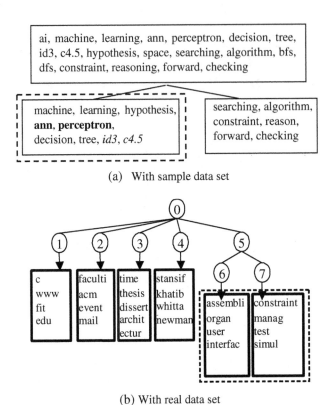

ai, machine, learning, ann, perceptron, decision, tree,
id3, c4.5, hypothesis, space, searching, algorithm, bfs,
dfs, constraint, reasoning, forward, checking

machine, learning, hypothesis,
ann, perceptron,
decision, tree, *id3, c4.5*

searching, algorithm,
constraint, reason,
forward, checking

(a)   With sample data set

c
www
fit
edu

faculti
acm
event
mail

time
thesis
dissert
archit
ectur

stansif
khatib
whitta
newman

assembli
organ
user
interfac

constraint
manag
test
simul

(b) With real data set

Fig. 2. Sample user interest hierarchies

To build the user profile, called UIH, we use the web pages in his/her bookmarks
[24,26] and the Divisive Hierarchy Clustering (DHC) algorithm [23]. A UIH organizes a user's interests from general to specific. Near the root of a UIH, general interests are represented by larger clusters of terms while towards the leaves, more specific
interests are represented by smaller clusters of terms. In this paper, "term" refers a
phrase that has one or more word. The root node contains all distinct terms in the
bookmarked web page. The leaf nodes contain more specifically interesting terms.
The relations between terms are calculated based on the co-occurrence in the same
web page.

Two examples of a UIH are shown in Fig. 2 – UIH (a) is generated from a sample
dataset in Table 1 and UIH (b) is generated from a user's real dataset. Each node
(cluster) contains a set of words. The root node contains all words that exist in a set of
web pages. Each node can represent a conceptual relationship if those terms occur
together at the same web page frequently, for example in Fig. 2 (a), 'perceptron' and
'ann' (in italics) can be categorized as belonging to neural network algorithms,
whereas 'id3' and 'c4.5' (in bold) cannot. Words in this node (in the dashed box) are
mutually related to some other words such as 'machine' and 'learning'. This set of
mutual words, 'machine' and 'learning', performs the role of connecting italicized
and bold words. In Fig. 2 (b), Cluster 1 represents the homepage of Computer Science

department. Cluster 3 illustrates academic degree programs. Cluster 4 contains names of faculty members. The tree has a node with two child clusters, Cluster 6 and 7, which contains words from course titles and hence represents the concepts of different courses (in the dashed box).

This paper mainly focuses on devising a scoring method that receives two inputs (UIH and retrieved results) and one output (personalized ranking). For completeness, we next briefly describe the DHC algorithm that learns an UIH from a set of web pages (bookmarks in our experiments).

4 Learning UIH

The divisive hierarchical clustering (DHC) algorithm [23] recursively partitions the words into smaller clusters, which represent more related words. We assume words occurring close to each other (within a window size) are related to each other.

DHC algorithm recursively divides clusters into child clusters until it meets the stopping conditions. In preparation for our clustering algorithm, we extract words from web pages that are interesting to the user, filter them through a stop list, and stem them. Fig. 3. illustrates the pseudo code for the DHC algorithm. Using a correlation function, we calculate the strength of the relationship between a pair of words in line 1. The WindowSize is the maximum distance (in number of words) between two related words in calculating their correlation value. After calculating a threshold to differentiate strong correlation values from weak correlation in line 2, we remove all weak correlation values in line 5. The FINDTHRESHOLD is a method that calculates the cutoff value for determining strong and weak correlation values. We then build a weighted undirected graph with each vertex representing a word and each weight denoting the correlation between two words. Since related words are more likely to appear in the same document than unrelated terms, we measure co-occurrence of words in a document. Given the graph, called a CorrelationMatrix, the clustering algorithm recursively partitions the graph into subgraphs, called Clusters, each of which represents a sibling node in the resulting UIH in line 6.

At each partitioning step, edges with "weak" weights are removed and the resulting connected components constitute sibling clusters (we can also consider cliques as clusters, but more computation is required). We treat the determination of what value is considered to be "strong" or "weak", as another clustering. The recursive partitioning process stops when one of the stopping criteria is satisfied. The first criterion is when the current graph does not have any connected components after weak edges are removed. The second criterion is a new child cluster is not formed if the number of words in the cluster falls below a predetermined threshold.

The CalculateCorrelationMatrix function takes a correlation function, cluster, and window size as parameters and returns the correlation matrix, where the window size affects how far two words (the number of words between two words) can be considered as related. The correlation function calculates how strongly two words are related. Since related words are likely to be closer to each other than unrelated words, we assume two words co-occurring within a window size are related to each other. To simplify our discussion, we have been assuming the window size to be the entire length of a document. That is, two words co-occur if they are in the same document.

Cluster: distinct words in a set of interesting web pages
to a user [with information of web page membership]
CORRELATIONFUNCTION: Calculates the "closeness" of two
words.
FINDTHRESHOLD: Calculates the cutoff value for determining
strong and weak correlation values.
WindowSize: The maximum distance (in number of words) between two related words in calculating their correlation value.

Procedure DHC (Cluster, CORRELATIONFUNCTION,
FINDTHRESHOLD, WindowSize)
1.   CorrelationMatrix ← CalculateCorrelationMatrix
(CORRELATIONFUNCTION, Cluster, WindowSize)
2.   Threshold ← CalculateThreshold(FINDTHRESHOLD, CorrelationMatrix)
3.   If all correlation values are the same or a threshold
is not found
4.   Return EmptyHierarchy
5.   Remove weights that are less than Threshold from CorrelationMatrix
6.   While (ChildCluster←NextConnectedComponent (CorrelationMatrix))
7.   If size of ChildCluster >= MinClusterSize
8.   ClusterHierarchy←ClusterHierarchy + ChildCluster + **DHC**(ChildCluster, CORRELATIONFUNCTION,
FINDTHRESHOLD, WindowSize)
9.   Return ClusterHierarchy
End Procedure

Fig. 3. DHC algorithm

We use AEMI (Augmented Expected Mutual Information) [6] as a correlation
function. Consider A and B in AEMI (A,B) are the events for the two words.
$P(A = a)$ is the probability of a document containing a and $P(A = \bar{a})$ is the
probability of a document not having term a. $P(B = b)$ and $P(B = \bar{b})$ is defined
likewise. $P(A = a, B = b)$ is the probability of a document containing both terms a and
b. These probabilities are estimated from documents that are interesting to the user.
AEMI (A,B) is defined as:

$$AEMI(A,B) = P(a,b)\log\frac{P(a,b)}{P(a)P(b)} - \sum_{(A=a,B=\bar{b})(A=\bar{a},B=b)} P(A,B)\log\frac{P(A,B)}{P(A)P(B)}$$

The first term computes supporting evidence that a and b are related and the second
term calculates counter-evidence.

The CalculateThreshold function takes a threshold-finding method and correlation matrix as parameters and returns the threshold. We examine methods that
dynamically determine a reasonable threshold value, in order to differentiate strong
from weak correlation values between a pair of terms. Weights with a weak correlation are removed from CorrelationMatrix and child clusters are identified.

The MaxChildren method selects a threshold such that maximum of child clusters are generated and is guided to generate a shorter tree. This way we divide the strongly correlated values from weakly correlated ones. This also ensures that the resulting hierarchy does not degenerate to a tall and thin tree (which might be the case for other methods). This preference also stems from the fact that topics are generally more diverse than detailed and the library catalog taxonomy is typically short and wide. For example, we want the trees in Fig. 2 to be shorter and wider. MaxChildren calculates the number of child clusters for each boundary value between two quantized regions. To guarantee the selected threshold is not too low, this method ignores the first half of the boundary values. This method recursively divides the selected best region until there are no changes on the number of child clusters.

Table 1 has words from ten sample web pages; after running the DHC algorithm, the UIH in Fig. 2a is produced. We next discuss how an UIH can be used to score a web page retrieved by a search engine.

5   Using UIH for Scoring Pages

In order to provide personalized, reordered search results to a user, we need to score each page depending on personal interests. Therefore, the goal is to assign higher scores to web pages that a user finds more interesting. This section explains how to score a retrieved web page using a user's UIH. First, we explain the basic characteristics for each matching term. Second, based on the characteristics, we propose functions to score a term. These functions determine how interesting a term is to a user. Third, based on the score and the number of the matching terms, we calculate an overall score for the page. Last, since the search engine provides a score/ranking for a web page, we incorporate this ranking into our final score of the web page.

5.1   Four Characteristics of a Term

Given a web page and a UIH, we identify matching terms (words/phrases) that reside both in the web page and in the UIH. The number of matching terms is defined m, which is less than the number of total distinct terms in the web page, n, and the number of total distinct terms in the UIH, l.

Each matching term, t_i, is analyzed according to four characteristics: the deepest level of a node where a term belongs to (D_{t_i}), the length of a term such as how many words are in the term (L_{t_i}), the frequency of a term (F_{t_i}), and the emphasis of a term (E_{t_i}). D and L can be calculated while building a UIH from the web pages in a user's bookmarks. Different web page has different values for F and E characteristics. We estimate the probability of these four characteristics and based on these probabilities, we approximate the significance of each matching term. Suppose a web page A has most of the terms bold formatted and the other web page B has only a few terms bold formatted. The bold formatted terms in B may be more significant than the bold formatted terms in A. The probability (0~1) of the bold formatted term can be used to represent the significance/emphasis of the term.

Level/depth of a UIH Node. A UIH represents general interests in large clusters of terms near the root of the UIH, while more specific interests are represented by smaller clusters of terms near the leaves. The root node contains all distinct terms and the leaf nodes contain small groups of terms that represent more specific interests. Therefore, terms in more specific interests are harder to match, and the deepest level (depth) where the term matches indicates significance. For example, a document that contains terms in leaf nodes will be more related to the user's interests than a document that contains the terms in a root node only. If a term in a node also appears in several of its ancestors, we use the level (depth) closest to the leaves.

There is research that indicates user-defined query scores can be used effectively [8,16,31]. From the acquisition point of view, it is not clear how many levels of importance users can specify if we ask a user directly. In I^3R [9], they used only two levels: important or default. Harper [16] used 5 levels of importance, and Croft and Das [8] used 4 levels. We calculate the scores of terms using the deepest level (depth) of a node in the UIH instead of explicitly asking the user.

The significance of a term match can be measured by estimating the probability, $P(D_{ti})$, of matching term t_i at depth (level) D_{ti} in the UIH. For example, $D_{ti}=0$ includes 100 terms (all terms), $D_{ti}=1$ has 20 terms, and $D_{ti}=2$ contains 10 terms. Then, $P(D_{ti}=1)$ will be 0.2 and $P(D_{ti}=2)$ becomes 0.1. A term that matches more specific interests (deeper in the UIH) has a lower $P(D_{ti})$ of occurring. Lower probability indicates the matching term, t_i, is more significant. The probability is estimated by:

$$P(D_{t_i}) = \frac{\text{number of distinct terms at depth } D_{ti} \text{ in the UIH}}{l}$$

Length of a Term. Longer terms (phrases) are more specific than shorter ones. If a web page contains a long search term typed in by a user, the web page is more likely what the user was looking for.

In general, there are fewer long terms than short terms. To measure the significance of a term match, the probability, $P(L_{ti})$, of matching term t_i of length L_{ti} in the UIH is calculated. L_{ti} is defined as MIN (10, the length of a term) (e.g., t_i = "apple computer", then $L_{ti} = 2$). We group the longer (greater than 10) phrases into one bin because they are rare. Longer terms has a smaller probability, $P(L_{ti})$, of occurring, which indicates a more significant match. The probability is estimated by:

$$P(L_{t_i}) = \frac{\text{number of distinct terms of length } L_{ti} \text{ in the UIH}}{l}$$

Frequency of a Term. More frequent terms are more significant/important than less frequent terms. Frequent terms are often used for document clustering or information retrieval [35]. A document that contains a search term many times will be more related to a user's interest than a document that has the term only once.

We estimate the probability, $P(F_{ti})$, of a matching term t_i at frequency F_{ti} in a web page to measure the significance of the term. However, in general, frequent terms have a lower probability of occurring. For example, in a web page most of the terms (without the terms in a stop list [12]) will occur once, some terms happen twice, and fewer terms repeat three times or more. Lower probabilities, $P(F_{ti})$, of a term t_i indicates the significance of a term. The probability is estimated by:

$$P(F_{t_i}) = \frac{\text{number of distinct terms with frequency } F_{ti} \text{ in a web page}}{n}$$

Emphasis of a Term. Some terms have different formatting (HTML tags) such as title, bold, or italic. These specially-formatted terms have more emphasis in the page than those that are formatted normally. A document that emphasizes a search term as a bold format will be more related to the search term than a document that has the term in a normal format without emphasis. If a term is emphasized by the use of two or more types of special formatting we assign a priority in the order of title, bold, and italic.

The significance for each type of format is estimated based on the probability, $P(E_{ti})$, of matching term t_i with the format type E_{ti} in a web page. Those format types are more significant/important if the format type has lower probability of occurring in a web page. Lower probability $P(E_{ti})$ of a matching term, t_i, indicates the term is more significant. The probability is estimated by:

$$P(E_{t_i}) = \frac{\text{number of distinct terms with emphasis } E_{ti} \text{ in a web page}}{n}$$

5.2 Scoring a Term

Uniform Scoring. $P(D_{ti}, L_{ti}, F_{ti}, E_{ti})$ is the joint probability of all four characteristics occurring in term t_i -- D_{ti} is the depth of a node where a term belongs to, L_{ti} is the length of a term, F_{ti} is the frequency of a term, and E_{ti} is the emphasis of a term. We can easily observe that there is no significant correlation among the four characteristics. Assuming independence among the four characteristics, we estimate:

$$P(D_{t_i}, L_{t_i}, F_{t_i}, E_{t_i}) = P(D_{t_i}) \times P(L_{t_i}) \times P(F_{t_i}) \times P(E_{t_i})$$

The corresponding log likelihood is:

$$\begin{aligned}\log P(D_{t_i}, L_{t_i}, F_{t_i}, E_{t_i}) = &\log P(D_{t_i}) + \log P(L_{t_i}) \\ &+ \log P(F_{t_i}) + \log P(E_{t_i})\end{aligned} \quad (1)$$

Smaller log likelihood means the term match is more significant. In information theory [27], $-\log_2 P(e)$ is the number of bits needed to encode event e, hence using $-\log_2$, instead of log, in Eq. 1 yields the total number of bits needed to encode the four characteristics. The uniform term scoring (US) function for a personalized term score is formulated as:

$$\begin{aligned}S_{t_i} = &-\log_2 P(D_{t_i}) - \log_2 P(L_{t_i}) \\ &- \log_2 P(F_{t_i}) - \log_2 P(E_{t_i})\end{aligned} \quad (2)$$

which we use as a score for term t_i. Larger S_{ti} means the term match is more significant.

Weighted Scoring. The uniform term scoring function uses uniform weights for each characteristic. It is possible that some characteristics are more important than the others. For instance, the depth of a node (D) may be more significant than frequency (F). Therefore, we attempted to differentiate the weights for each characteristic. F and E characteristics represent the relevance of a web page. Longer terms (greater L) represent a user's interest more specifically; however, longer terms do not mean that a user is more interested in that term. Therefore, those L, F, and E characteristics do not fully reflect a user's interests. It is more reasonable to emphasize D characteristic more than other characteristics, because D (depth) represents the strength of a user's interests.

A simple heuristic is used in this paper that assumes the depth of a node is at least two times more important than other characteristics. Based on this heuristic, the weights $w_1=0.4$, $w_2=0.2$, $w_3=0.2$, and $w_4=0.2$ are assigned. The weighted term scoring (WS) function for a personalized term score is formulated as:

$$S_{t_i} = -w_1 \log_2 P(D_{t_i}) - w_2 \log_2 P(L_{t_i})$$
$$- w_3 \log_2 P(F_{t_i}) - w_4 \log_2 P(E_{t_i}) \tag{3}$$

The performance of WS may depend on how the weights for each characteristic are assigned. We will examine this further in the future.

5.3 Scoring a Page

The *personal* page score is based on the number of interesting terms and how interesting the terms are in a web page. If there are many terms in a web page that are interesting to a user, it will be more interesting to the user than a web page that has fewer interesting terms. If there are terms in a page that are more interesting to a user, the web page will be more interesting to the user than a web page that has less interesting terms.

The personalized page scoring function for a web page S_{pj} adds all the scores of the terms in the web page and can be formulated as:

$$S_{p_j} = \sum_{i=1}^{m} S_{t_i} \tag{4}$$

where m is the total number of matching terms in a web page and S_{t_i} is the score for each distinct term. The time complexity of scoring a page is $O(n)$, where n is the number of "distinct" terms in a web page. D and L characteristics can be calculated during the preprocessing stage of building a UIH. F and L characteristics can be calculated while extracting distinct terms from a web page.

5.4 Incorporating Public Page Score

Personal page scoring is not sufficient for some search engines. The success of using *public* scoring in popular search engines, such as Google's PageRank, indicates the importance of using a public page-popularity measure to determine what page a user is interested in. Many existing methods determine the public popularity of a page by determining the number pages that link to it [18,19]. Many collaborative filtering approaches also use the popularity of a web page for recommendation [11,20]. Section 4.3 described our personal web page scoring function. We wish to incorporate the *public* scoring into our page scoring function so both the popularity of a page and individual interests are taken into account. We use the rank order returned by Google as our *public* score. $GOOGLE_{p_j}$ is the score of a web page p_j based on the page rank returned by Google for a search term. Users tend to find the answers they are looking for with Google [10], so we decide to use the Google's rank as the *public* page score. The use of Google's page rank makes our experimental comparison with Google clearer, because any improvement in the ordering is due to the contribution of our *personal* page score. For a given web page, p_j, the *personal* and *public* page score (*PPS*) equation can be written as:

$$PPS_{p_j} = c \times R\ (S_{p_j}) + (1-c) \times R\ (GOOGLE_{p_j}) \tag{5}$$

where function $R(GOOGLE_{p_j})$ return the rank of a web page, p_j, with the *public* page score of $GOOGLE_{p_j}$, and $R(S_{p_j})$ is the rank of a web page, p_j, with the *personal* page score, S_{p_j}. If the function R returns the rank in an ascending order, more interesting web pages will have lower *PPS* values. Therefore, the function R reverses the rank. The *personal* page score and the *public* page score are weighted by the value of the constant c. In this paper, both functions are weighed equally: $c = 0.5$.

The performance of US or WS may depend on how much we weigh the *personal* page score over the *public* page score. The experiment with various c will be our future work.

6   Experiments

In our experiments data were collected from 34 different users. Of the 34 human subjects, 27 were undergraduate students and 7 were graduate students. In terms of major, 23 were in Business/Computer Information Systems, 7 were Computer Sciences, 2 were Aeronautical Sciences, 1 was Chemical Engineering, and 1 was Marine Biology. Our earlier study included 22 search terms from 11 users; this study has expanded to 46 search terms from 34 users. Each user submitted one or two search terms. The search terms can contain any Boolean operators. Some examples of the search terms used are {review forum +"scratch remover", cpu benchmark, aeronautical, Free cross-stitch scenic patterns, neural networks tutorial, DMC(digital media center), artificial intelligence , etc.}

Then, we used Google to retrieve 100 related web pages for each search term. Those collected web pages (about 4,600 in total) were classified/labeled by user based on two categories: *interest* and *potential interest*. The data set for *interest* has more authority because it indicates direct relevance to the current search query. The data set for *potential interest* reflects the user's general personal interests, which might not be directly relevant at the time of query. The areas of a user's *potential interests* often go beyond the boundary of a search term's specific meaning. Sometimes users find interesting web pages while searching for different subjects. These unexpected results help the user as well. Therefore, it is also a contribution if a method shows higher precision in finding potentially interesting web pages.

In order to build UIHs, we also requested each volunteer to submit the web pages in their bookmarks. If there were fewer than 50 web pages in their bookmarks, we asked them to collect more pages up to around 50. The minimum number of web pages was 29 and the maximum number was 72. Web pages from both bookmarks and Google were parsed to retrieve only texts. The terms (words and phrases) in the web pages are stemmed and filtered through the stop list [12]. A phrase-finding algorithm [22] was used to collect variable-length phrases. Words in selection boxes/menus were also removed because they did not appear on the screen until a user clicks on them. Unimportant contexts such as comments and style were also removed. Web pages that contain non-text (e.g., ".pdf" files, image files, etc.) were excluded because we are handling only text. To remove any negative bias to Google, broken links that were still ranked high erroneously by Google were excluded from the test, since those web pages will be scored "Poor" by the user for sure. The data used in this study is available upon request. Microsoft .NET language was used, and the program ran on an Intel Pentium 4 CPU.

Users categorized the *interest* as "Good", "Fair", and "Poor"; the *potential interest* is categorized as "Yes" and "No". A web page was scored as "Good", "Fair", and "Poor" depending on each individual's subjective opinion based on the definition of *interest*. We are interested in the small number of "Good" web pages, since users tend to open only the top several web pages. That is why we use the three scales instead of two scales such as "related" and "not related". It was also marked as "Yes" or "No" based on the user's *potential interest*. We evaluated a ranking method based on how many interesting (categorized as "Good") or potentially interesting web pages (categorized as "Yes") the method collected within a certain number of top links [2] (called "Top link analysis"). It is realistic in a sense many information retrieval systems are interested in the top 10 or 20 groups. Precision/recall graph [35] is used for evaluation as well (called "precision/recall analysis"). It is one of the most common evaluation methods in information retrieval. However, traditional precision/recall graphs are very sensitive to the initial rank positions and evaluate entire rankings [8]. The formula for precision and recall were:

```
Precision = Number of "Good" or "Yes" pages retrieved in the set /
            Size of the set
Recall = Number of "Good" or "Yes" pages retrieved in the set /
         Number of "Good" or "Yes" pages in the set
```

where the "set" is the group of top ranked web pages. In this paper we study five groups: Top 1, 5, 10, 15, and 20.

7 Analysis

We compare four ranking methods: Google, Random, US, and WS. Google is the ranking provided by Google. Random arbitrarily ranks the web pages. US and WS are the two proposed methods based on a personal UIH learned from a user's bookmarks. For Random, US, and WS, the top 100 pages retrieved by Google are re-ranked based on the method. Each method is analyzed with two data sets: a set of web pages chosen as interesting and another chosen as potentially interesting by the users. Top link analysis, precision/recall analysis, the sensitivity of personal score weight c (Section 4.4) are discussed.

7.1 Interesting Web Page

Web search engine users are usually interested in the links ranked within top 20 [7]. We compare each method only with Top 1, 5, 10, 15, and 20 links on the interesting web page data set and present the results in Table 2. The first column is the methods; the next five columns present the precision values of each method with respect to the five Top links. The values in each cell are the average of 46 search terms' precision values. High precision value indicates high accuracy/performance. Precision values higher than Google's are formatted as bold and the percentage of improvement is within parentheses. The highest precision value in each column is underscored.

The results show that our WS method was more accurate than Google in three Top links (Top 1, 10, and 15) and the percentages of improvements are 1% or 13%, while WS ties with Google for Top 10 and US ties with Google for Top 1. In terms of the highest precision, US showed the highest performance in two columns; Google showed in two columns. WS showed higher precision in Top 1 than both US and Google, where the Top 1 is the most important link. This indicates that WS could improve the performance of Google. Random was the lowest as we expected, showing the lowest precisions in all five columns.

Precision/recall analysis visualizes the performance of each method in graphs as shown in Fig. 4. The x-axis is recall and y-axis is precision. The line closer to the upper ceiling has higher performance. Even though WS and US showed higher performance in the Top link analysis, Google seemed to show higher performance in Precision/recall analysis.

Table 2. Precision in Top 1, 5, 10, 15 and 20 for interesting web pages

	Top 1	Top 5	Top 10	Top 15	Top 20
Google	0.326	<u>0.378</u>	0.328	0.339	<u>0.332</u>
Random	0.304	0.248	0.252	0.249	0.259
US	**0.326**	0.335	**<u>0.330</u>** (1%)	**<u>0.343</u>** (1%)	0.328
WS	**<u>0.370</u>** (13%)	0.335	**0.328**	**0.341** (1%)	0.329

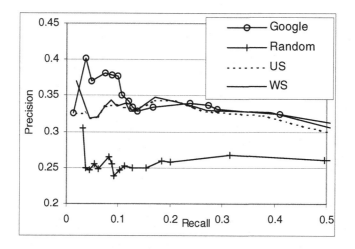

Fig. 4. Precision/recall graph for interesting web pages

We also wanted to know which search terms yielded higher precision with WS than with Google and analyzed the precision for Top 10 with respect to each individual search term. Out of 46 search terms, WS achieved higher precision for 18 search terms (39%), Google did for 22 search terms (48%), and they were even for 6 search terms (13%). US achieved higher precision for 23 search terms (50%), Google did for 21 search terms (46%), and they were even for 2 search terms (4%). Since the UIH is built from a user's bookmarks, we analyse the bookmarks to understand the search terms that did not perform well using WS. When we compare the bookmarks with the "good" retrieved web pages, we found that they are unrelated. For example, a volunteer used"woodworking tutorial" as a search term, but he never bookmarked web pages related to that term. This implies bookmarks are useful for building user profiles, but they are not sufficient. We will discuss enhancements in the conclusion.

7.2 Potentially Interesting Web Page

We compare our four methods with Top 1, 5, 10, 15, and 20 links on the potentially interesting web page data set and present the results in Table 3. The values in each cell are the average of 46 search terms' precision values. The ways of reading this table and the table for interesting web pages are similar.

WS showed higher performances than Google in four Top links (Top 1, 5, 10, and 20). Two precisions (Top 1 and 5) achieved by WS are the highest values as well. The percentages of improvements are between 1% and 9%. Random showed the lowest in all five Top links. The reason for the improvement of WS is, we predict, because the UIH that was derived from a user's bookmarks supported the user's *potential interest*. It might be difficult for Google that used the *global/public* interest to predict individual user's broad *potential interests*.

The results from precision/recall graph for potentially interesting web pages in Fig. 5 and the Top link analysis in Table 3 are similar to each other. WS was closer to the upper ceiling than Google, US, and Random over all. WS outperformed other methods on potentially interesting web pages data set.

We also counted what search terms yielded higher precision with WS than with Google. WS achieved higher performance for 24 search terms (52%), Google made for 13 search terms (28%), and they were even for 9 search terms (20%) out of 46 search terms. US achieved higher performance for 23 search terms (50%), Google made for 13 search terms (28%), and they were even for 10 search terms (22%). The reason for the low performance of some search terms might be because there is no relation between his/her bookmarks and the search terms.

Table 3. Precision in Top 1, 5, 10, 15 and 20 for potentially interesting web pages

	Top 1	Top 5	Top 10	Top 15	Top 20
Google	0.522	0.535	0.528	<u>0.532</u>	0.509
Random	0.457	0.430	0.424	0.422	0.430
US	**0.522**	**0.578** (8%)	<u>**0.541**</u> (2%)	0.529	<u>**0.516**</u> (1%)
WS	<u>**0.565**</u> (8%)	<u>**0.583**</u> (9%)	**0.537** (2%)	0.520	**0.513** (1%)

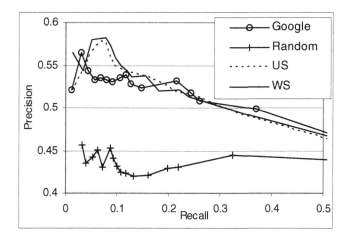

Fig. 5. Precision/recall graph for potentially interesting web pages

8   Conclusion

In order to devise a new method of ranking web search results to serve each individual user's interests, a user profile called UIH is learned from his/her bookmarks using the DHC algorithm [23]. For scoring a term in a web page that matches a term in the UIH, we identified four characteristics: the depth of tree node in the UIH that contains the term, the length of the term, the frequency of the term in the web page, and the html formatting used for emphasis. Our approach uses the terms filtered though stop list in web pages [12]. This approach removes the process of selecting important/significant terms unlike other information retrieval techniques [30]. We evaluated methods based on how many interesting web pages or potentially interesting web pages each algorithm found within certain number of top links [2]. Traditional precision/recall graphs [35] were also used for evaluation. We counted which search term showed higher performances with WS than with Google as well.

We compared four ranking methods: Google, Random, US, and WS. Google is the most popular search engine and posts the best ordering results currently. Random method was chosen to see the improved performance of Google and our new methods. We used two data sets: interesting web pages that are relevant to the user search term and potentially interesting web pages that could be relevant in the future. On interesting web pages, the results indicate that Google seemed outperformed US and WS, even though WS showed higher precision than Google for Top 1 and 15. It is because Google drew a line closer to the ceiling in the Prcison/recall analysis in general. However, WS showed the higher performance than Google in Top 1, which is the most important. Out of 46 search terms, US achieved higher precision than Google for 23 search terms (50%) where they are even for 2 search terms. On potentially interesting web pages, WS achieved the higher performance in four Top links (Top 1, 5, 10, and 20) with improvement over Google between 1% and 9%. It also outperformed the other methods in the precision/recall graph. The analysis of individual search terms showed that WS achieved higher performance for 24 search terms

(52%), Google made for 13 search terms (28%), and they were even for 9 search terms (20%) out of 46 search terms. These results conclude that WS can provide more accurate ranking than Google on average for potentially interesting web pages.

The improvement of WS was not statistically significant because the precision values of Google had large variance. The reason for the low performance of some search terms might be because there is no relation between his/her bookmarks and the search terms. We may be able to relieve this problem by incorporating interesting web pages based on implicit interest indicators such as mouse movements [21] in addition to bookmarking. There is a downside to using bookmarks because it relies on users deleting old bookmarks that they no longer consider relevant, so the data may become polluted with uninteresting documents with time. Therefore, we may have to adjust the time as the fifth characteristic. In this work, we used two characteristics of a term for personalization. The effect of these qualitatively different features should be evaluated in the future as well.

During the experiment, we observed that users do not tend to measure index pages as "Good". It is because index pages usually contain long lists of hyperlinks with little description for a user to find interesting. To identify index pages automatically, we count the number of "outside words" (the text outside anchor tags), which usually provide the subject content. However, our approach of penalizing the index pages did not make much improvement in our initial experiments. We will examine this approach further in the future.

References

1. Anderson, C.R.: A Machine Learning Approach to Web Personalization, Ph.D. thesis. University of Washington, Department of Computer Science and Engineering (2002)
2. Ben Schafer, J., Konstan, J.A., Riedl, J.: Electronic commerce recommender applications, Journal of Data Mining and Knowledge Discovery, 5 (2001) 115-152
3. Bharat, K., Mihaila, G. A.: When experts agree: using non-affiliated experts to rank popular topics. In Proc. of the 10th Intl. World Wide Web Conference (2001)
4. Brin, S., Motwani, R., Page, L., Winograd, T.: What can you do with a web in your pocket. In Bulletin of the IEEE Computer Society Technical Committee on Data Engineering (1998)
5. Cadez, I., Heckerman, D., Meek, C., Smyth, P., White, S.: Visualization of navigation patterns on web site using model based clustering. Technical Report MSR-TR-00-18, Microsoft Research, Microsoft Corporation, Redmond, WA (2000)
6. Chan, P.K.: A non-invasive learning approach to building web user profiles, In KDD-99 Workshop on Web Usage Analysis and User Profiling (1999) 7-12
7. Chen, L., Sycara, K.: WebMate: A personal agent for browsing and searching. In Proc. of the 2nd Intl. conf. on Autonomous Agents (1998) 132-139
8. Croft, W. B., Das, R.: Experiments with query acquisition and use in document retrieval systems. In Proc. of 13th ACM SIGIR (1989)
9. Croft, W. B., Thompson, R. T.: I3R: A new approach to the design of document retrieval systems. Journal of the Americal Society for Information Science, 38 (1987) 389-404
10. Delaney, K. J.: Study questions whether google really is better. Wall Street Journal. (Eastern edition). New York, May 25 (2004) B.1 http://proquest.umi.com/pqdweb?RQT=309&VInst=PROD&VName=PQD&VType=PQD&sid=5&index=45&SrchMode=1&Fmt=3&did=000000641646571&clientId=15106

11. Eirinaki, M., Lampos, C., Paulakis, S., Vazirgiannis M.: Web personalization integrating content semantics and navigational patterns. In Workshop on Web Information and Data Management (2004) 72 – 79
12. Frakes, W.B., Baeza-Yates, R.: Information Retrieval: Data Structures and Algorithms, Prentice-Hall (1992)
13. Fu, X., Budzik, J., Hammond, K.J.: Mining navigation history for recommendation, In Proc. 2000 Conference on Intelligent User Interfaces (2000)
14. Google co. (2004) http://www.google.com/
15. Grossman, D., Frieder, O., Holmes, D., Roberts, D.: Integrating structured data and text: A relational approach. Journal of the American Society for Information Science, 48, 2 (1997)
16. Harper, D. J.: Relevance Feedback in Document Retrieval Systems: An Evaluation of Probabilistic Strategies. Ph.D. Thesis, Computer Laboratory, University of Cambridge (1980)
17. Haveliwala, T. H.: Efficient computation of PageRank. Technical Report, Stanford University Database Group (1999) http://dbpubs.stanford.edu/pub/1999-31
18. Haveliwala, T. H.: Topic-sensitive PageRank. In Proc. of the 11th Intl. World Wide Web Conference, Honolulu, Hawaii (2002)
19. Jeh, G., Widom, J.: Scaling personalized web search. In Proc. of the 12th Intl. Conference on World Wide Web, Budapest, Hungary (2003) 20-24
20. Kim, D., Atluri, V., Bieber, M., Adam, N., Yesha, Y.: A clickstream-based collaborative filtering personalization model: towards a better performance. In Workshop on Web Information and Data Management (2004)
21. Kim, H., Chan, P. K.: Implicit indicator for interesting web pages. In International Conference on Web Information Systems and Technologies (2005) 270-277
22. Kim, H., Chan, P. K.: Identifying variable-length meaningful phrases with correlation functions, In IEEE International Conference on Tools with Artificial Intelligence, IEEE press (2004) 30-38
23. Kim, H., Chan, P. K.: Learning implicit user interest hierarchy for context in personalization. In International Conference on Intelligent User Interfaces (2003) 101-108
24. Li, W. S., Vu, Q., Agrawal, D., Hara, Y., Takano, H.: PowerBookmarks: A System for personalizable web information organization, sharing, and management. In Proc. of the 8th Intl. World Wide Web Conference, Toronto, Canada (1999)
25. Liu, F., Yu, C., Meng, W.: Personalized web search by mapping user queries to categories. In CIKM'02, ACM Press, Virginia, USA (2002)
26. Maarek, Y.S., Ben-Shaul, I.Z.: Automatically organizing bookmarks per contents, In Proc. 5th International World Wide Web Conference (1996)
27. Mitchell, T. M.: Machine Learning. New York: McGraw Hill (1997)
28. Mobasher, B., Cooley, R., Srivastava, J.: Creating adaptive web sites through usage-based clustering of URLs, In Proc. 1999 IEEE Knowledge and Data Engineering Exchange Workshop (1999) 19-25
29. Page, L., Brin, S., Motwani, R., Winograd, T.: The PageRank citation ranking: Bringing order to the web. Technical Report, Stanford University Database Group (1998) http://citeseer.nj.nec.com/368196.html
30. Pazzani, M., Billsus, D.: Learning and revising user profiles: The identification of interesting web sites. Machine Learning, 27, 3 (1997) 313-331
31. Salton, G., Waldstein, R. G.: Term relevance weights in on-line information retrieval. Information Processing and Management, 14 (1978) 29-35

32. Shahabi, C., Banaei-Kashani, F.: Efficient and anonymous web-usage mining for web personalization. INFORMS Journal on Computing-Special Issue on Data Mining, 15, 2 (2003)
33. Stefani, A., Strapparava, C.: Exploiting nlp techniques to build user model for web sites: The use of worldnet in SiteIF project, In Proc. 2nd Workshop on Adaptive Systems and User Modeling on the WWW (1999)
34. Teevan, J., Dumais, S.T., Horvitz, E.: Personalizing search via automated analysis of interests and activities, In Proc. SIGIR (2005)
35. van Rijsbergen, C. J.: Information Retrieval. Butterworths, London (1979) 68–176
36. Vivisimo co. 2004 http://www.vivisimo.com
37. Voorhees, E. M.: Implementing agglomerative hierarchic clustering algorithms for use in document retrieval. Information Processing & Management, 22, 6 (1986) 465-476
38. Wexelblat, A., Maes, P.: Footprints: History-rich web browsing, In Proc. Conference on Computer-Assisted Information Retrieval (RIAO) (1997) 75-84
39. Yan, T.W., Jacobsen, M., Garcia-Molina, H., Dayal, U.: From user access patterns to dynamic hypertext linking, In Proc. 5th International World Wide Web Conference (1996)
40. Zukerman, I., Albrecht, D. W., Nicholson, A. E.: Predicting users' requests on the WWW. In Proc. of the 7th Intel. Conference on User Modeling (UM), Banff, Canada (1999) 275-284

Author Index

Lecture Notes in Artificial Intelligence (LNAI)

Vol. 4031: M. Ali, R. Dapoigny (Eds.), Advances in Applied Artificial Intelligence. XXIII, 1353 pages. 2006.

Vol. 4029: L. Rutkowski, R. Tadeusiewicz, L.A. Zadeh, J.M. Zurada (Eds.), Artificial Intelligence and Soft Computing – ICAISC 2006. XXI, 1235 pages. 2006.

Vol. 4027: H.L. Larsen, G. Pasi, D. Ortiz-Arroyo, T. Andreasen, H. Christiansen (Eds.), Flexible Query Answering Systems. XVIII, 714 pages. 2006.

Vol. 4021: E. André, L. Dybkjær, W. Minker, H. Neumann, M. Weber (Eds.), Perception and Interactive Technologies. XI, 217 pages. 2006.

Vol. 4020: A. Bredenfeld, A. Jacoff, I. Noda, Y. Takahashi (Eds.), RoboCup 2005: Robot Soccer World Cup IX. XVII, 727 pages. 2006.

Vol. 4013: L. Lamontagne, M. Marchand (Eds.), Advances in Artificial Intelligence. XIII, 564 pages. 2006.

Vol. 4012: T. Washio, A. Sakurai, K. Nakajima, H. Takeda, S. Tojo, M. Yokoo (Eds.), New Frontiers in Artificial Intelligence. XIII, 484 pages. 2006.

Vol. 4008: J.C. Augusto, C.D. Nugent (Eds.), Designing Smart Homes. XI, 183 pages. 2006.

Vol. 4005: G. Lugosi, H.U. Simon (Eds.), Learning Theory. XI, 656 pages. 2006.

Vol. 3978: B. Hnich, M. Carlsson, F. Fages, F. Rossi (Eds.), Recent Advances in Constraints. VIII, 179 pages. 2006.

Vol. 3963: O. Dikenelli, M.-P. Gleizes, A. Ricci (Eds.), Engineering Societies in the Agents World VI. XII, 303 pages. 2006.

Vol. 3960: R. Vieira, P. Quaresma, M.d.G.V. Nunes, N.J. Mamede, C. Oliveira, M.C. Dias (Eds.), Computational Processing of the Portuguese Language. XII, 274 pages. 2006.

Vol. 3955: G. Antoniou, G. Potamias, C. Spyropoulos, D. Plexousakis (Eds.), Advances in Artificial Intelligence. XVII, 611 pages. 2006.

Vol. 3949: F. A. Savacı (Ed.), Artificial Intelligence and Neural Networks. IX, 227 pages. 2006.

Vol. 3946: T.R. Roth-Berghofer, S. Schulz, D.B. Leake (Eds.), Modeling and Retrieval of Context. XI, 149 pages. 2006.

Vol. 3944: J. Quiñonero-Candela, I. Dagan, B. Magnini, F. d'Alché-Buc (Eds.), Machine Learning Challenges. XIII, 462 pages. 2006.

Vol. 3930: D.S. Yeung, Z.-Q. Liu, X.-Z. Wang, H. Yan (Eds.), Advances in Machine Learning and Cybernetics. XXI, 1110 pages. 2006.

Vol. 3918: W.K. Ng, M. Kitsuregawa, J. Li, K. Chang (Eds.), Advances in Knowledge Discovery and Data Mining. XXIV, 879 pages. 2006.

Vol. 3913: O. Boissier, J. Padget, V. Dignum, G. Lindemann, E. Matson, S. Ossowski, J.S. Sichman, J. Vázquez-Salceda (Eds.), Coordination, Organizations, Institutions, and Norms in Multi-Agent Systems. XII, 259 pages. 2006.

Vol. 3910: S.A. Brueckner, G.D.M. Serugendo, D. Hales, F. Zambonelli (Eds.), Engineering Self-Organising Systems. XII, 245 pages. 2006.

Vol. 3904: M. Baldoni, U. Endriss, A. Omicini, P. Torroni (Eds.), Declarative Agent Languages and Technologies III. XII, 245 pages. 2006.

Vol. 3900: F. Toni, P. Torroni (Eds.), Computational Logic in Multi-Agent Systems. XVII, 427 pages. 2006.

Vol. 3899: S. Frintrop, VOCUS: A Visual Attention System for Object Detection and Goal-Directed Search. XIV, 216 pages. 2006.

Vol. 3898: K. Tuyls, P.J. 't Hoen, K. Verbeeck, S. Sen (Eds.), Learning and Adaption in Multi-Agent Systems. X, 217 pages. 2006.

Vol. 3891: J.S. Sichman, L. Antunes (Eds.), Multi-Agent-Based Simulation VI. X, 191 pages. 2006.

Vol. 3890: S.G. Thompson, R. Ghanea-Hercock (Eds.), Defence Applications of Multi-Agent Systems. XII, 141 pages. 2006.

Vol. 3885: V. Torra, Y. Narukawa, A. Valls, J. Domingo-Ferrer (Eds.), Modeling Decisions for Artificial Intelligence. XII, 374 pages. 2006.

Vol. 3881: S. Gibet, N. Courty, J.-F. Kamp (Eds.), Gesture in Human-Computer Interaction and Simulation. XIII, 344 pages. 2006.

Vol. 3874: R. Missaoui, J. Schmidt (Eds.), Formal Concept Analysis. X, 309 pages. 2006.

Vol. 3873: L. Maicher, J. Park (Eds.), Charting the Topic Maps Research and Applications Landscape. VIII, 281 pages. 2006.

Vol. 3864: Y. Cai, J. Abascal (Eds.), Ambient Intelligence in Everyday Life. XII, 323 pages. 2006.

Vol. 3863: M. Kohlhase (Ed.), Mathematical Knowledge Management. XI, 405 pages. 2006.

Vol. 3862: R.H. Bordini, M. Dastani, J. Dix, A.E.F. Seghrouchni (Eds.), Programming Multi-Agent Systems. XIV, 267 pages. 2006.

Vol. 3849: I. Bloch, A. Petrosino, A.G.B. Tettamanzi (Eds.), Fuzzy Logic and Applications. XIV, 438 pages. 2006.

Vol. 3848: J.-F. Boulicaut, L. De Raedt, H. Mannila (Eds.), Constraint-Based Mining and Inductive Databases. X, 401 pages. 2006.

Vol. 3847: K.P. Jantke, A. Lunzer, N. Spyratos, Y. Tanaka (Eds.), Federation over the Web. X, 215 pages. 2006.

Vol. 3835: G. Sutcliffe, A. Voronkov (Eds.), Logic for Programming, Artificial Intelligence, and Reasoning. XIV, 744 pages. 2005.

Vol. 3830: D. Weyns, H. V.D. Parunak, F. Michel (Eds.), Environments for Multi-Agent Systems II. VIII, 291 pages. 2006.

Vol. 3817: M. Faundez-Zanuy, L. Janer, A. Esposito, A. Satue-Villar, J. Roure, V. Espinosa-Duro (Eds.), Nonlinear Analyses and Algorithms for Speech Processing. XII, 380 pages. 2006.

Vol. 3814: M. Maybury, O. Stock, W. Wahlster (Eds.), Intelligent Technologies for Interactive Entertainment. XV, 342 pages. 2005.

Vol. 3809: S. Zhang, R. Jarvis (Eds.), AI 2005: Advances in Artificial Intelligence. XXVII, 1344 pages. 2005.